BELLTOWN EXPOSED

CHIN MUSIC PRESS • SEATTLE, WASHINGTON

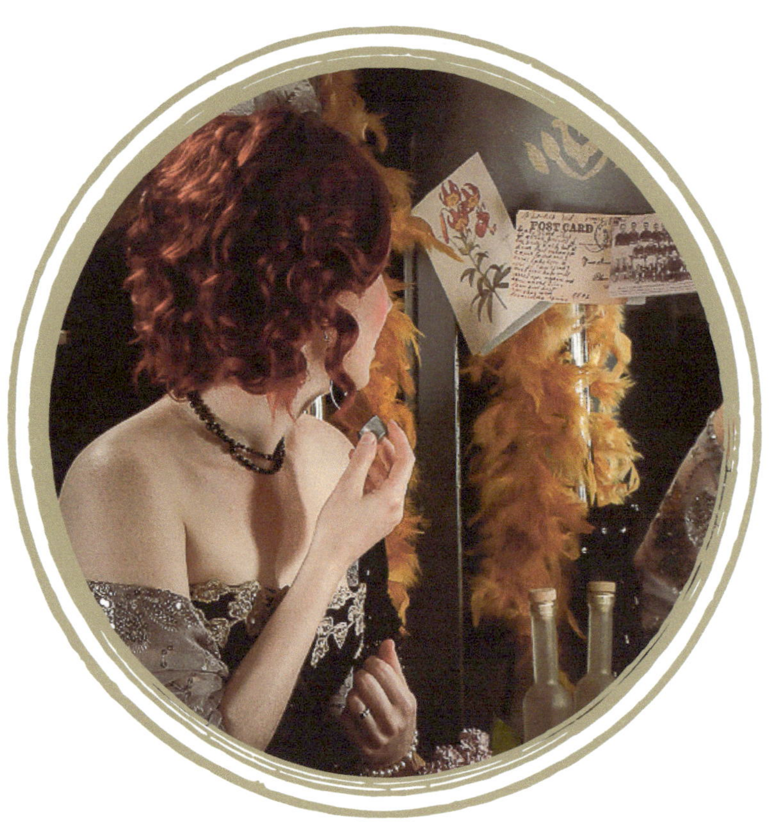

Copyright © 2019 by Staci Bernstein

First [1] edition

All rights reserved

ISBN: 9781634059176

Library of Congress Cataloging-in-Publication data available.

Book and cover design by Dan D Shafer

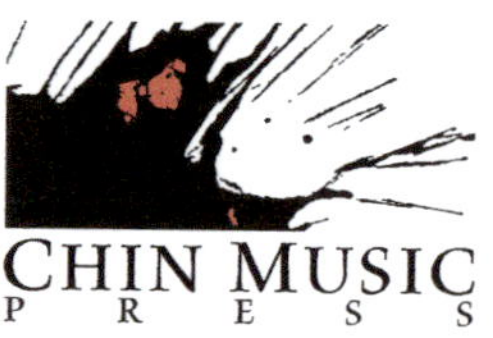

CHIN MUSIC
PRESS

PUBLISHER
Chin Music Press
1501 Pike Place #329
Seattle, WA 98101
www.chinmusicpress.com

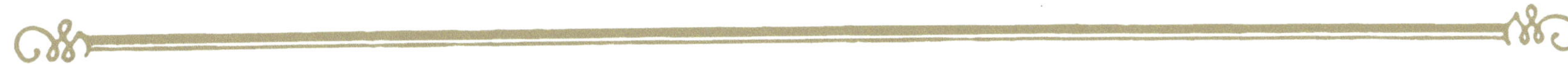

BELLTOWN EXPOSED

STACI BERNSTEIN

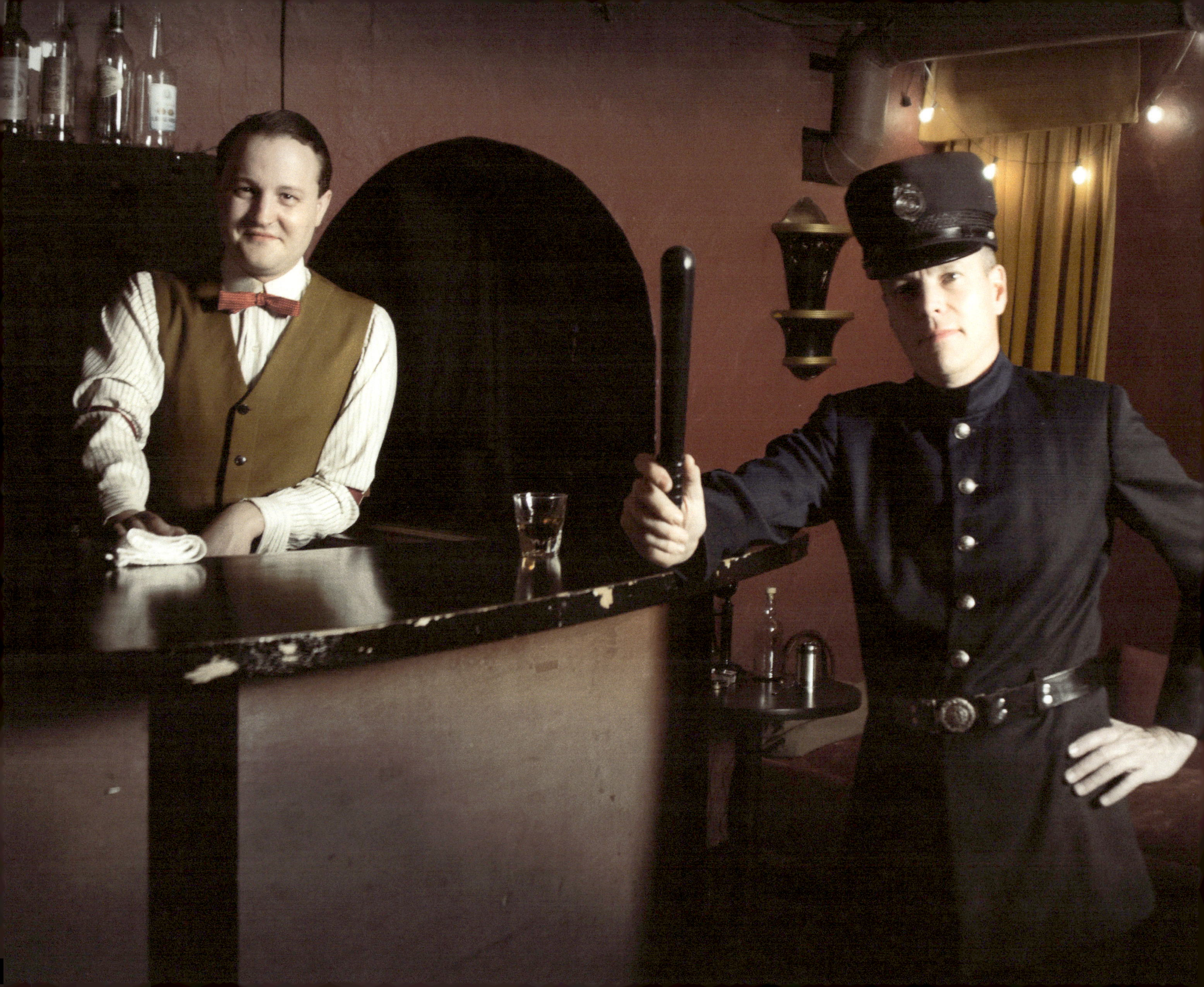

TABLE OF CONTENTS

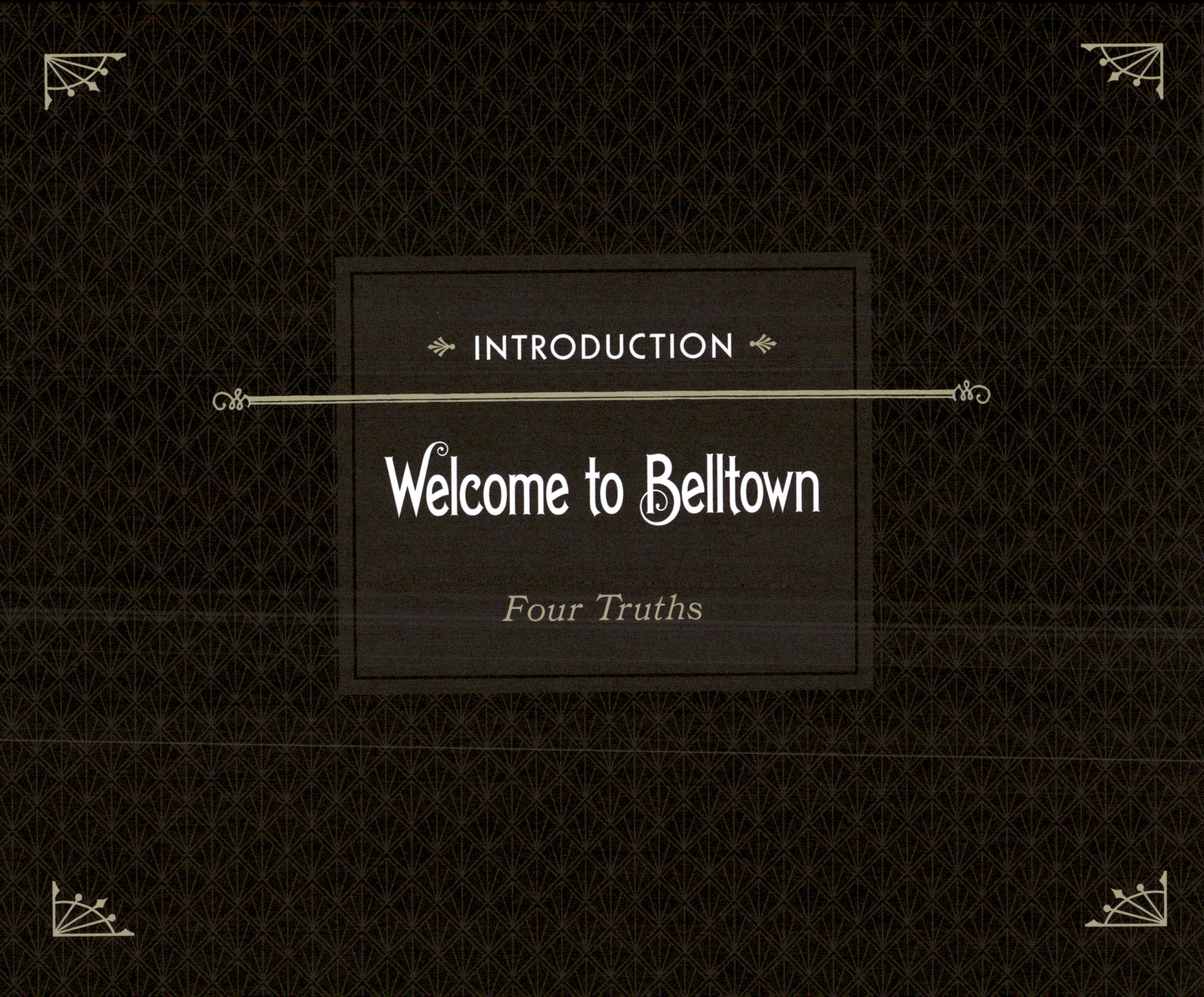

Welcome to Belltown

Four Truths

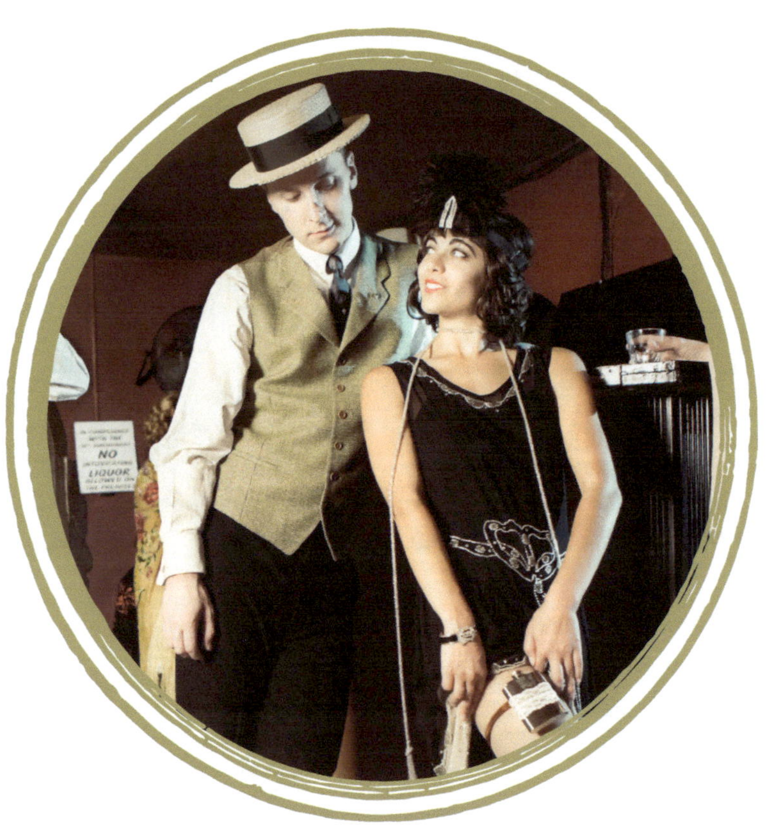

You are about to explore a photographic tour of the history of Belltown, one of Seattle's most lively neighborhoods. Coupled with the tableaux vivant photography of Staci Bernstein are some vignettes about the neighborhood. Your job, if you choose to accept it, is to ferret out the lies from the truths. Do your best historical detective work, then check the key in the back to see how you fared. And don't miss the completely true histories of the neighborhood from HistoryLink in the back of this collection.

OK, sleuths, here we go. We'll start you off with a few truths to get you ready for what "lies" ahead.

LONGHOUSES ON THE PRAIRIES

The foot of Bell Street was the site of a Native village called *Baqbaq bab,* or "Little Prairies." Historians say the name probably refers to the fields of salal berries, which were grown here for thousands of years. Little Prairie was home to several longhouses. The Feds burned the last one to the ground in the 1800s. The Little Prairies village made something of a comeback in 1865, when the city evicted Native Americans from current-day Pioneer Square. Many of the displaced people resettled in Belltown. Native people from different tribes came from all over the Puget Sound to Belltown, building a community for themselves that lasted until the 1890s.

STURDY OUTHOUSES

Belltown is named for William Nathaniel Bell, a shadowy figure who didn't spend much time in the neighborhood that is named after him. He arrived with his wife, Sarah Ann, in 1851 on the Schooner Exact, and eventually staked his claim in today's Belltown. In 1856, in the Battle of Seattle, the Native Americans attacked the city after becoming fed up with the terms of treaties that were forced on them by Governor Isaac Stevens. When the fighting had subsided, Bell had nothing left of his home but his outdoor bathrooms. He wrote to Arthur Denny: "My house was burned on my claim during the action but the outhouses are still standing but your house in town was robbed of flour and perhaps other things." Bell took his sick wife and daughters and left town for California. In fact, many white settlers left Seattle after the battle. Bell didn't come back until 1870, when he found that the land he still owned had become quite lucrative. Bell named the streets Olive and Virginia after his daughters and Stewart after his son-in-law.

BRING OUT YOUR DEAD

Back in the Gold Rush days, Belltown was a seedy neighborhood where criminals would prey on the unsuspecting nouveau riche miners back from Alaska with their gold-dust fortunes. The local *Seattle Post-Intelligencer* newspaper would report how much gold the miners found in Alaska and when they were expected back in town. Ne'er-do-wells would hunt those miners down, kill them, and steal their fortunes. Butterworth and Sons ran a lucrative funeral business out of the Butterworth Building on First Avenue. The murders coupled with the bouts of plague that were sending people to an early grave meant that the morticians had more work than they could handle. The city offered citizens fifty dollars, equal to a year's salary, if they would collect the dead bodies in one of the Butterworth's hearses and return them to the funeral home. People rushed to be the first to find dead bodies and collect the reward, a practice that became known as the "Butterworth hearse races."

HE BUILT THIS CITY

James Moore had a huge impact on early Seattle. He built the Moore Theater (still in business today), the New Washington Hotel, developed parts of Lake Union and Rainier Beach. He was even instrumental in supporting the channel that now connects Lake Washington and Lake Union. But in the end, misfortune and perhaps a bit too much ambition got the better of the man. He had a plan to turn Irondale (near Port Townsend) into the "Pittsburgh of the West," envisioning a booming center of steel production with easy access to the Pacific. That plan ultimately failed and left him in debt. He then fled to Florida, where he set up a subdivision called Moore Haven near Lake Okeechobee. A hurricane in 1926 wiped out the nearby dike, and two hundred people in the subdivision drowned. Moore, financially and emotionally ruined, traveled back to California, where he died in 1929. He didn't have enough money to pay for his own burial.

Yep, all those stories are **TRUE**.

Now good luck figuring out the rest of them!

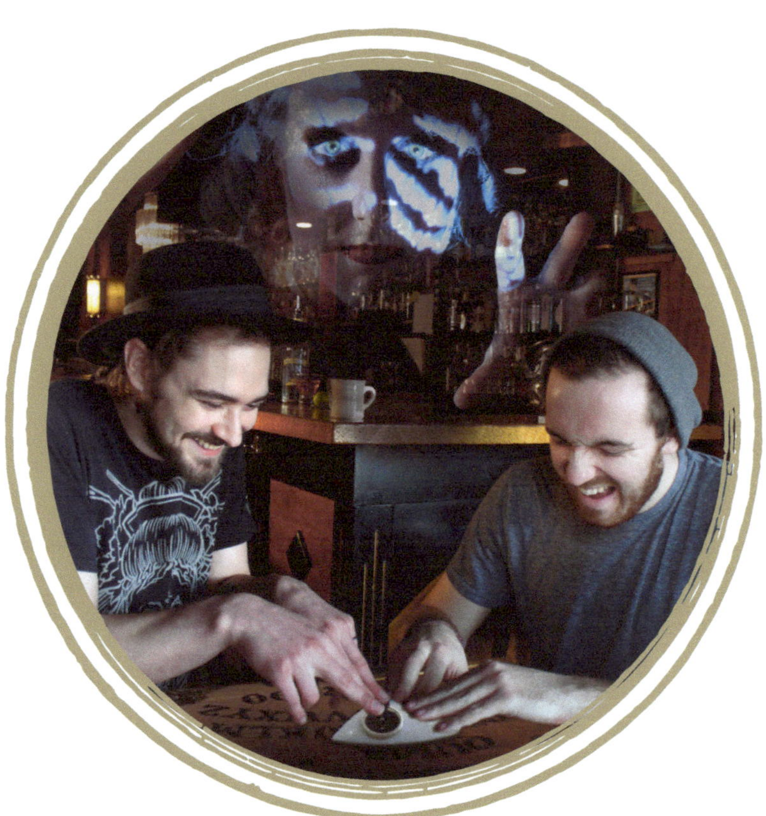

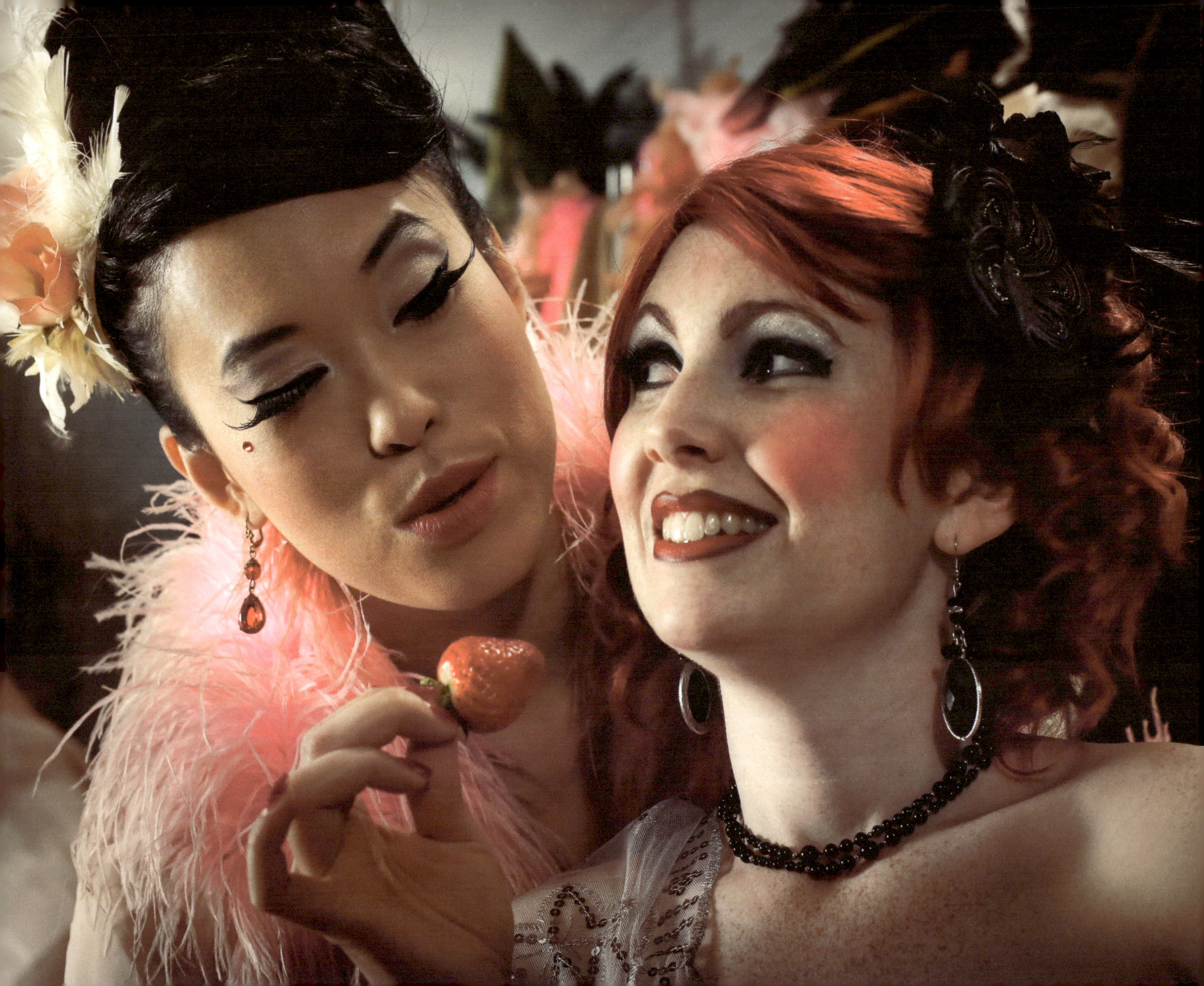

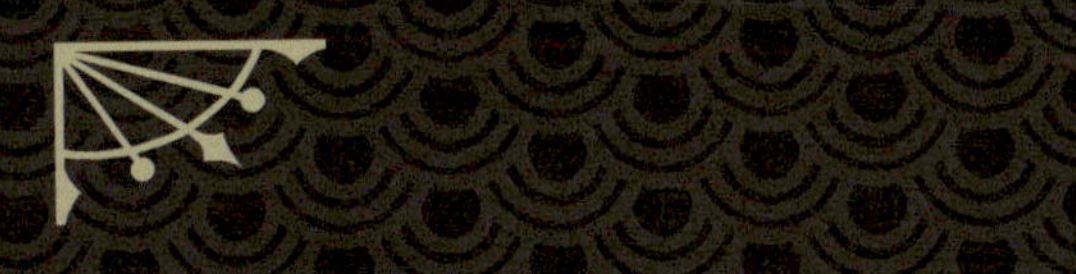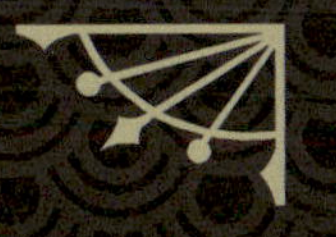

CHAPTER ONE

The Vaudeville Days

Two Lies and a Truth

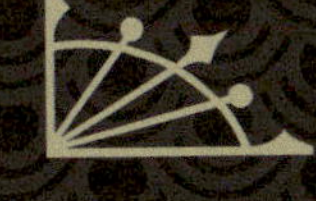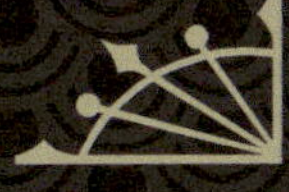

A.

Nancy "Fancy" Malone (née Hetty Brickman of North Platte, Nebraska) started as a chorus hoofer in some of the seedier joints in town, but soon worked her way up to principal dancer. She also gave the world one of the Vaudeville era's signature dance moves. At the young age of eight, Nancy contracted a bout of rheumatic fever that left the right side of her body weakened. As a result, Nancy's turns and spins tended to be counterclockwise, the opposite direction from the national standard. This reversal caught on in the Puget Sound area and spread east, becoming known as the "Seattle Swivel." Nancy herself eventually married a Congregationalist minister and had six daughters.

B.

The Vaudeville era Rendezvous kept a list of words comics could only use later in the night. One memorable stage manager, Ted "Trusty" Berns, was knows to pull out his pocket watch with a flourish and announce, "It is now nine o'clock! Time to let the Hells and Damns out of their cage."

C.

Cecilia Augspurger Schultz booked the acts for the Moore Theater from 1934 to 1949. She was a colorful dame who the local newspapers described as a "cold blooded businesswoman" who could "squeeze more money out of a dollar than a leech." But she wasn't afraid to drop a wad of cash on big name performers. She brought in dancer Martha Graham, a traveling Shakespeare troupe, piano virtuoso Arthur Rubenstein and even (if you can believe it) Robert Ripley of Ripley's Believe it or Not. Seattle fell in love with Cecilia's eccentric, unpredictable programming. Her poor husband, Gustav, however, would endlessly fret about how much she was spending. One season she invested a hundred grand on the entertainment line up. When Gustav found out, it is reported that he lost thirty pounds in three days!

TWO *are lies.*
Which one is **TRUE**?

[ANSWER KEY ON PAGE 86]

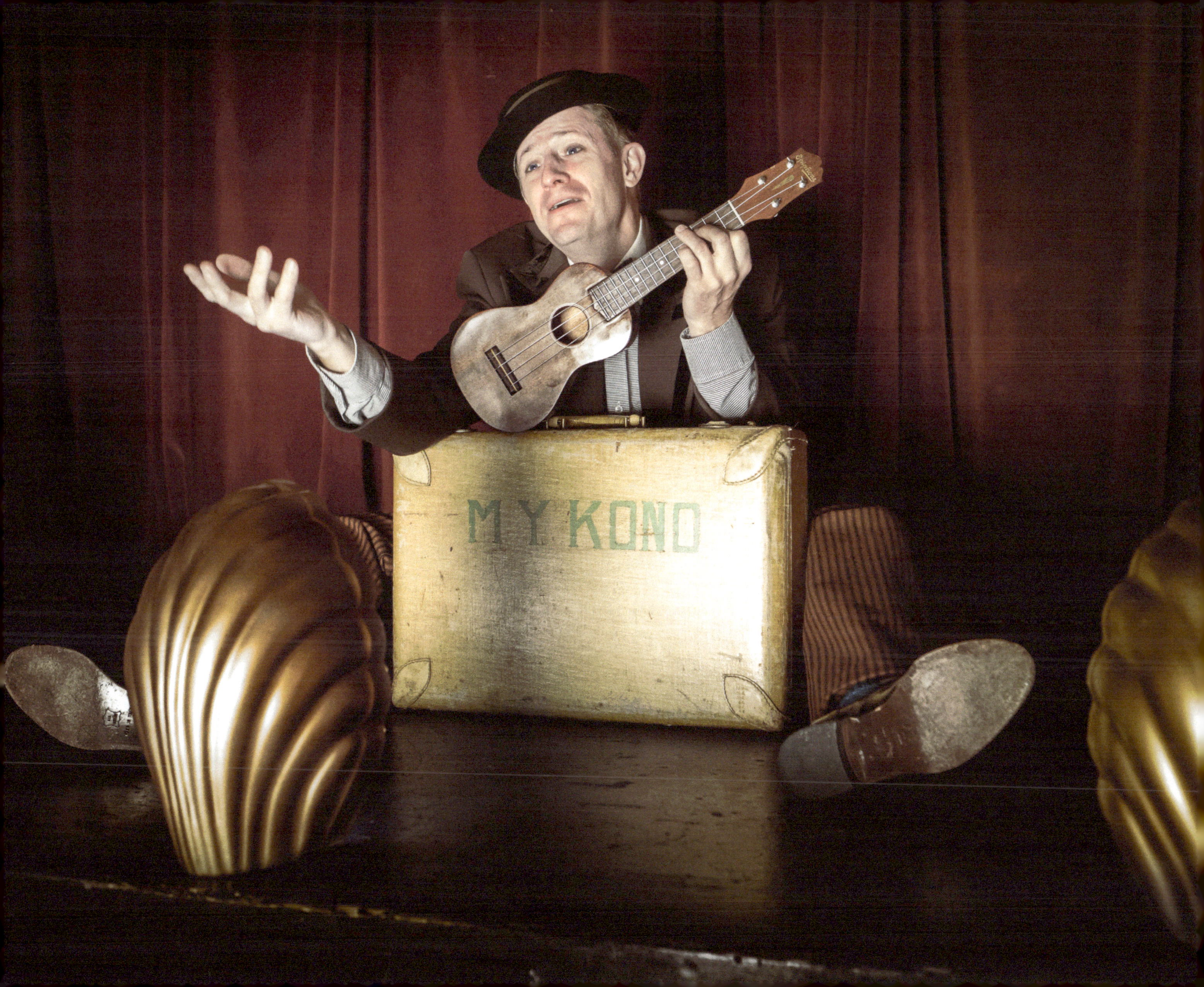
M Y K O N O

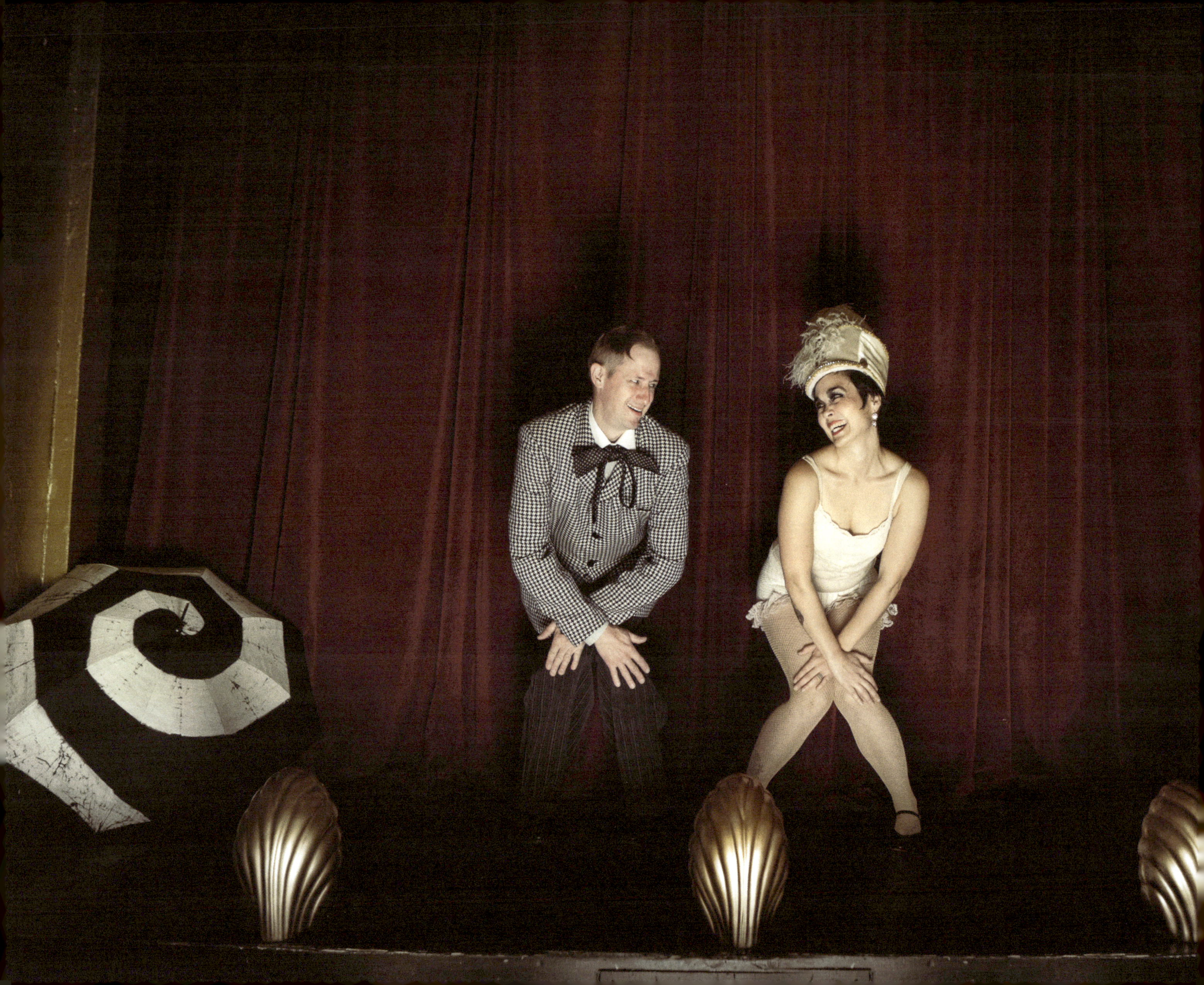

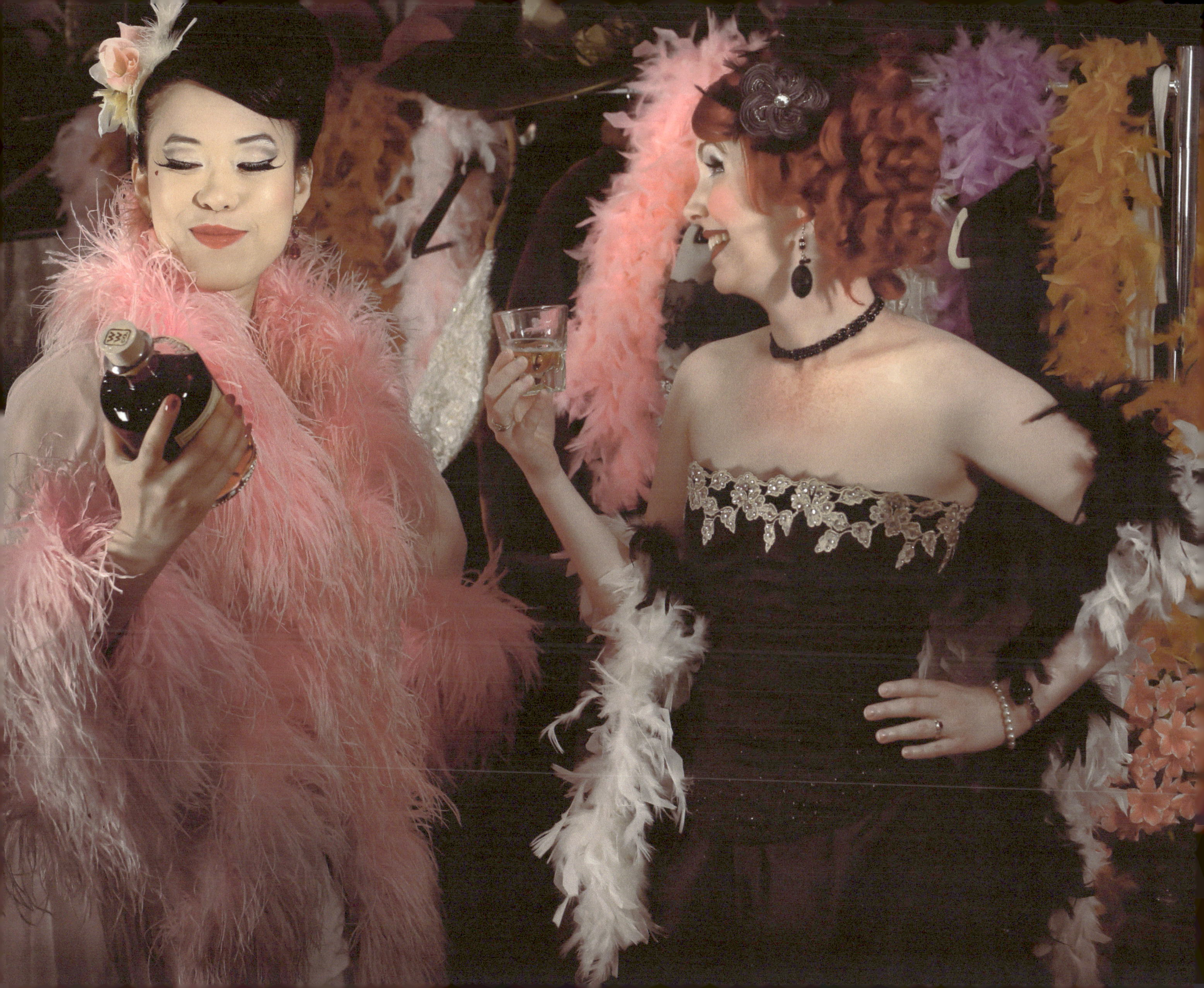

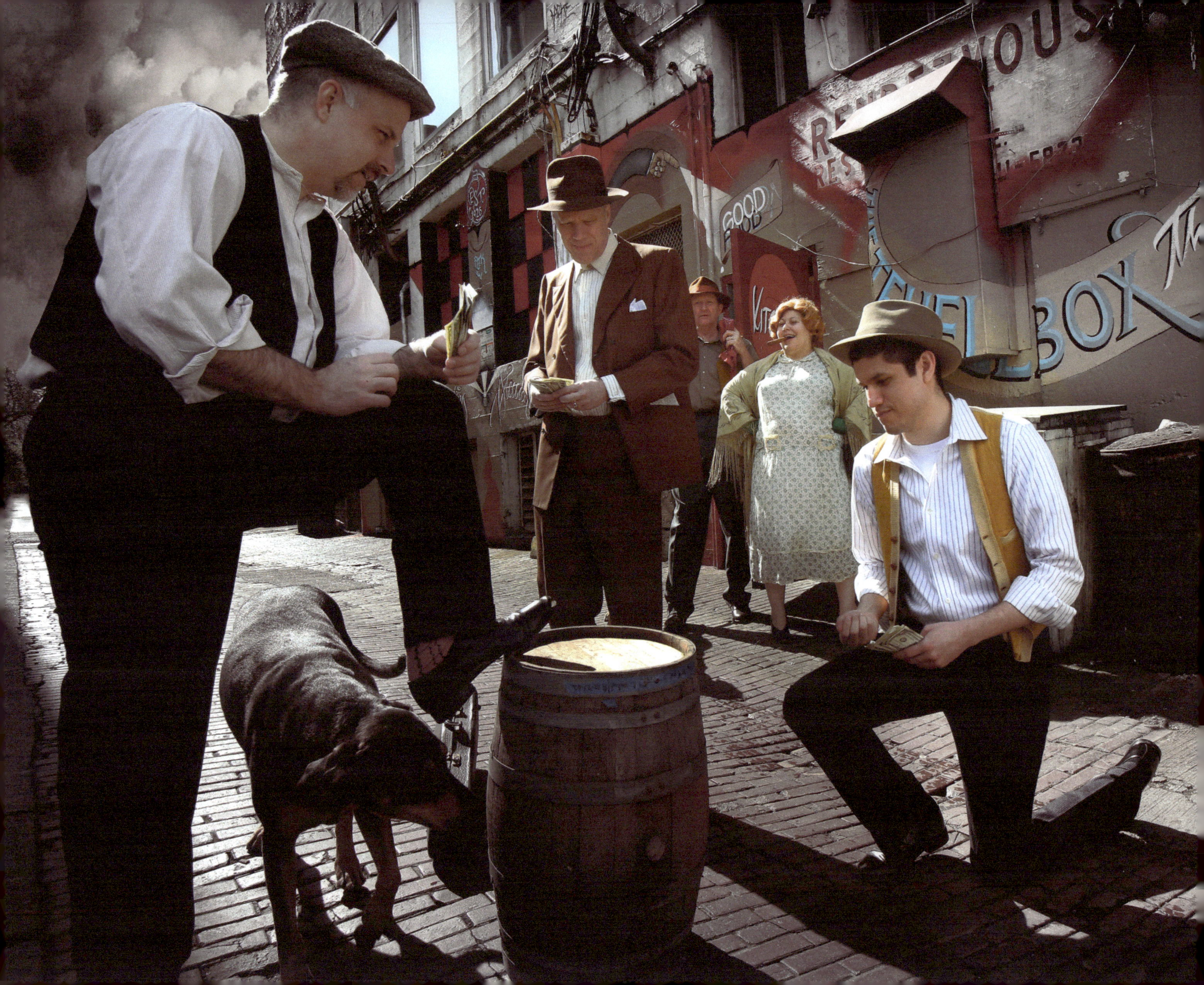
RENDEZVOUS
RENDEZVOUS
RES
GOOD
THE JEWEL BOX The

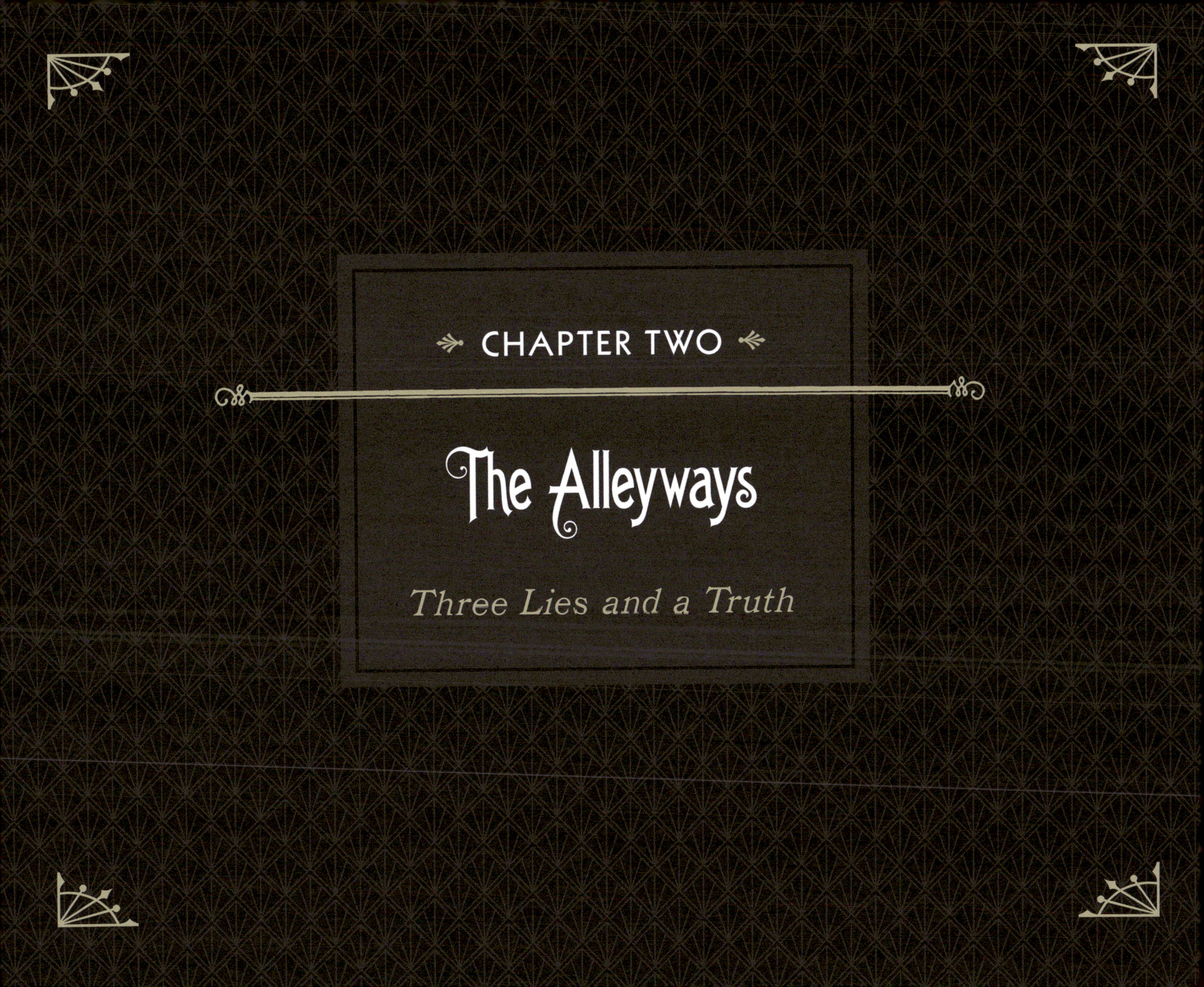

The Alleyways

Three Lies and a Truth

A.

In the 1940s, the infamous alleys of Belltown hosted the longest running floating craps game in the city. The euphemism "Going to visits Aunt Sue" arose from the founder of these ongoing games of chance, Suzanne "Snake Eyes" Trumble. Rumor has it that when the cops showed up, she'd tuck the dice and the cash into her hollowed-out wooden leg.

B.

A vibrant culture of vice flourished for decades in the alleys of Belltown. A bustling but discreet "Ask No Questions" Night Market existed for years, selling goods that were likely smuggled in by sea or "fallen off a truck." Because a fixed location would have meant a swift shut down, an elaborate language of chalk marks developed. Folks in the know could glance at a wall of scribbles and read exactly where and when to pick up their desired contraband. Everyone knew what you meant when you said, "I'm gonna check out the chalkies."

C.

Before the era of modern sanitation, every Sunday night the restaurants and cafes of Belltown would empty their deep fat fryers out the backdoor into the alley. This gave rise to a tradition amongst the area youngsters of Monday Morning Grease Hockey.

D.

At one point in the 1970s, well after the dice and gambling had been replaced by drug-dealing, some alleyway denizens decided to turn the area into a shooting gallery. They'd set up cans and bottles and take aim. The cops turned a blind eye, and most people knew to stay far away from the alley. One fellow who is still alive to talk about it swears he saw an alleyway sharpshooter shoot a can right off of a fella's head.

THREE *are lies. Which one is* **TRUE**?

[ANSWER KEY ON PAGE 86]

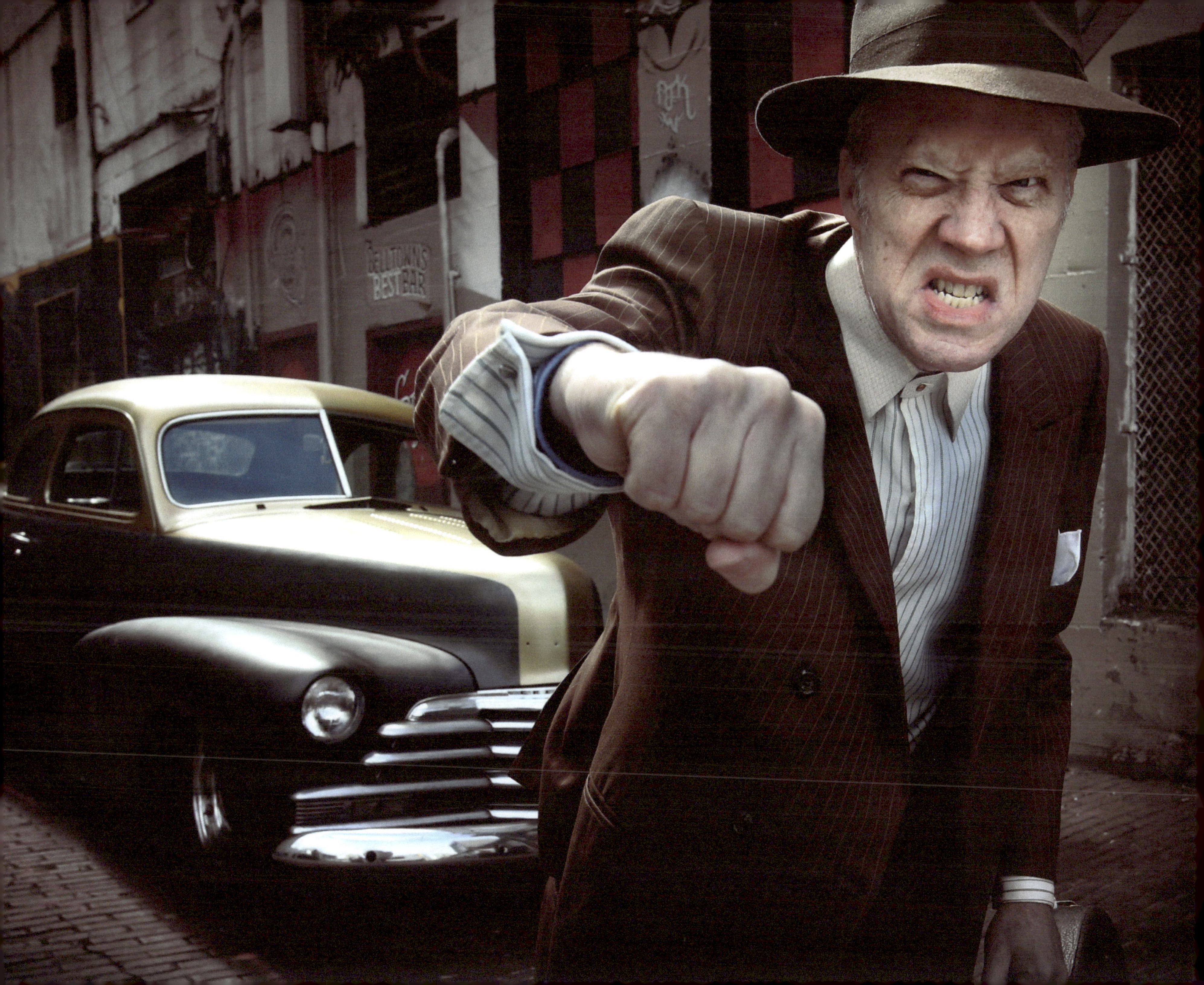

BELLTOWN'S
BEST BAR

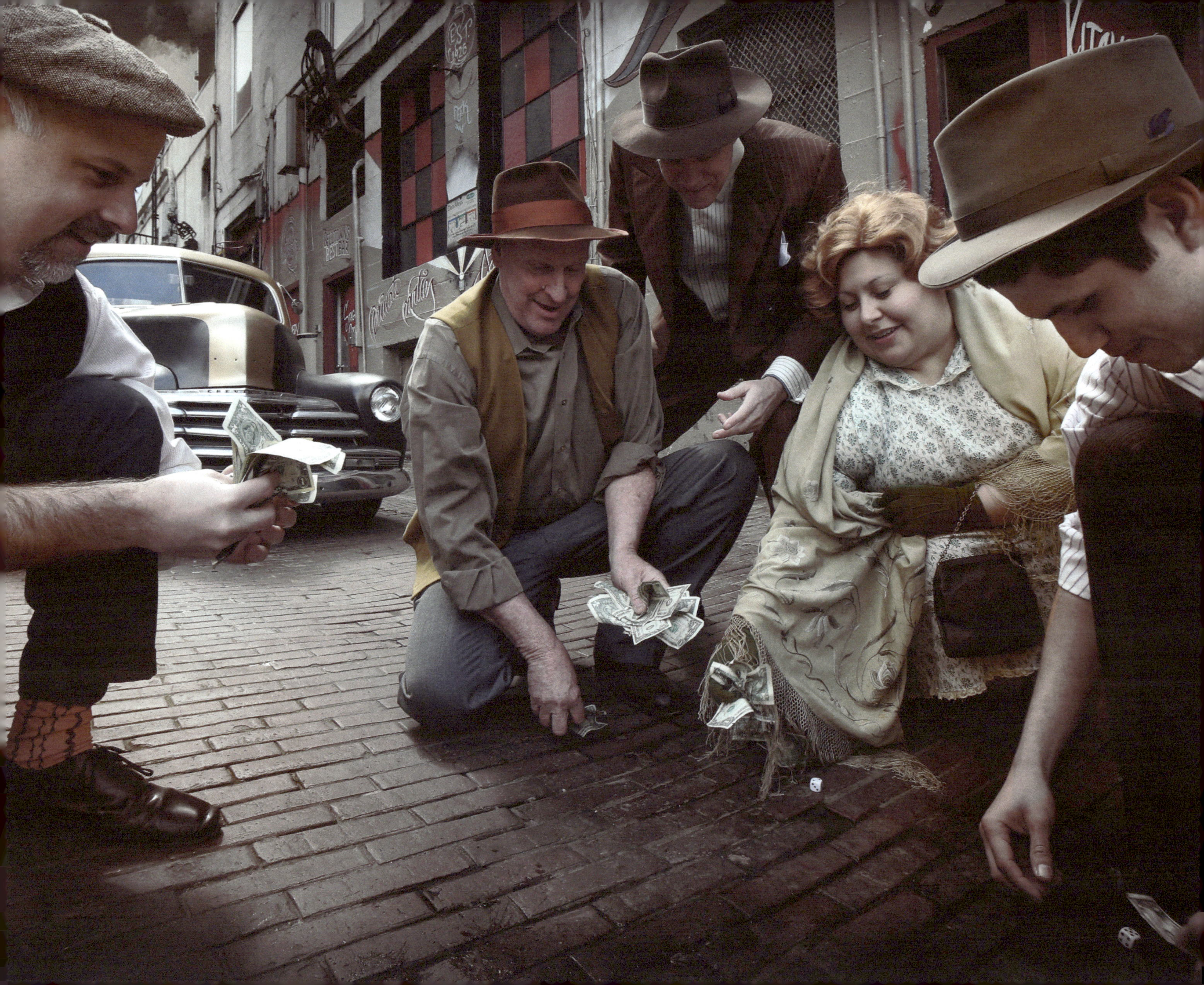

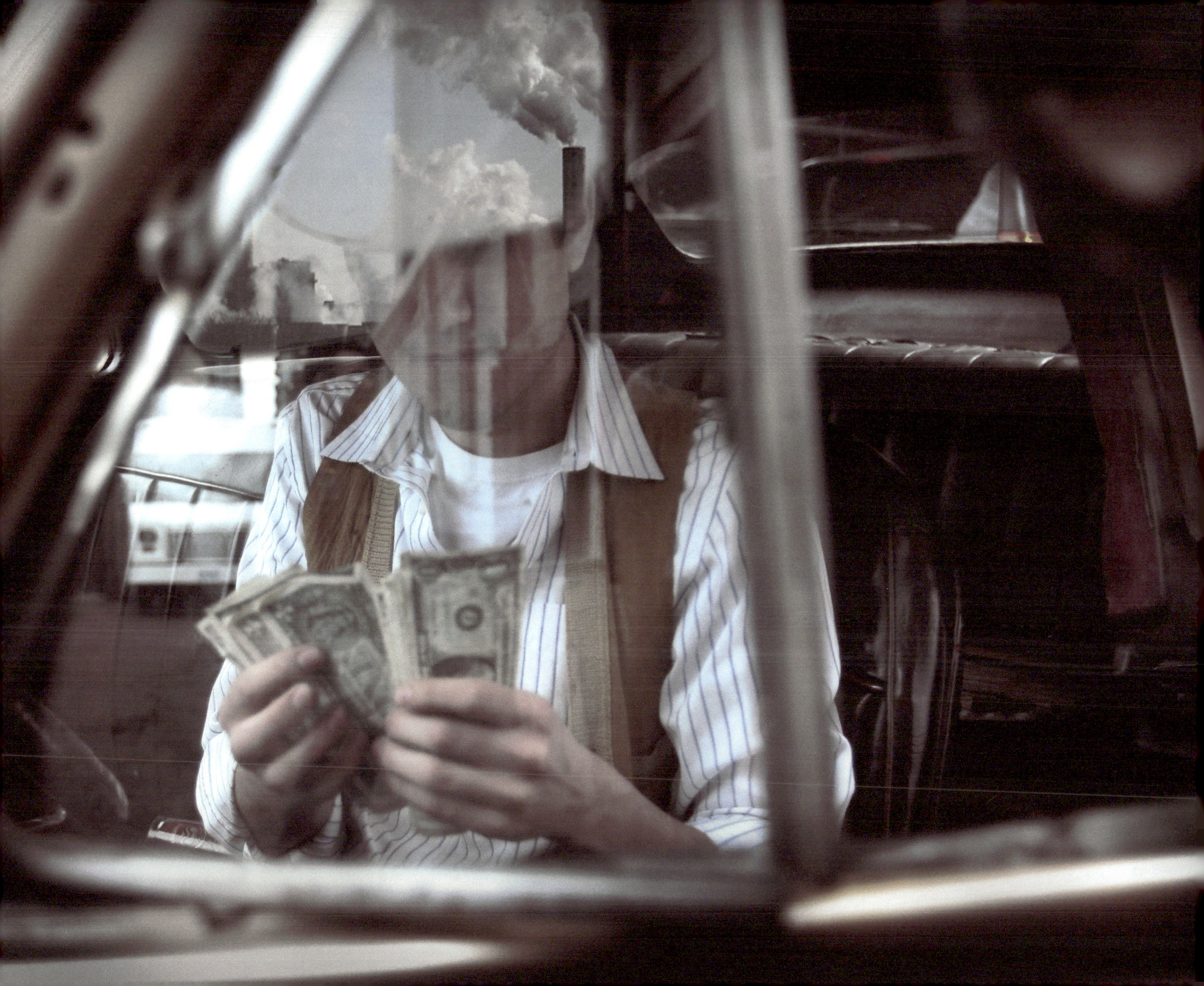

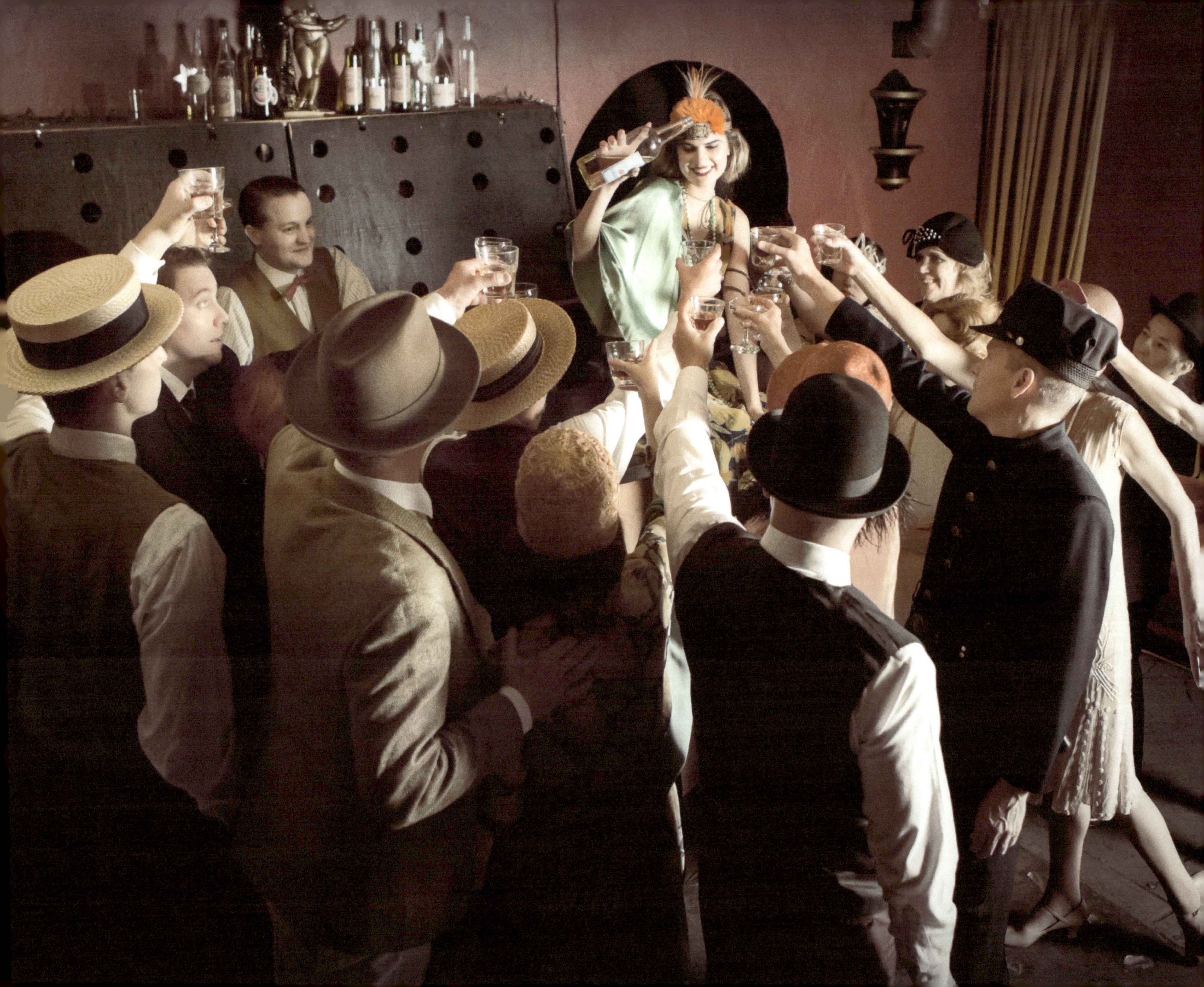

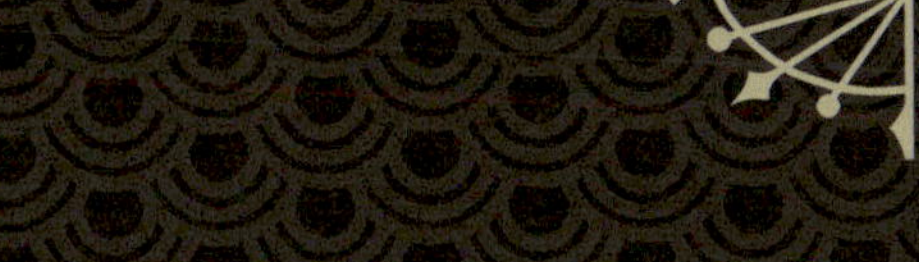

CHAPTER THREE

The Speakeasies

Three Lies and a Truth

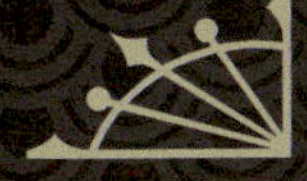

A.

MGM Bigwigs had an office on the second floor above the Rendezvous. Said office had a secret staircase that led straight to The Grotto speakeasy in the basement. This discreet passage allowed the Hollywood execs and stars to access the illicit bar without having to mingle with the hoi polloi that filled the restaurant on the ground floor. The Grotto was decorated in the fashion of a classic Hollywood speakeasy to make the LA folks feel right at home. That, along with the Spanish Colonial style of the Lorraine Hotel across the street (where now stands the City Hostel) made the corner of 2nd and Bell a little pocket of sunny Southern California right in the heart of cloudy Seattle.

B.

One publisher/bootlegger in Vancouver, BC, used to send spirits south tucked into hollowed out dictionaries. This worked well until one shipment made its way to the nascent Belltown Public Library. Nelda Kempler, a savvy teetotaling librarian, sold the smuggled goods to finance a fine set of sturdy bookshelves.

C.

Everybody has heard of the Prohibition era's famous bathtub gin. But what many don't know is that the homemade hooch had connoisseurs who claimed that the kind of bathtub used had big impact on the final product. One Belltown imbiber was quoted as saying, "A fine porcelain tub makes for a smooth gin that can be sipped bare naked. But zinc tub will always leave a bit of a metallic tang; this variety is best enjoyed with tonic and good portion of lime."

D.

The grimmest Prohibition story might just be that of Canadian embalmer Travis Jeets. If an American died up north, Jeets would fill their veins with whisky before shipping them down to a partner who kept the Jeets funeral home at First and Wall.

THREE *are lies. Which one is* **TRUE**?

[ANSWER KEY ON PAGE 86]

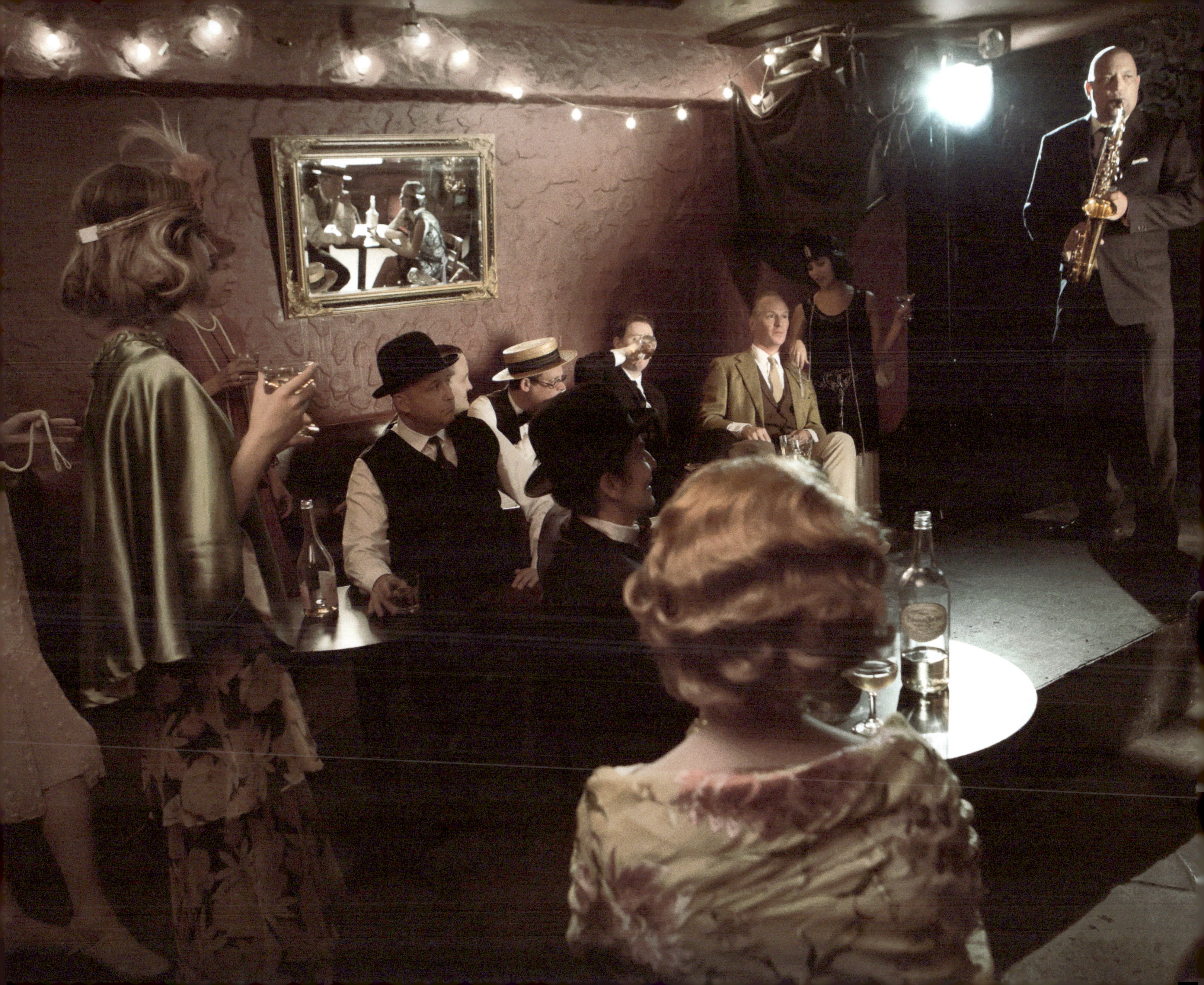

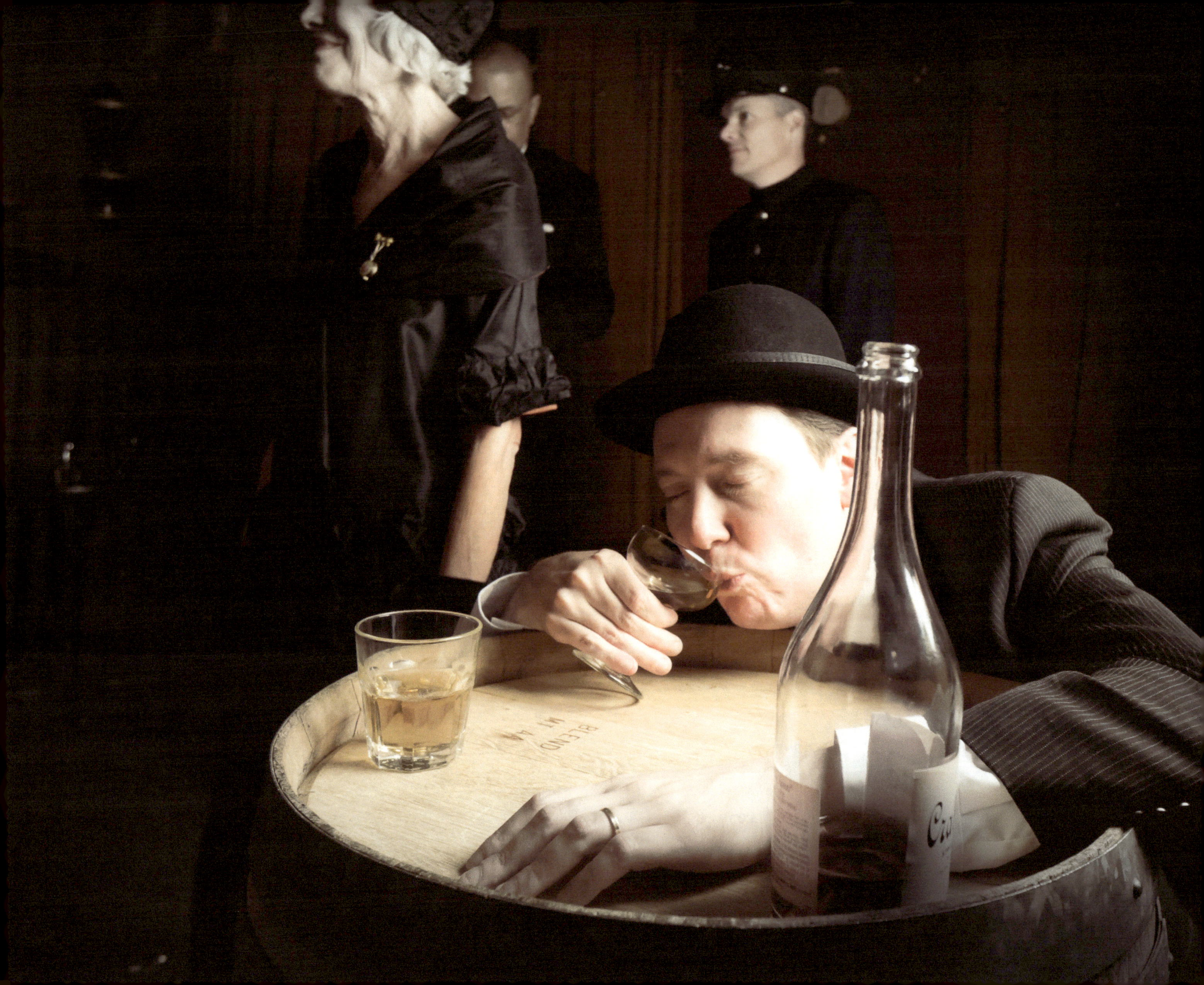

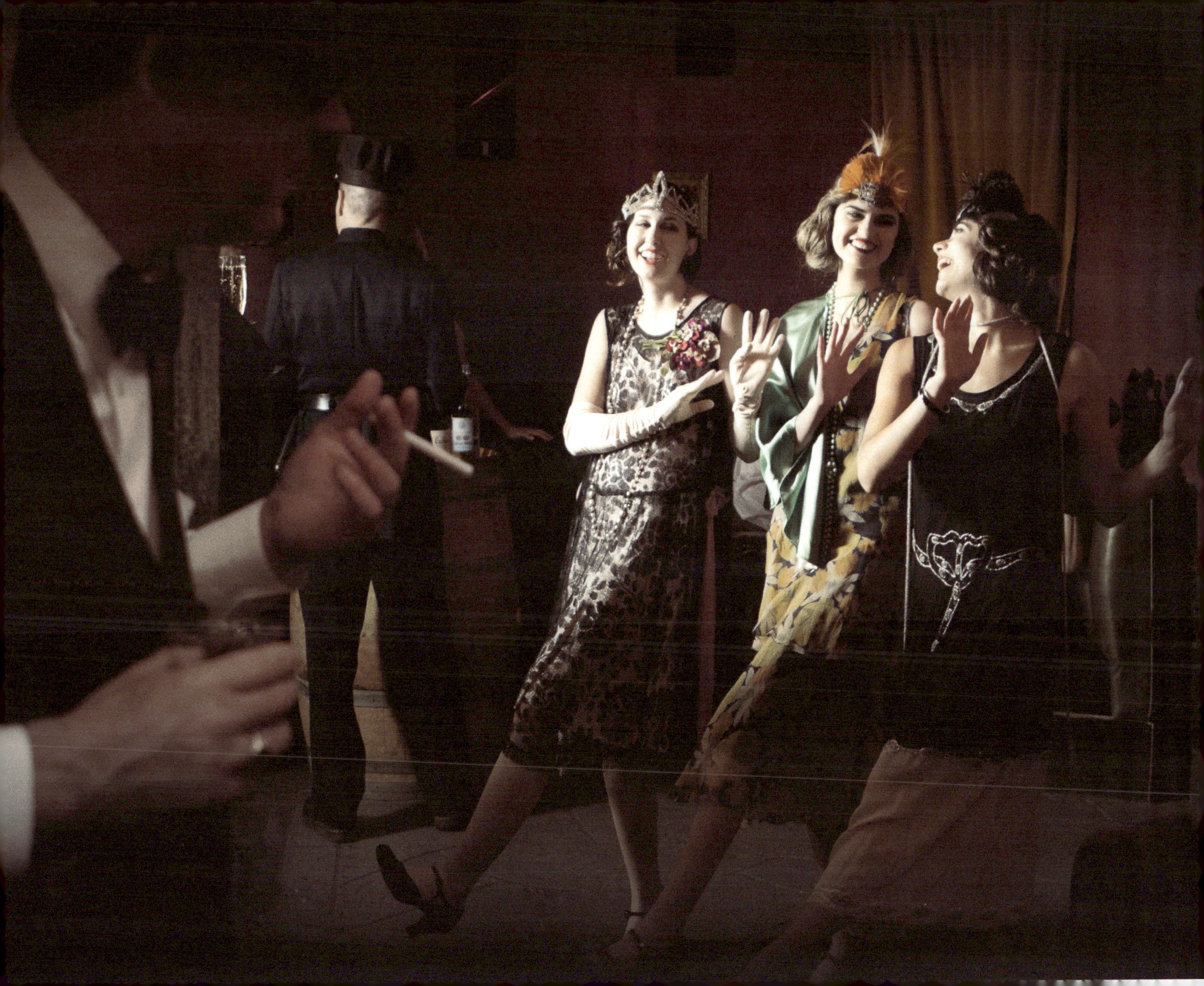

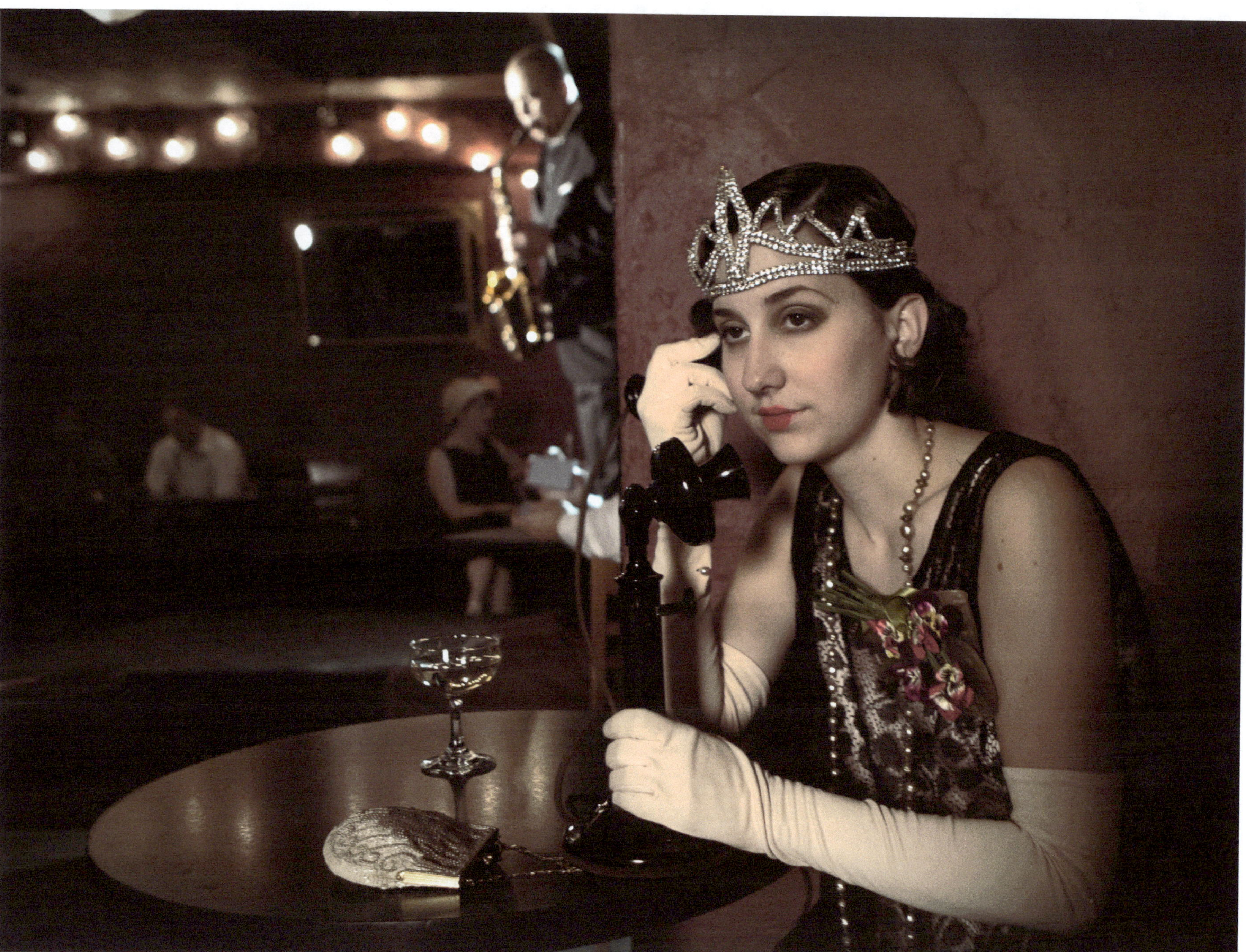

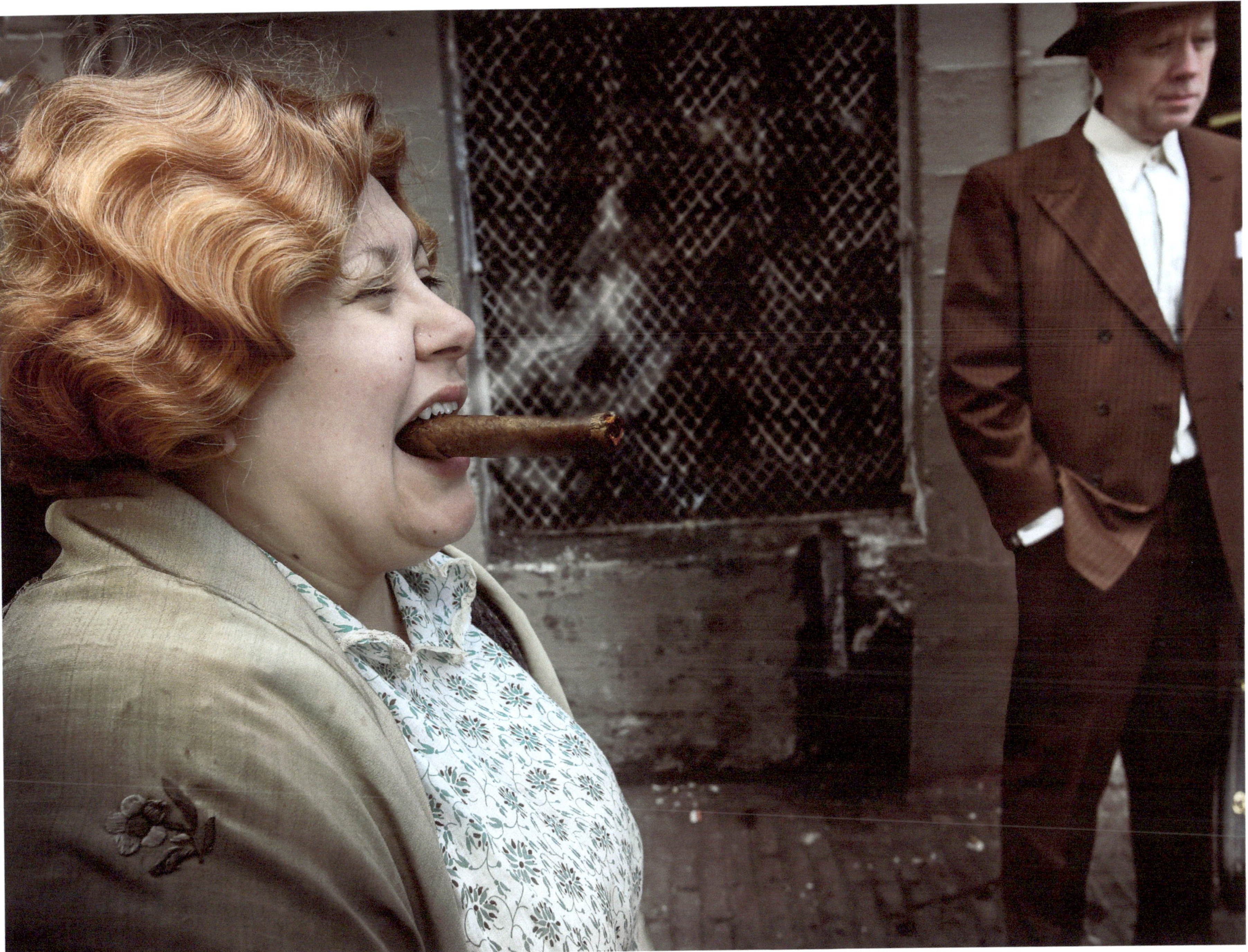

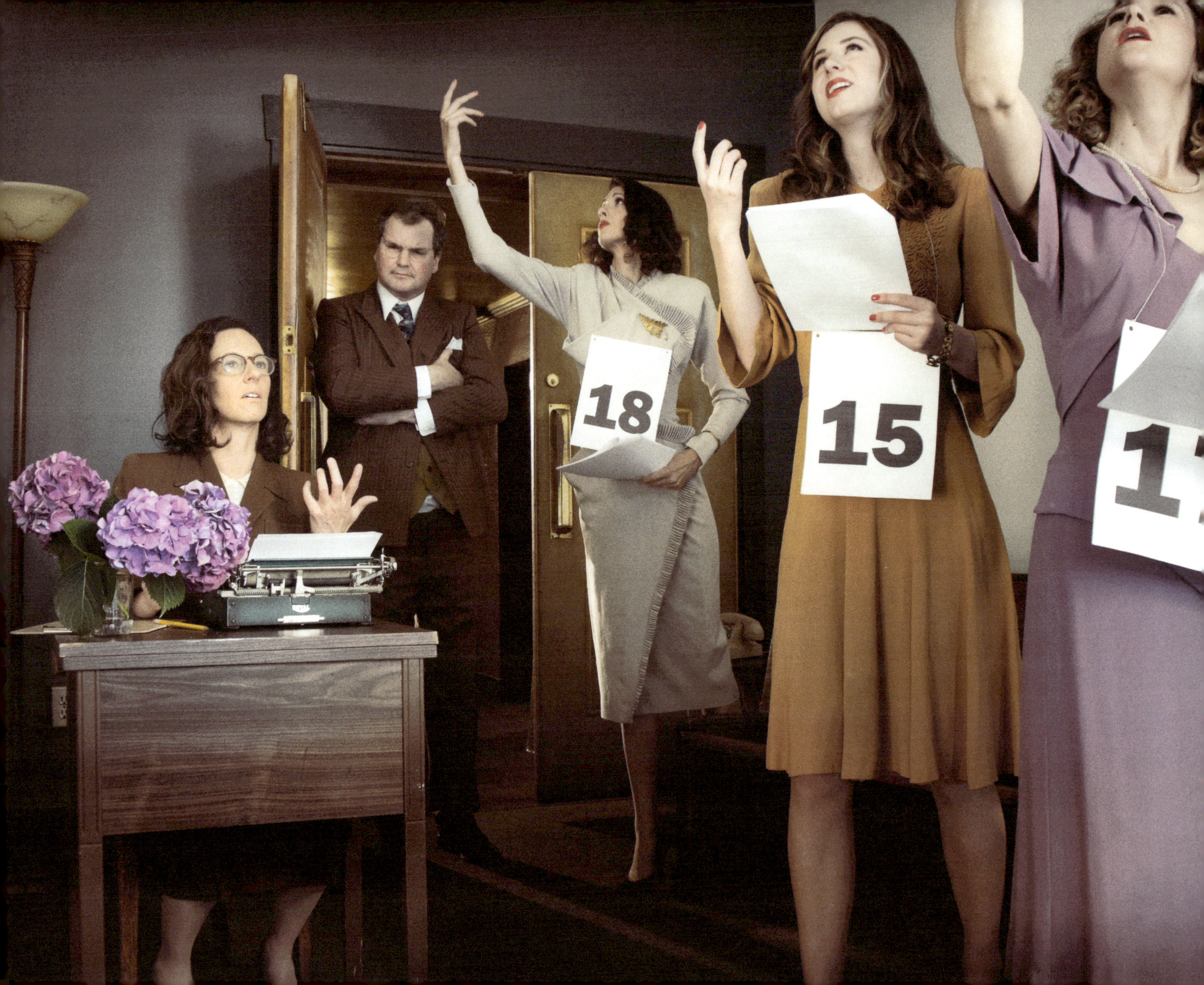
18
15

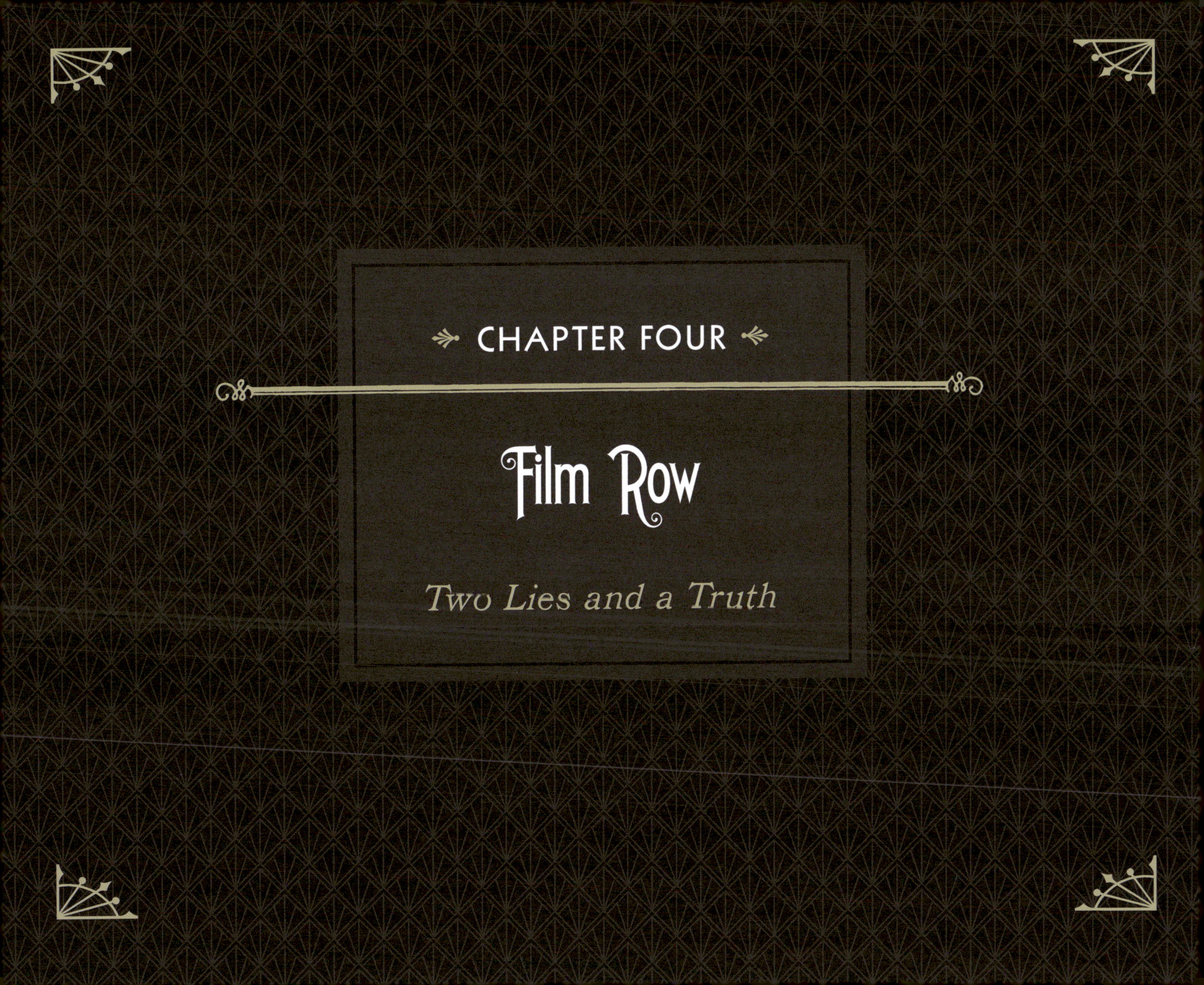

CHAPTER FOUR

Film Row

Two Lies and a Truth

A.

In the early days of the twentieth century, Belltown and Hollywood were in bed together. Before these digital days, movies lived on nitrocellulose film that was extremely flammable, ready to burst into flame if you looked at it funny! Belltown became the place to ship these films for storage because back in the Twenties, the neighborhood was more sparsely populated than nearby downtown, which meant fewer folks to burn if something went terribly wrong.

B.

Theater owners and screen bookers came from all over the region to check out films, making the decisions about what movies would play at their local bijous. The general public was not allowed into the viewings. However, the pros were welcome to bring a guest with them. These plus-ones became a hot commodity among Seattleites. The visiting movie businessmen were often showered with drinks and food and attention. Women who traded their company for sneak peeks were called "plussies."

TWO *are lies.*
Which one is TRUE?

[ANSWER KEY ON PAGE 86]

C.

The projectionists' union (Local #111) was dominated by Polish and Ukrainian immigrants, most of them single men. At any one time a good dozen or so would be living at the Flickerton Arms, an apartment building located about where the Space Needle now stands. The Flicks, as it was known, had a reputation for the wildest parties and for the best discussions of cinematic theory. Rumor has it they had a still on the roof and ran pipes down so that some of the apartments had a vodka tap.

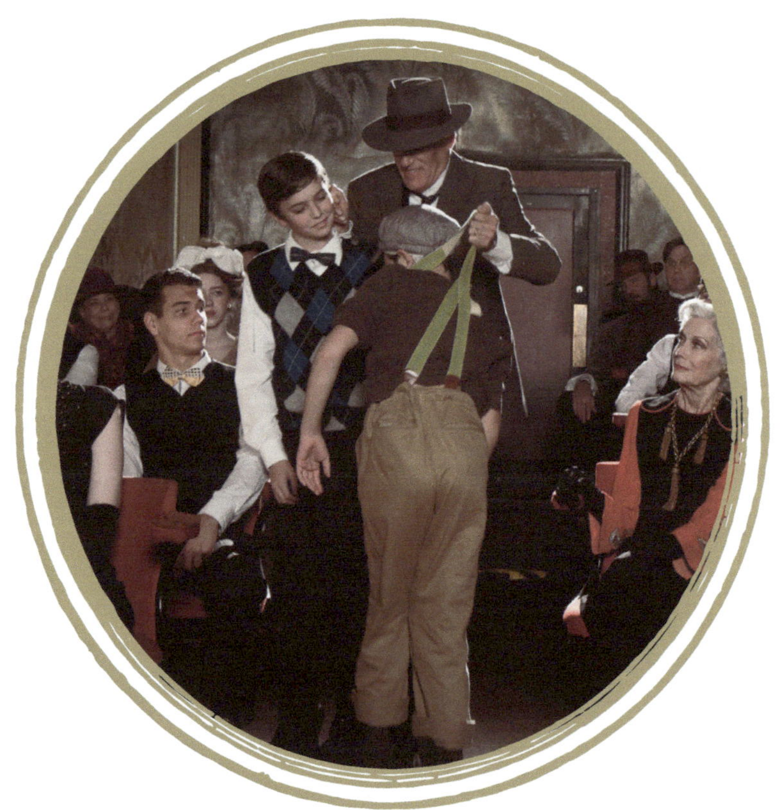

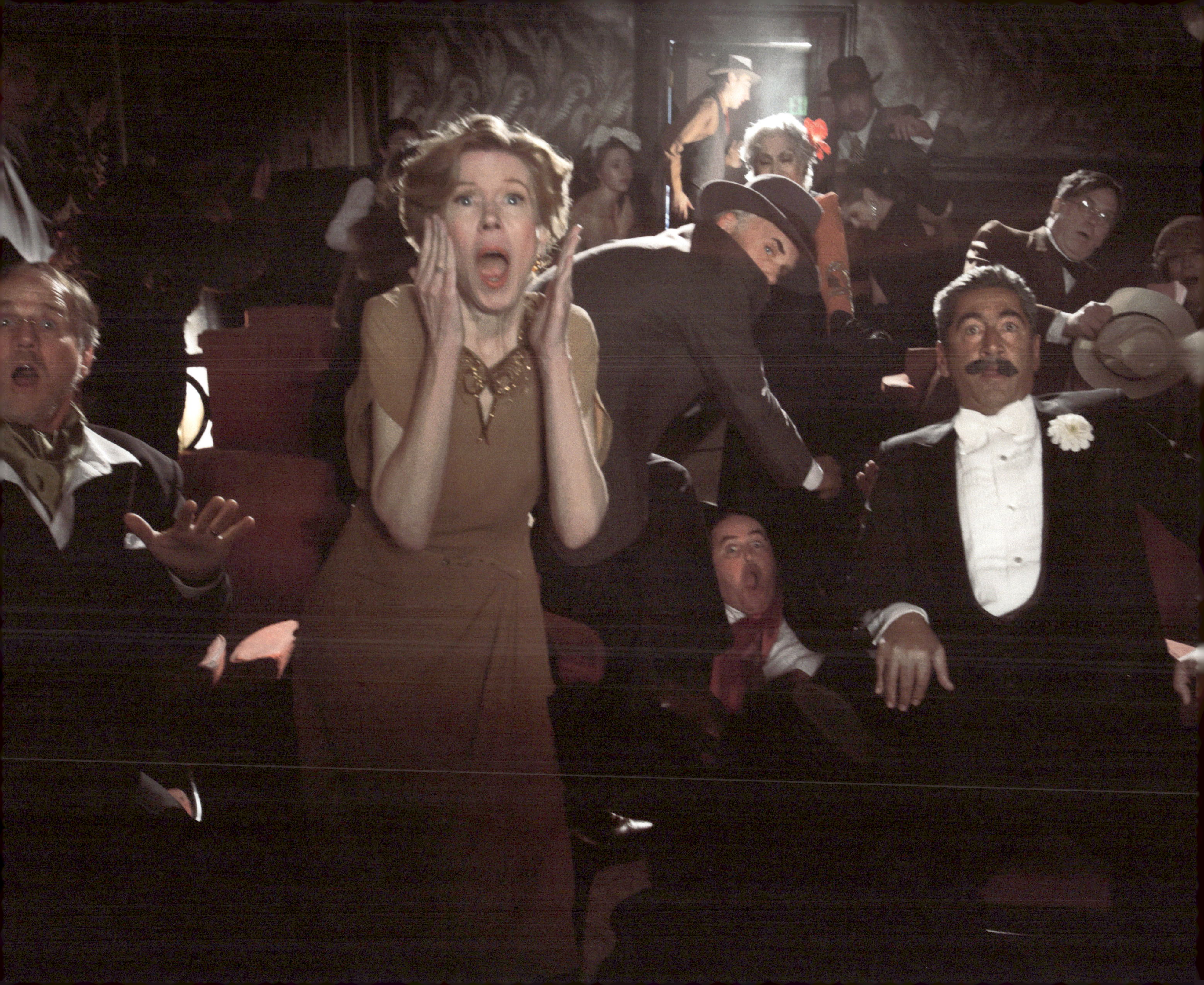

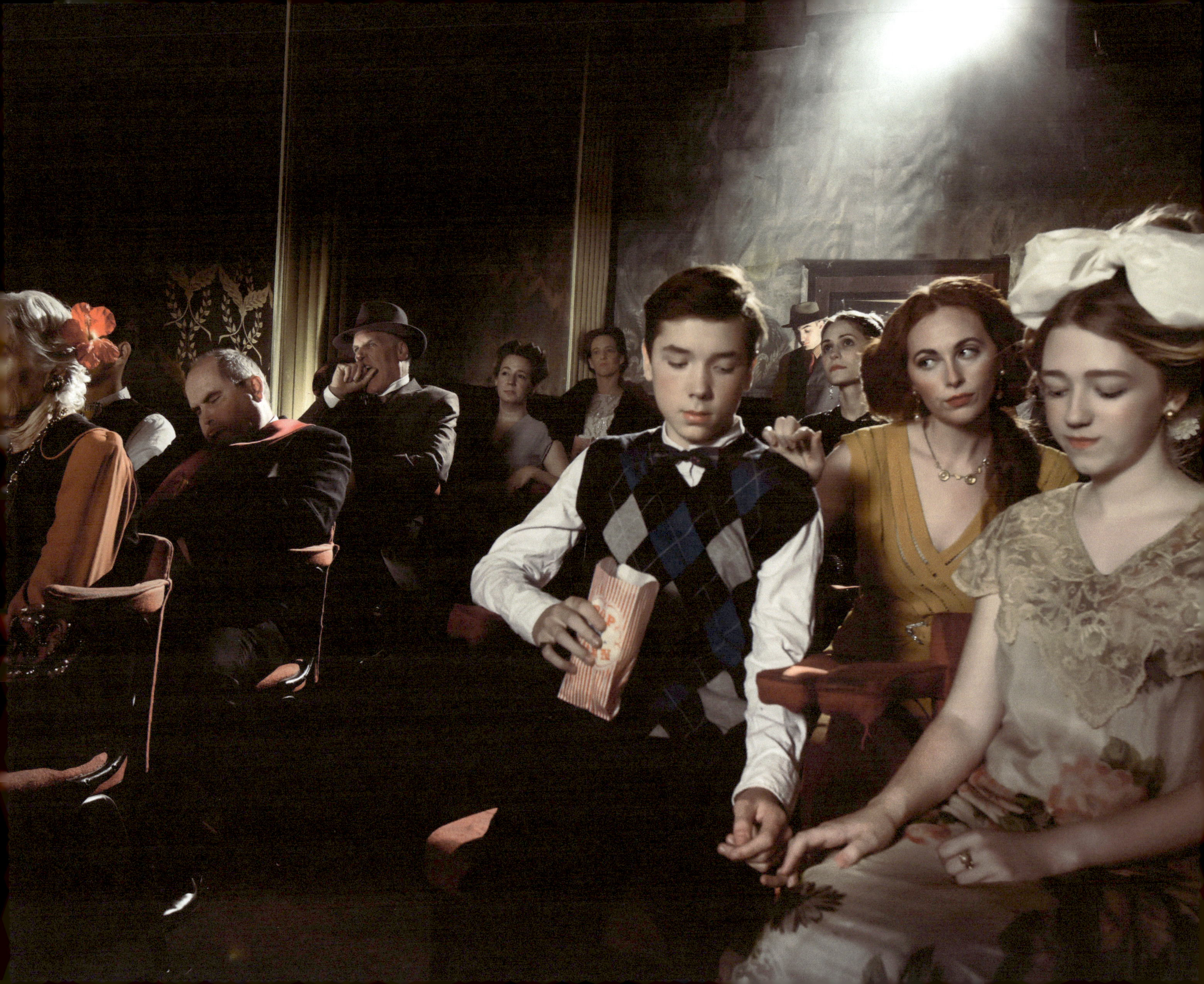

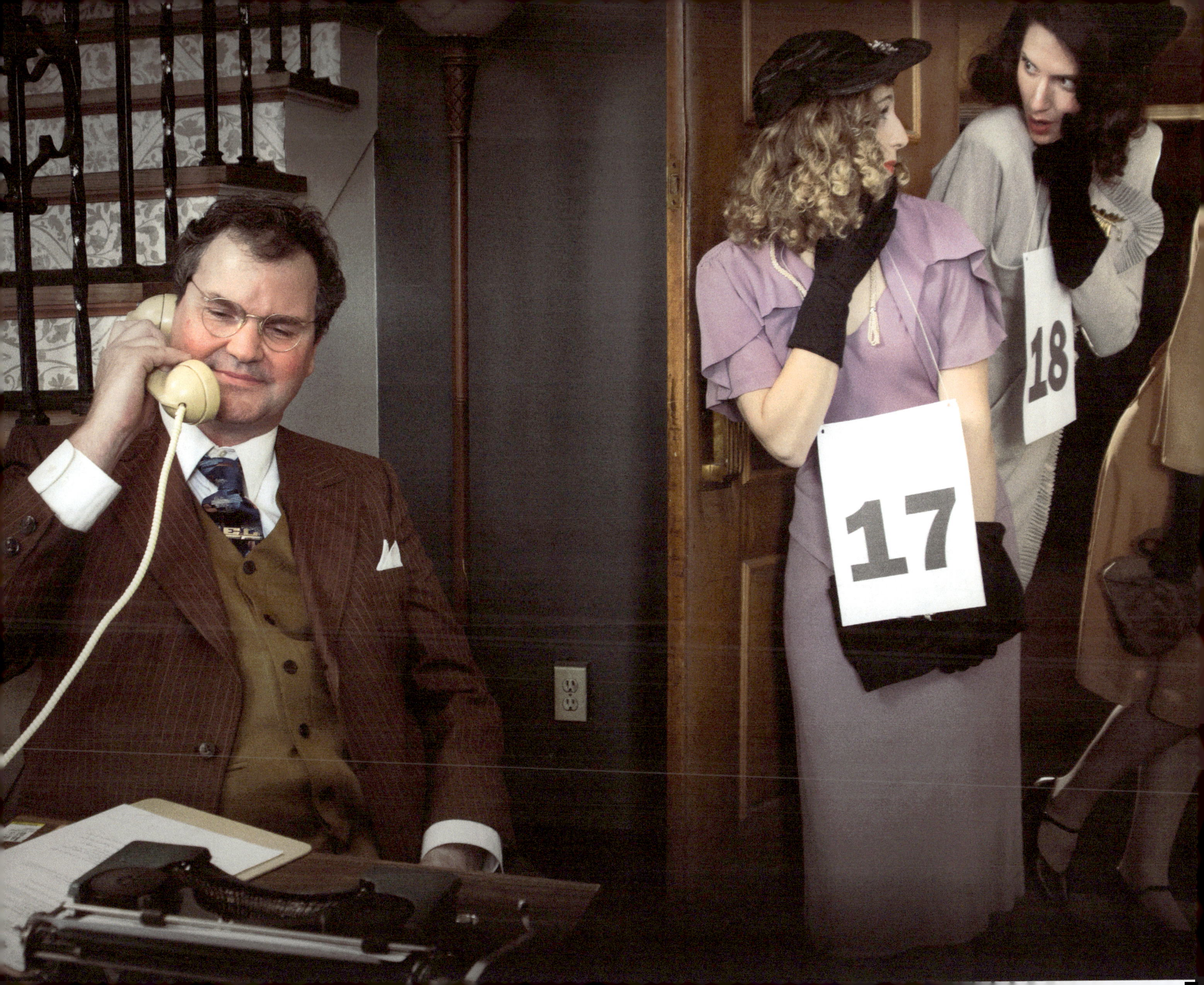

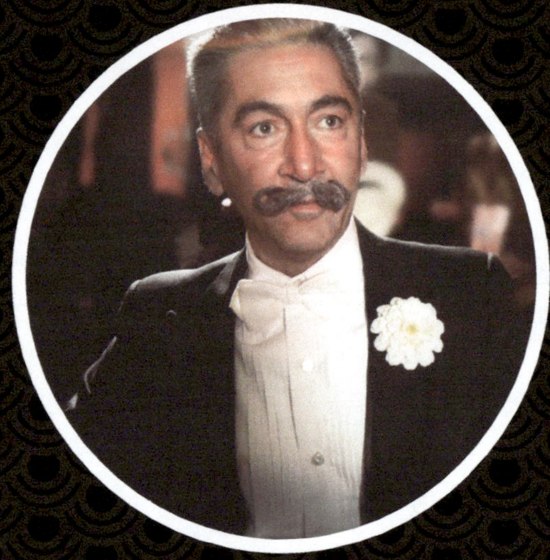

THE
Theatre Owner

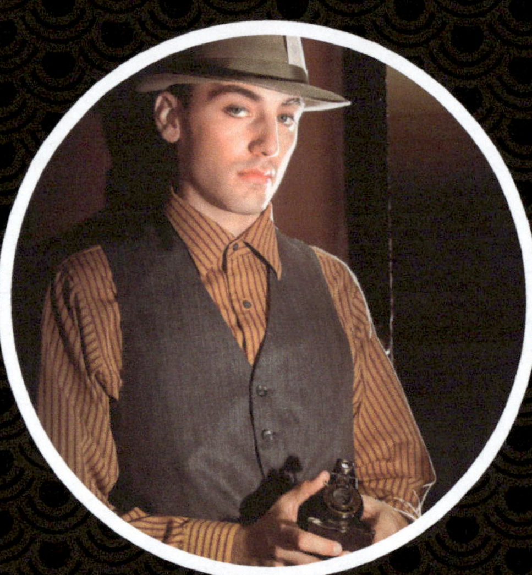

THE
Aspiring Auteur

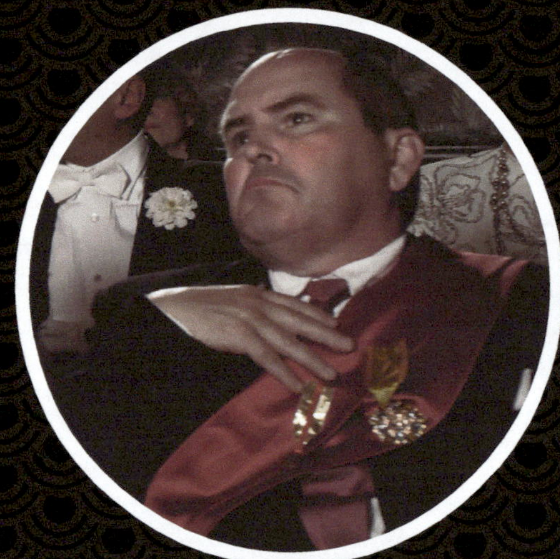

THE
Diplomat

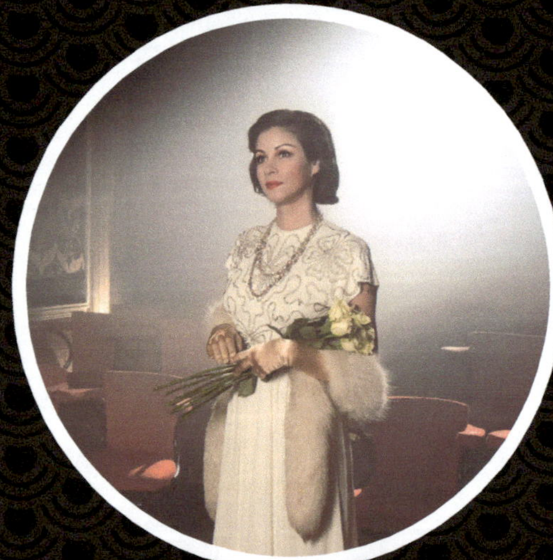

THE
Starlet

THE
Producers

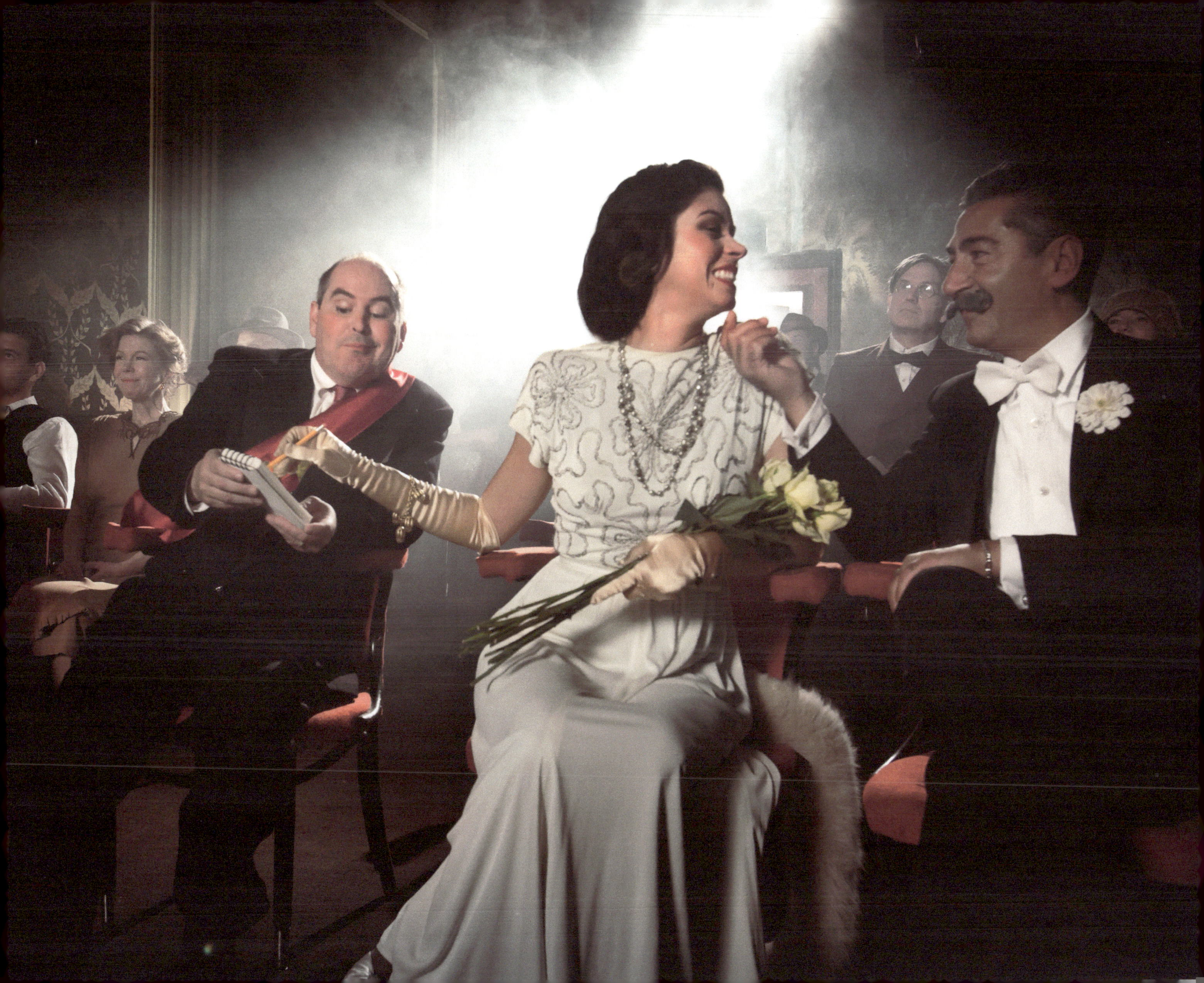

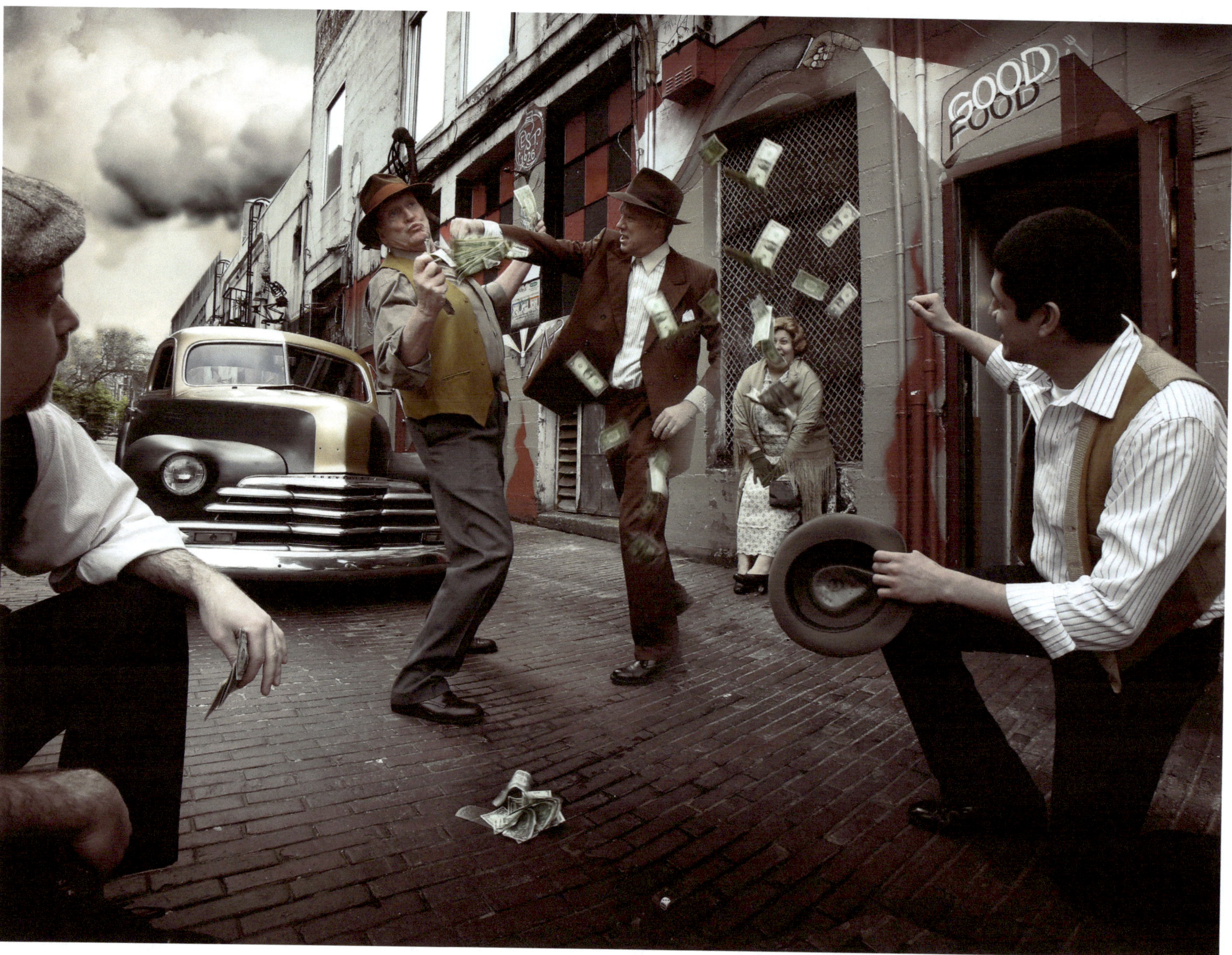

GOOD
FOOD

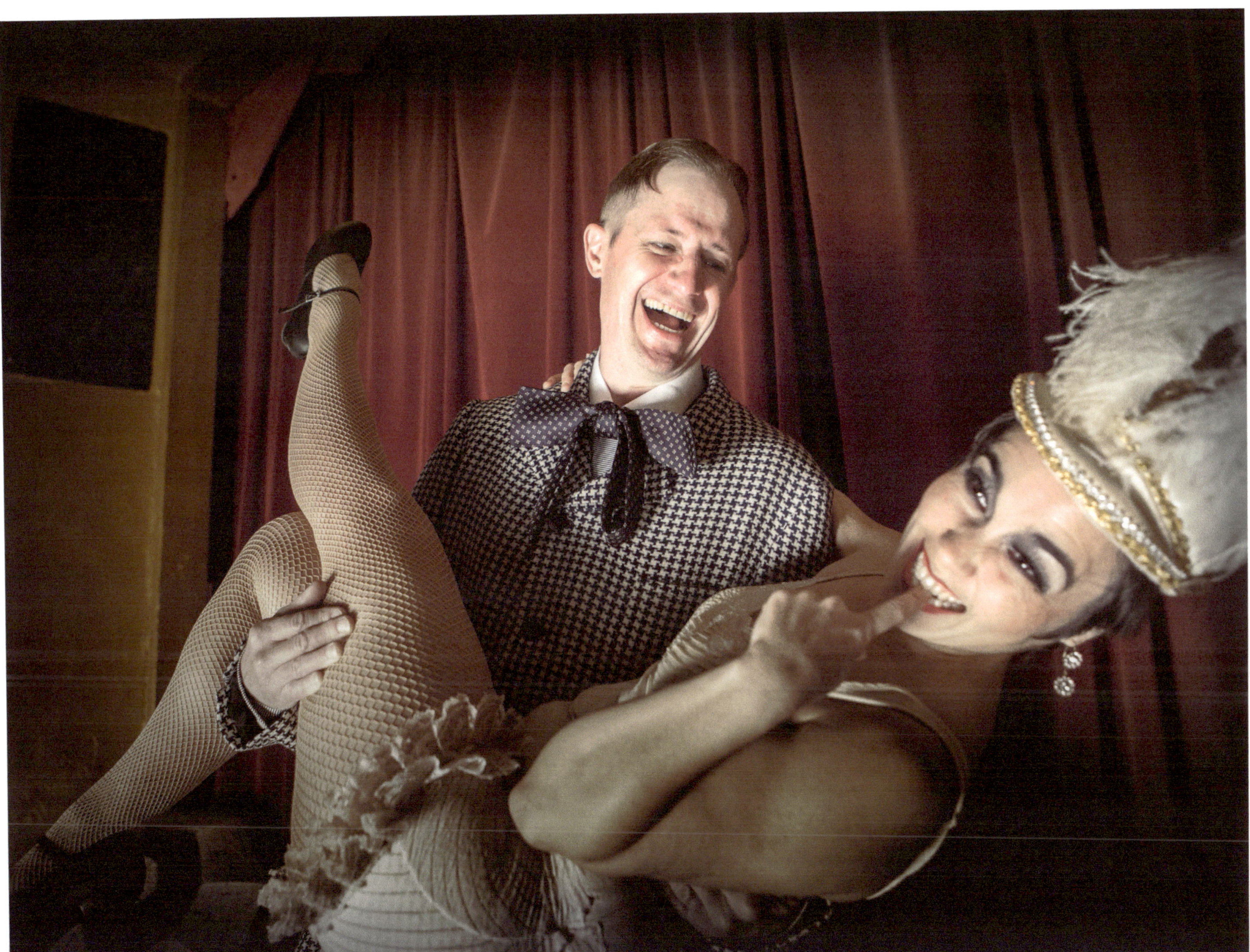

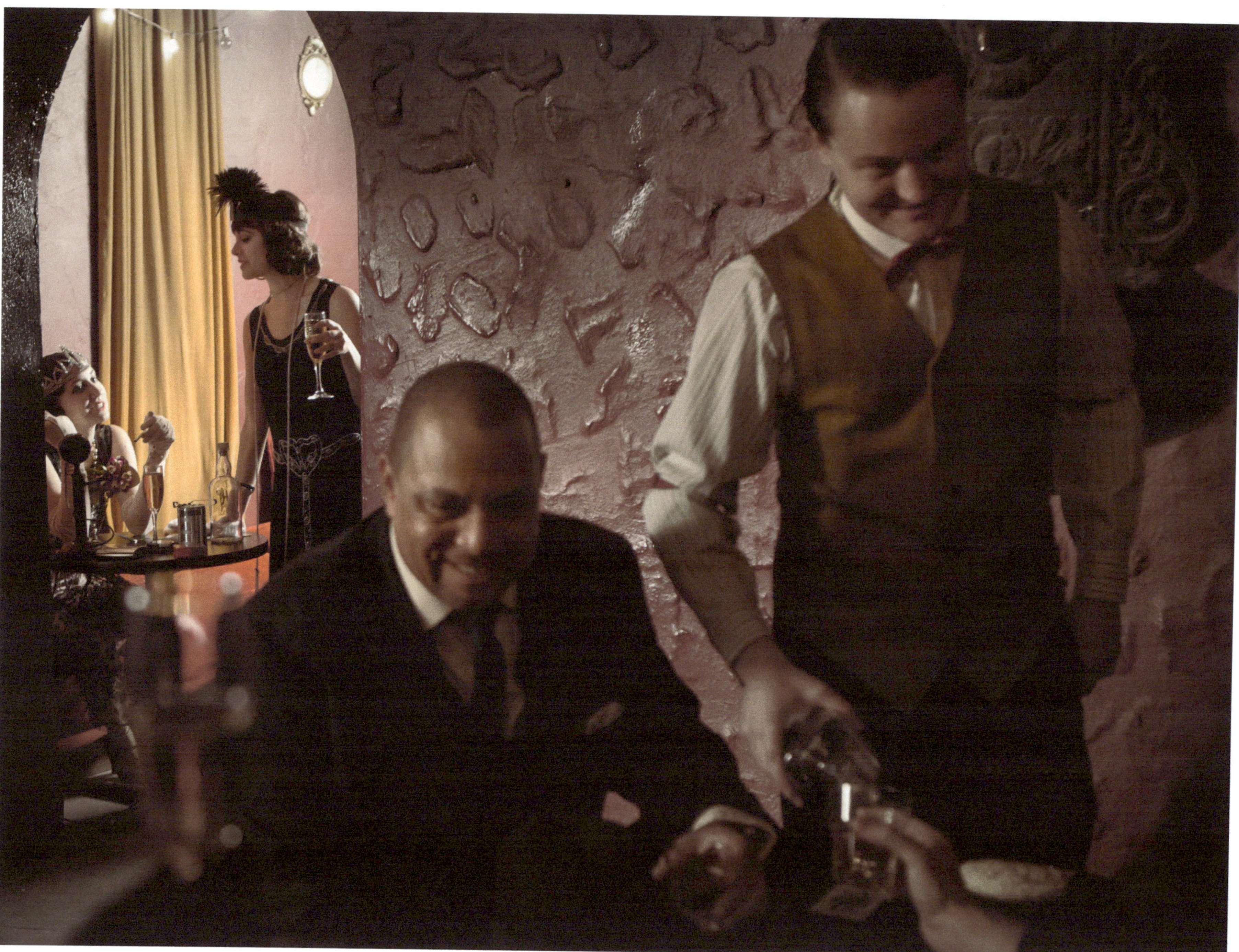

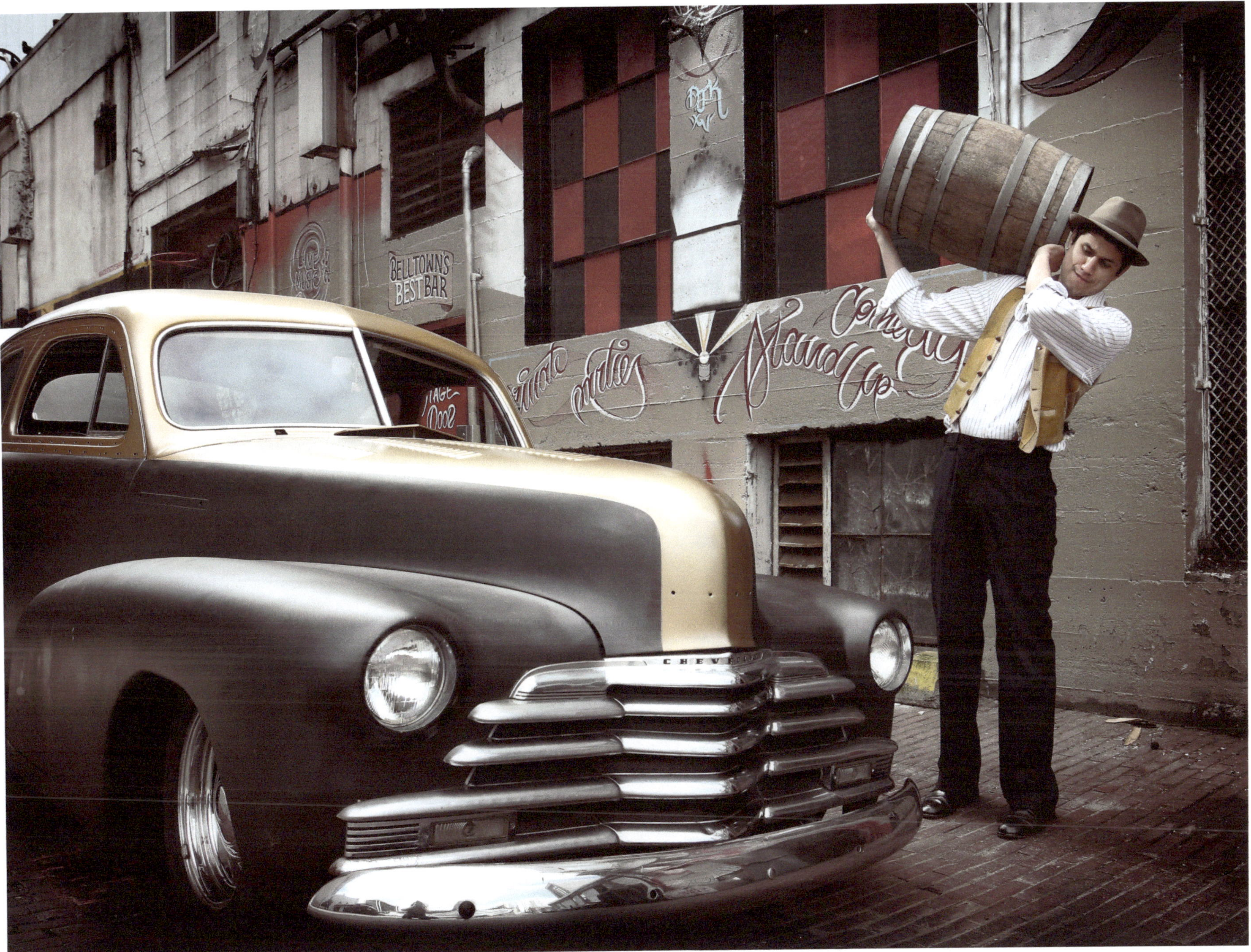

BELLTOWN'S
BEST BAR
Comedy
Stand Up
CHEV

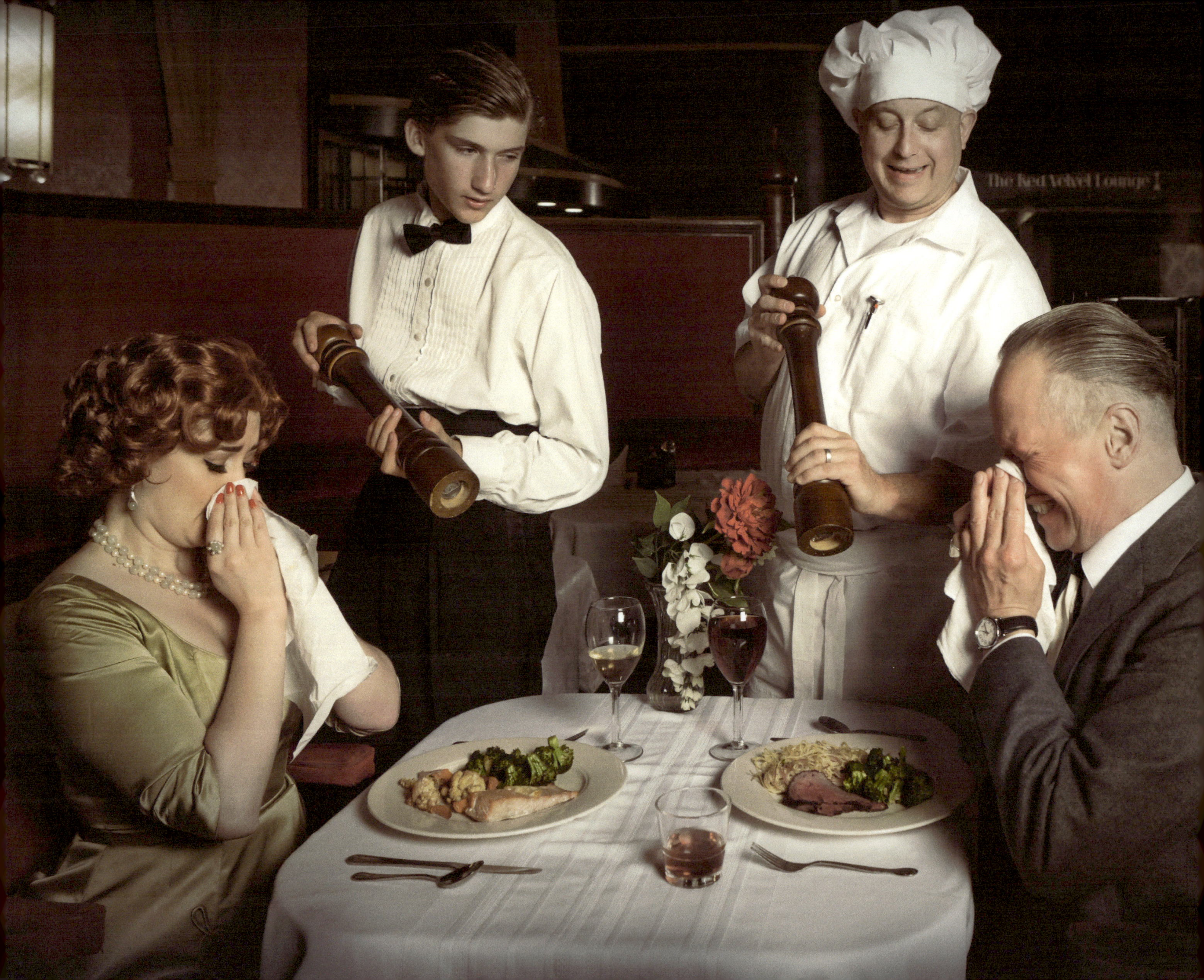
The Red Velvet Lounge

Fine Dining

Three Lies and One Truth

Saturday   July 15th

THE RENDEZVOUS CAFE

A LA CARTE

Rice Tomato Soup   .10

COCKTAILS
Fresh Crab or Shrimp .25   Crab All Legs .35
Olympia Oyster .35

ENTREES
Baked Ham, Applesauce,
     Cream Style Corn, Boiled Potato   .45
Cold Prime Ribs of Beef, Sliced Tomatoes   .35
Griddle Cakes, Maple Syrup, Melted Butter   .20
Brown Beef Stew, Vegetables, Potatoes   .35
Corned Beef Hash, Poached Egg   .25

SPECIAL SANDWICHES
Hot Dry Ham, Applesauce   .20
Hormel's Spiced Ham   .10
Hormel's Lunch Meat   .10
Thick Cheeseburger on a Bun   .20
Thin Steack on a Bun   .20

DESSERTS
Raspberry Pie .10, Apricot Pie .10,
Apple Pie .10, Pudding .10, Jello .10,
Assorted Ice Cream .10, Sundaes .15,
Fresh Fruit in Season   Iced Tea .10
Layer Cake .10, Pound Cake .10

**************   **************

.35   SPECIAL LUNCH   .35

Roll & Butter   Rice Tomato Soup
Potatoes

Brown Beef Stew
Corned Beef Hash
Assorted Cold Cuts, Potato Salad

Pudding, Jello, Vanilla or Chocolate Ice Cream
Coffee, Milk, Buttermilk
****

A.

Belltown has always been a bit of a buyer-beware neighborhood. The Trident staked its reputation on its seafood. Its menu listed seven varieties of salmon, all of which were actually cod with a bit of diluted beet juice to pink them up a bit

B.

The Vous, as the Rendezvous was affectionately called, was one of the swankiest restaurants in Seattle in the Forties and Fifties. There was even a gossip columnist (sort of a poor person's Hedda Hopper) who wrote about "lunching at the Vous" and gave readers all the inside dirt on who was lunching with whom!

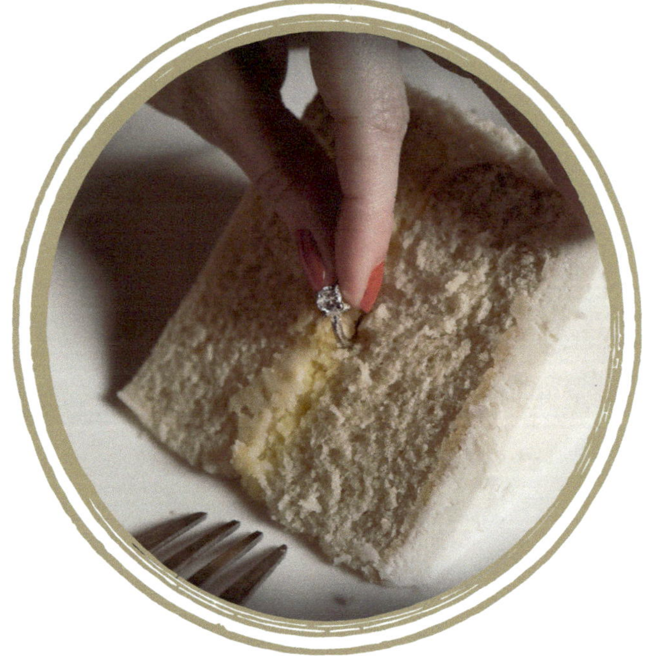

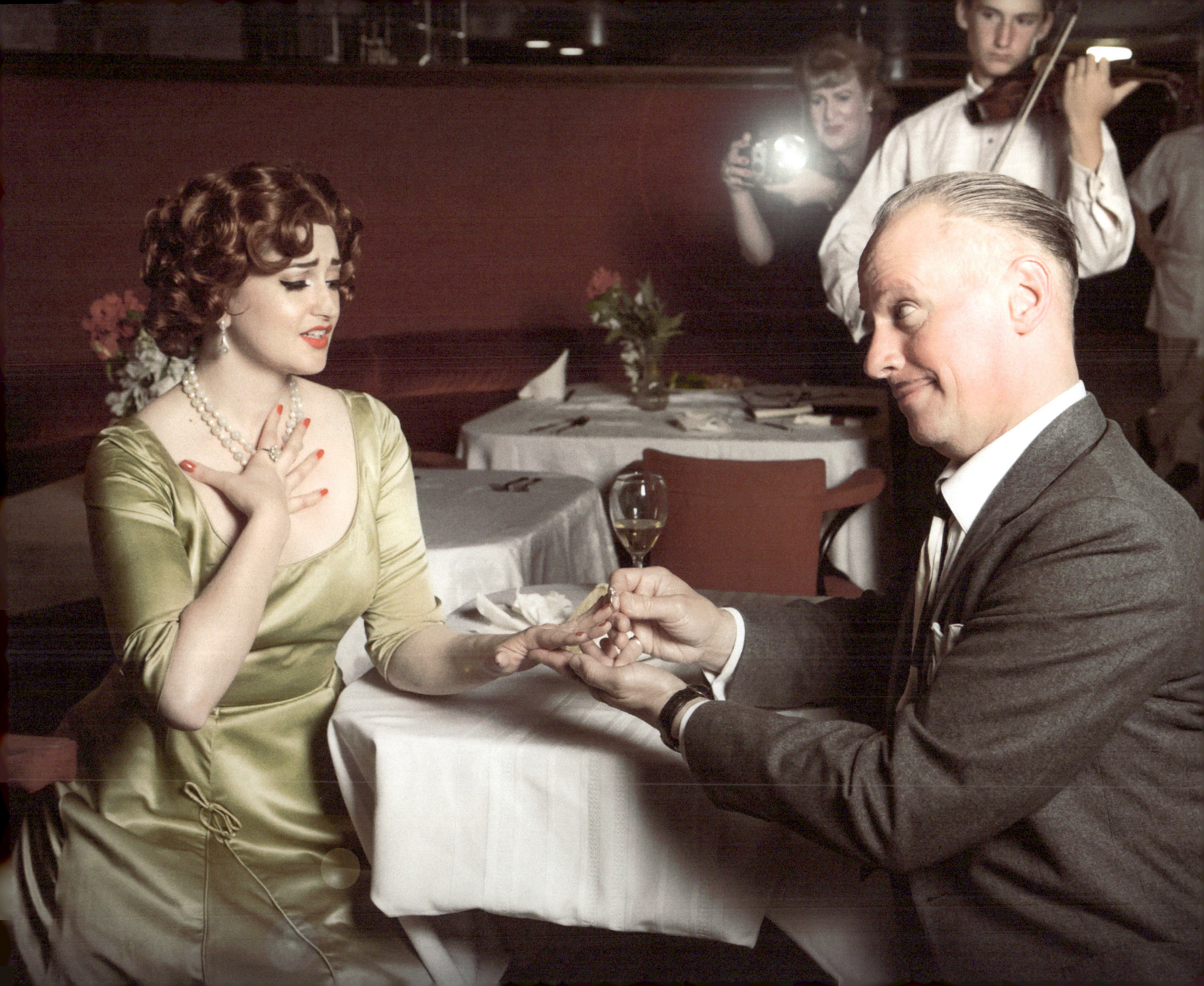

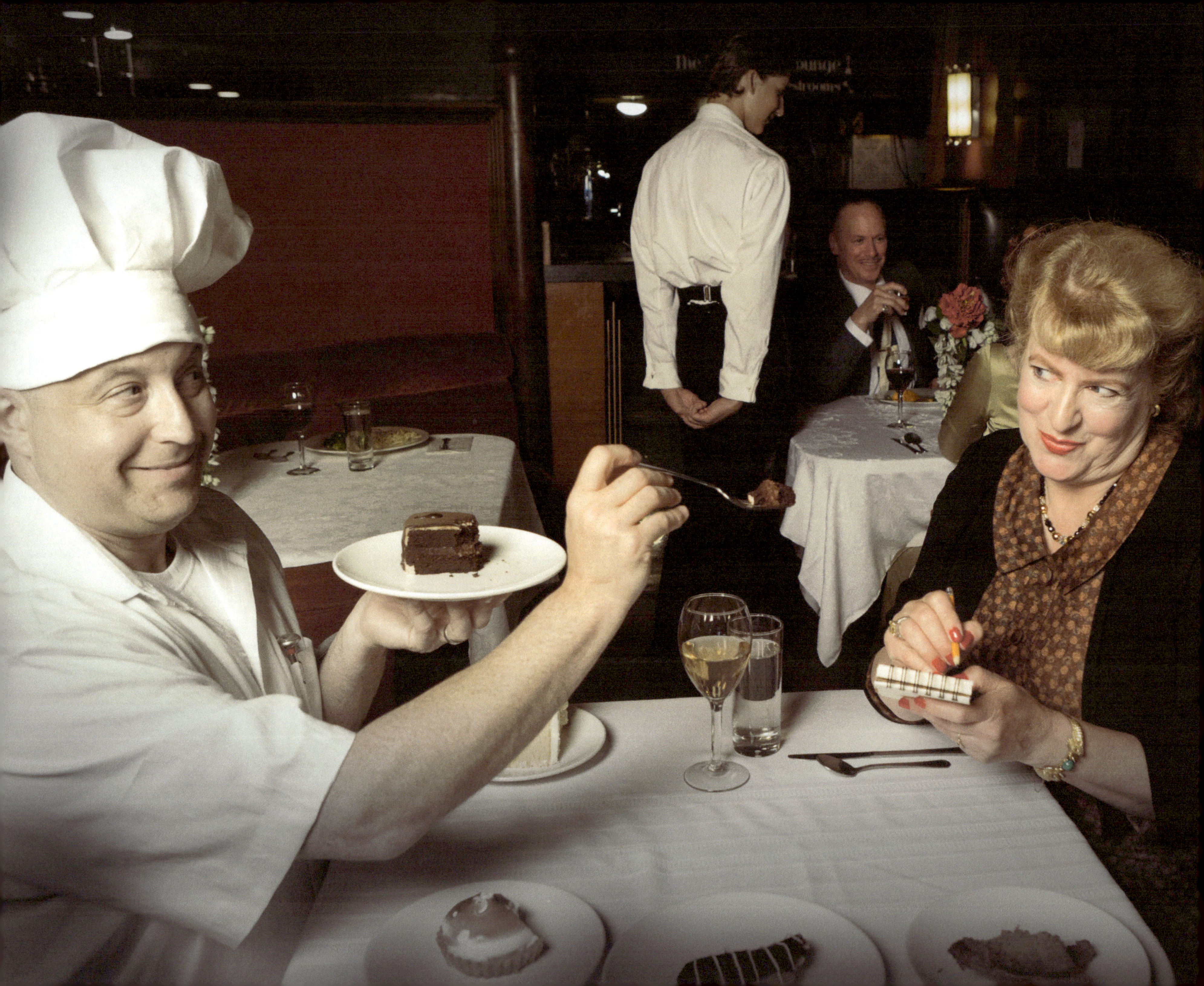

C.

Back in the Thirties, a Seattle health inspector's official wages were quite paltry. However, the bribes they took made them among the highest-paid public servants in the city. They were often seen driving new cars and wearing very nice suits.

D.

Eateries in Seattle have always been eager to cash in on the occasional economic booms that hit the region. Just before the crash of '29 a wave of fancy restaurants tried to capitalize on the river of cash flowing through town. One greasy silver spoon advertised that they had recruited a chef named Alfonse D'orge from Galaufex, France. Only problem was, there is no such town and the chef's real name was Al Dorgman.

3 *are lies* & 1 *is true.*
Can you tell the difference?

[ANSWER KEY ON PAGE 86]

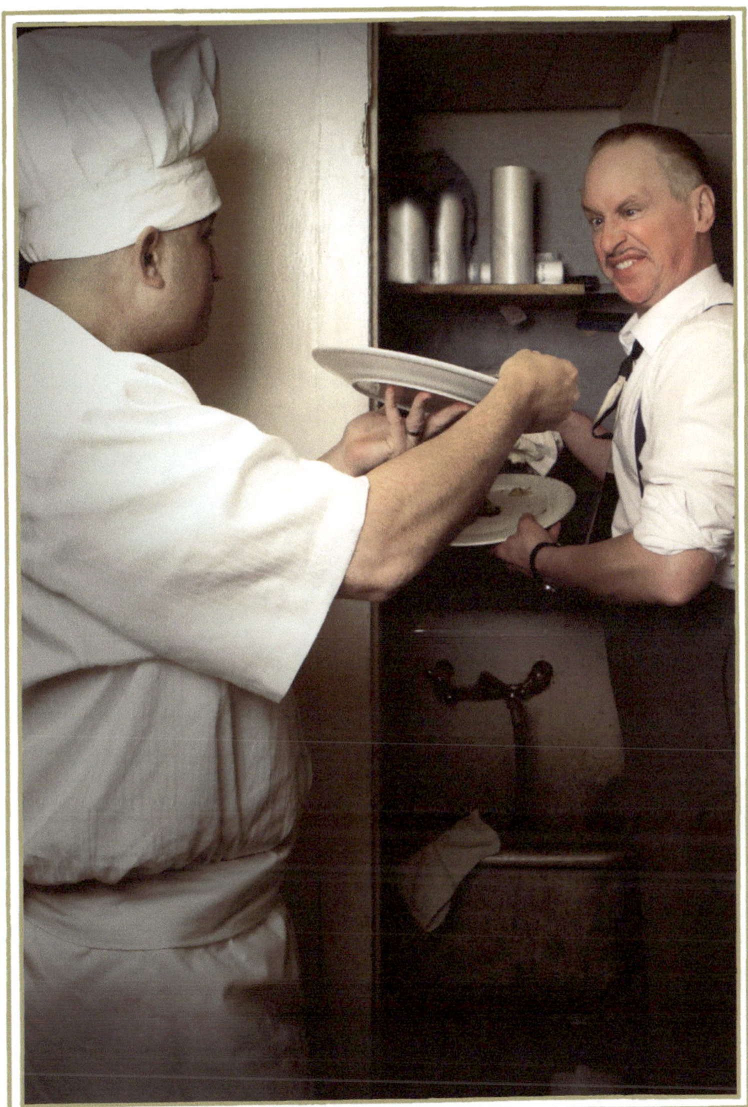

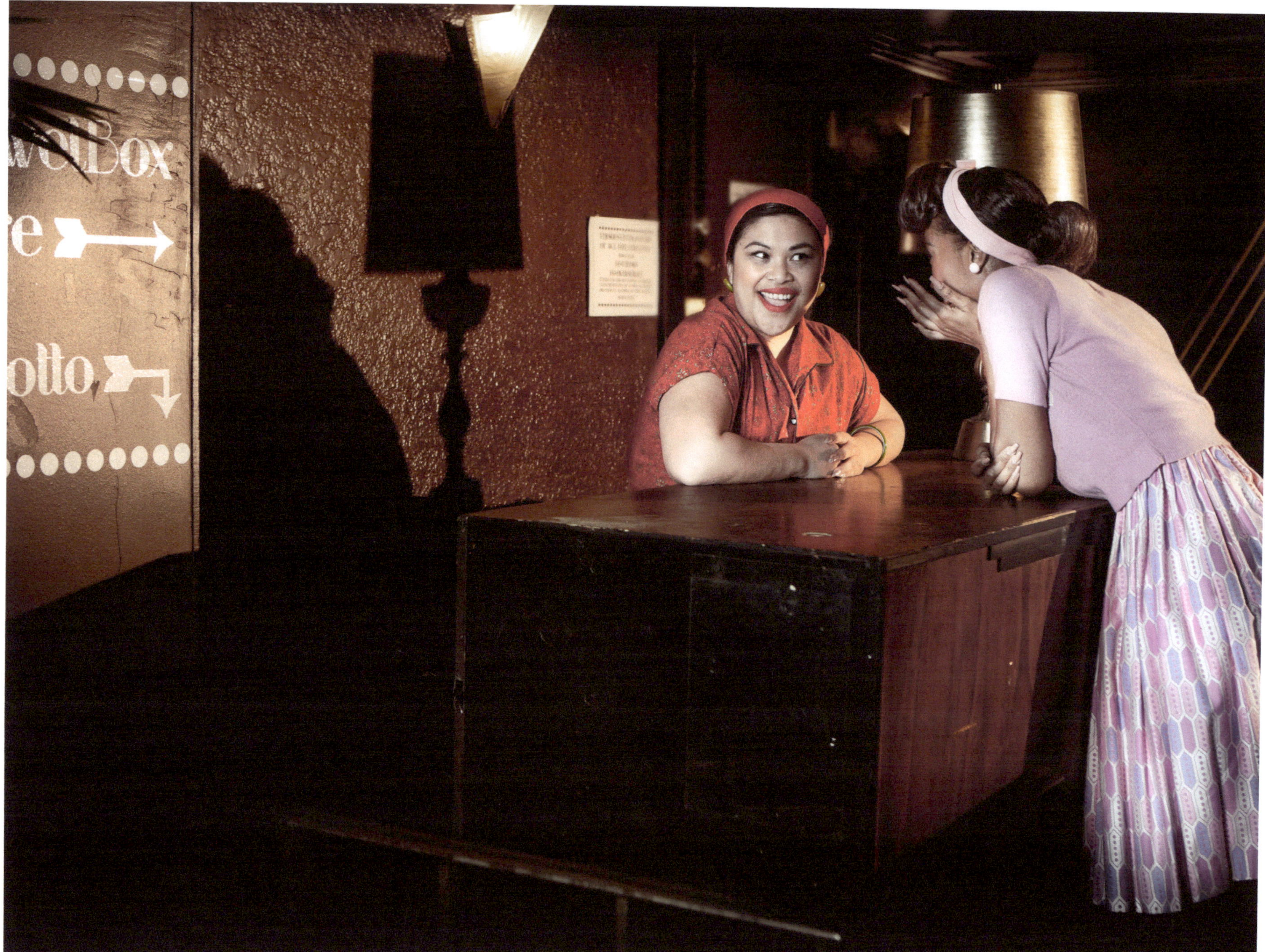
wellBox
re →
otto →

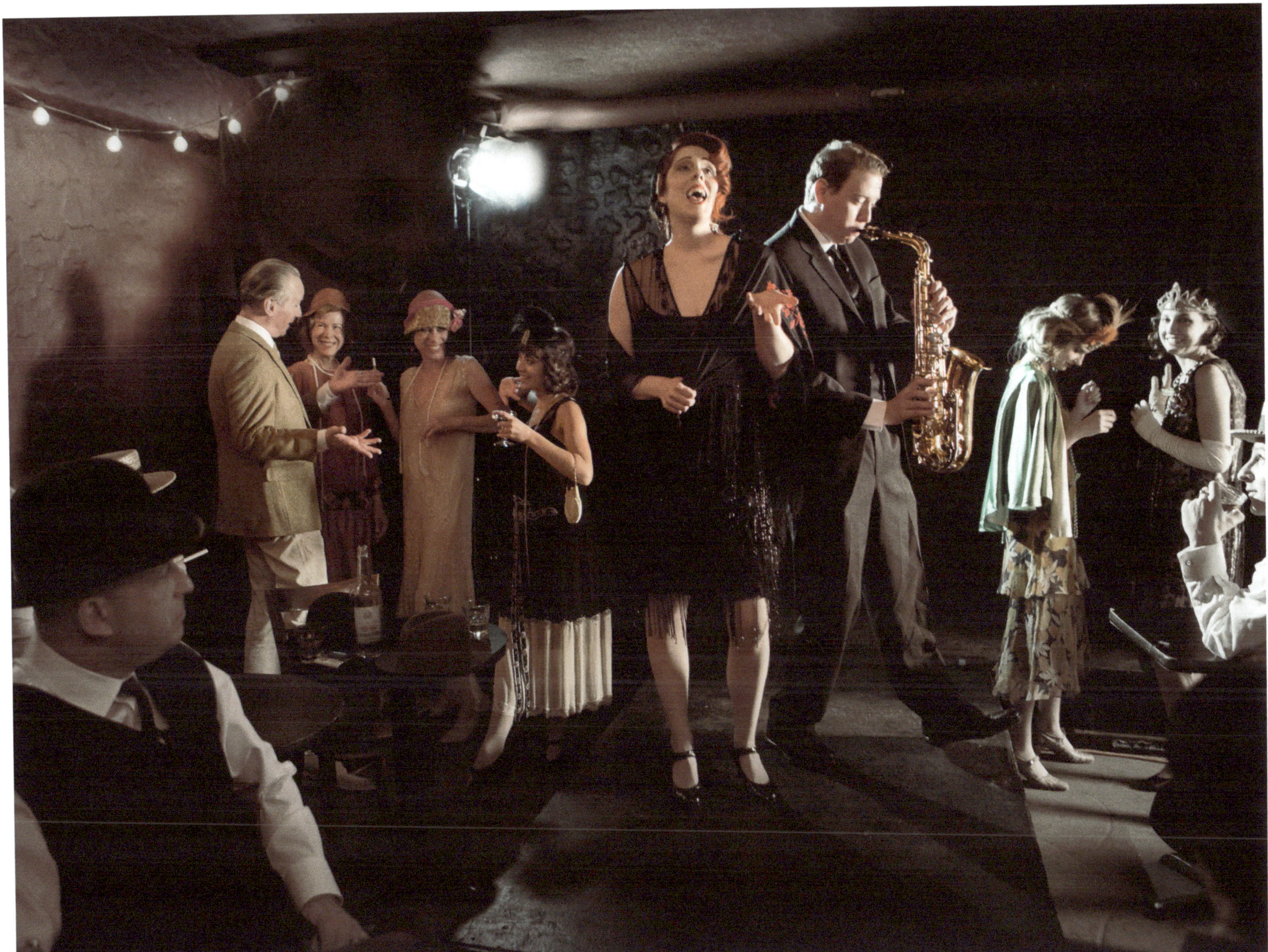

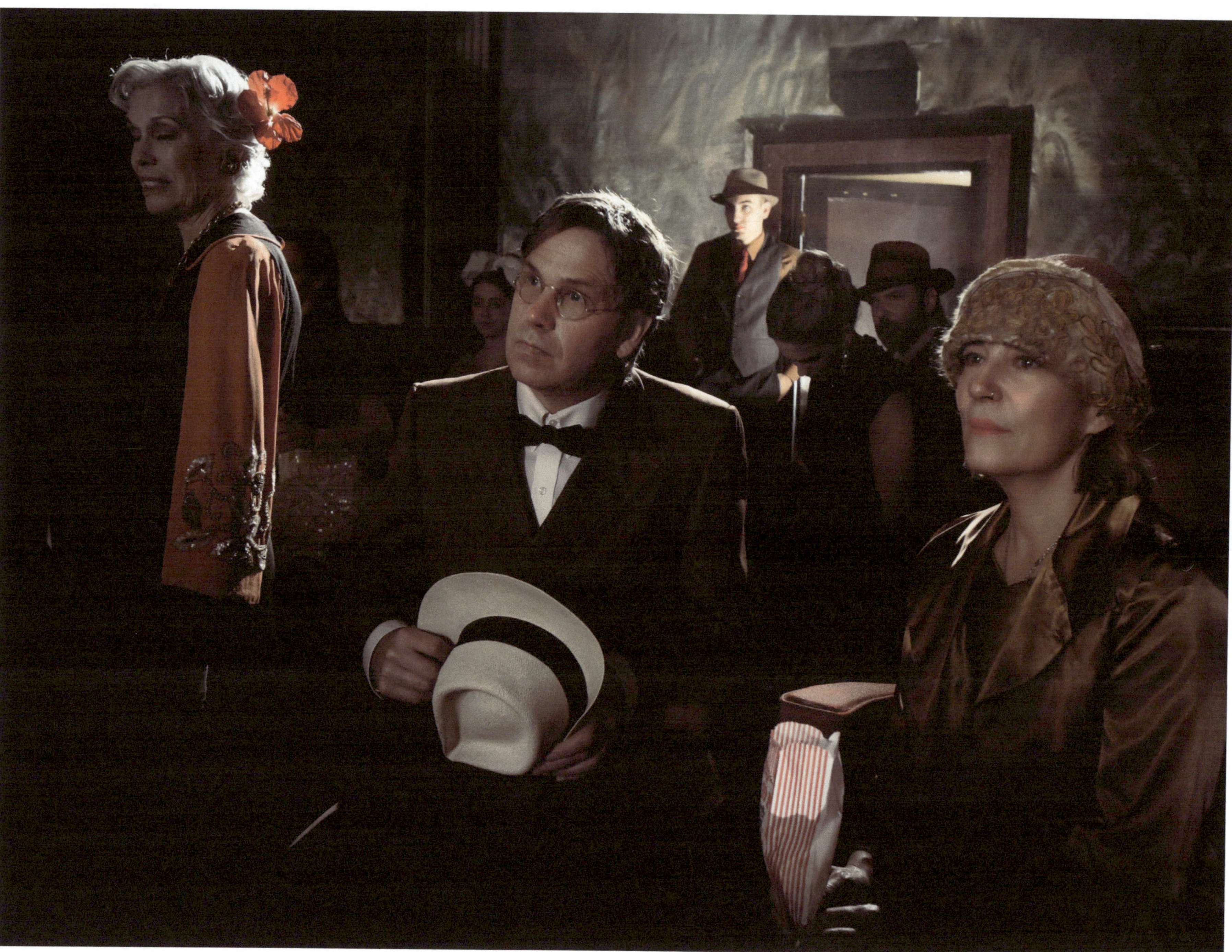

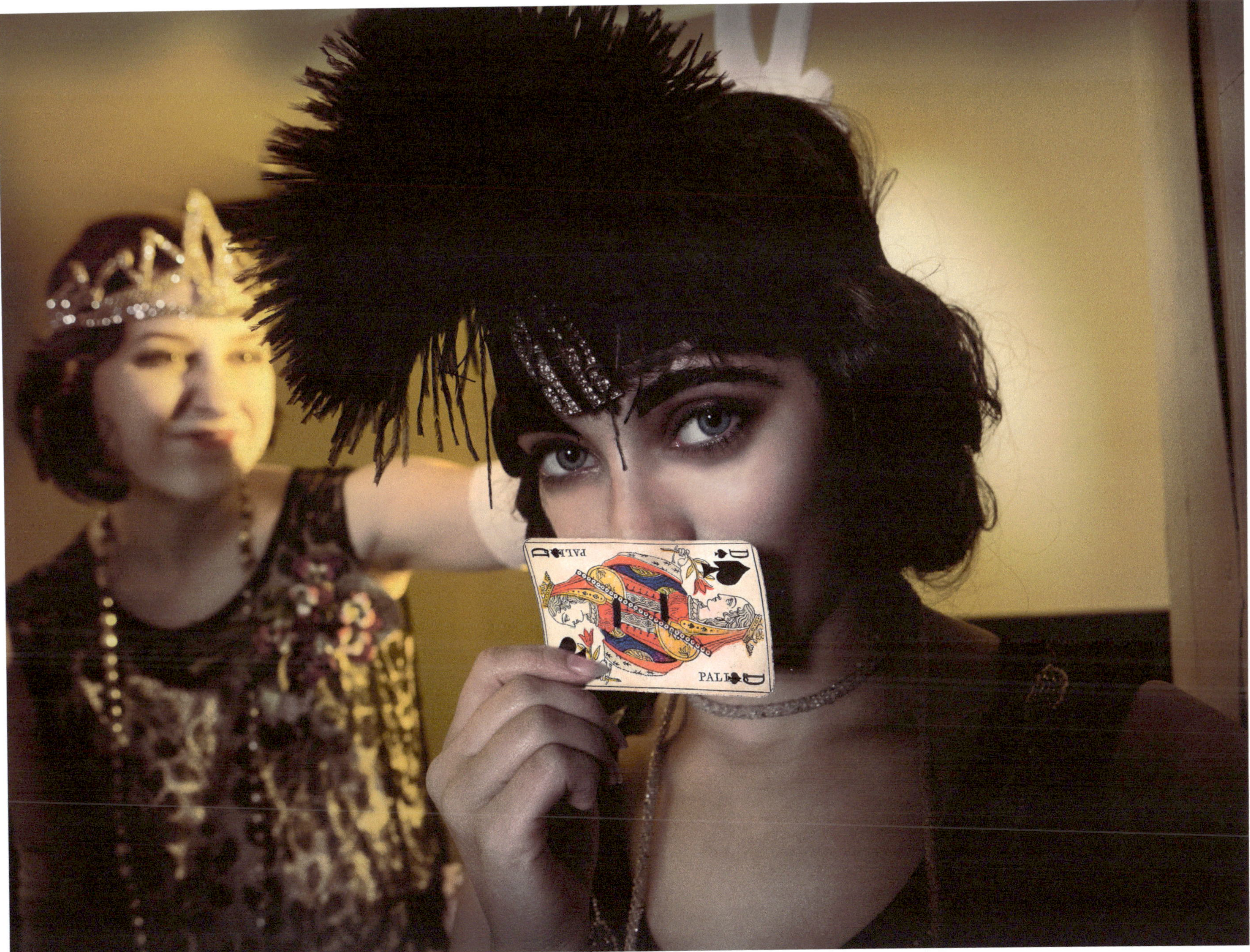

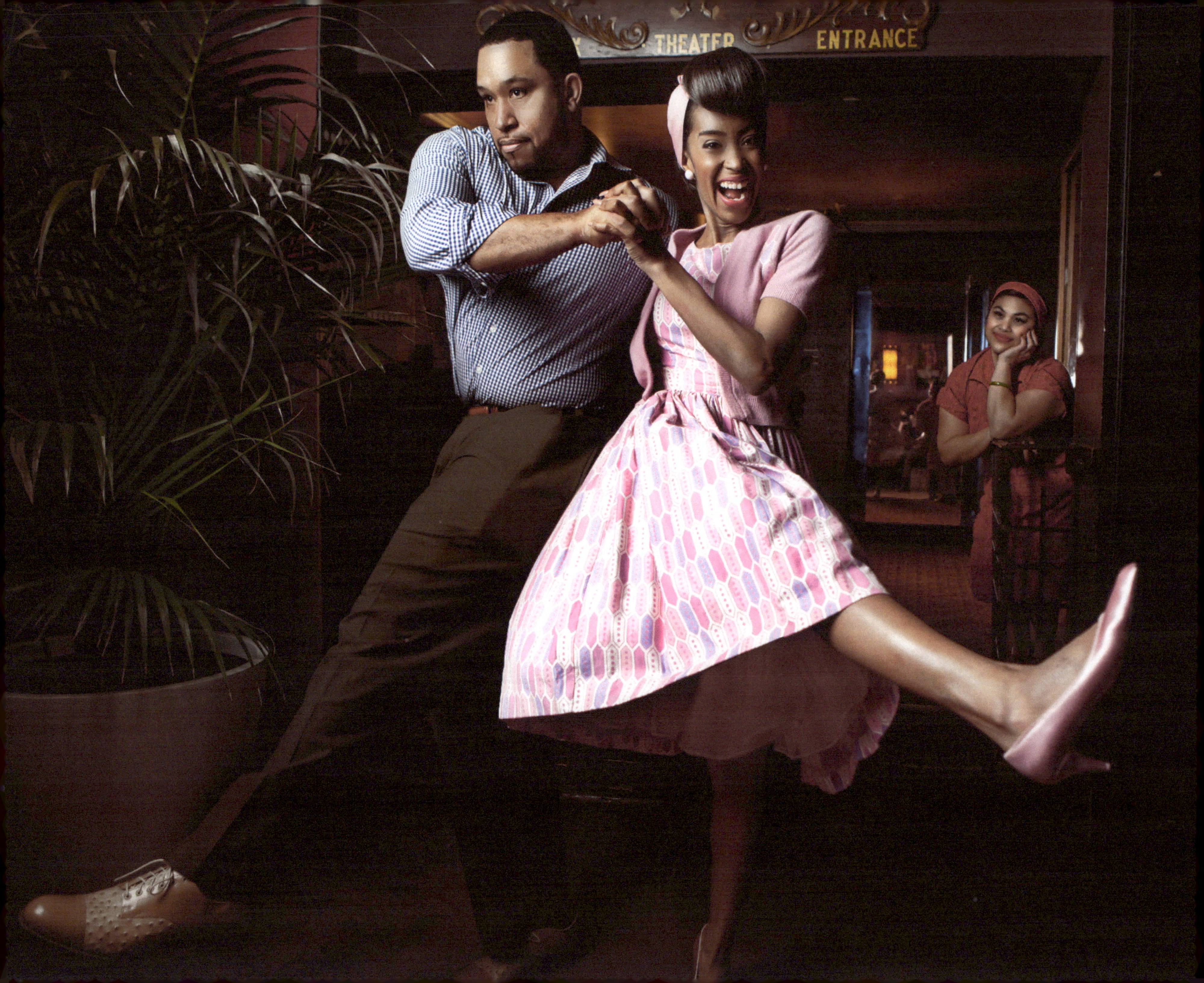

THEATER   ENTRANCE

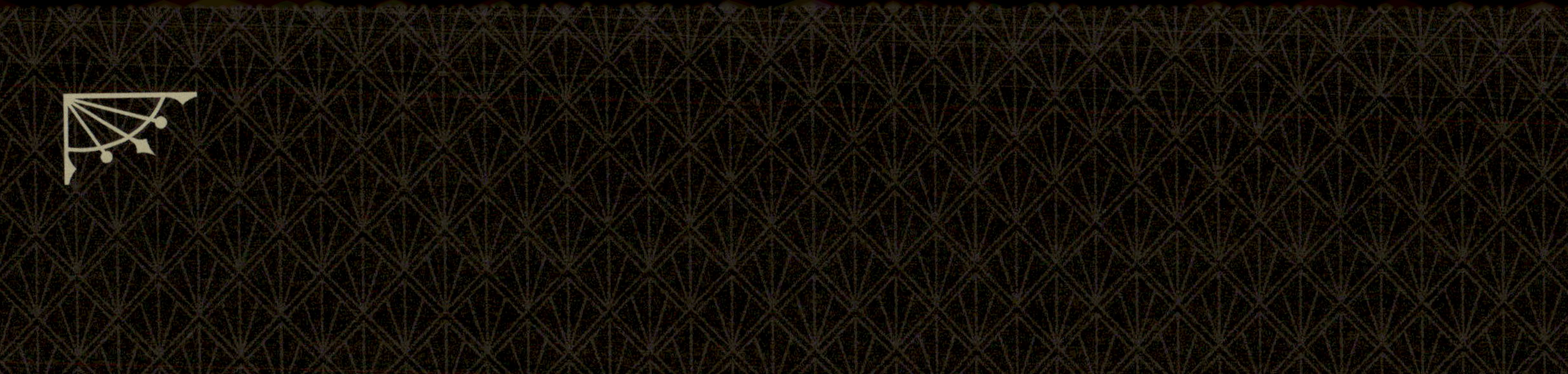

The Fight for Civil Rights

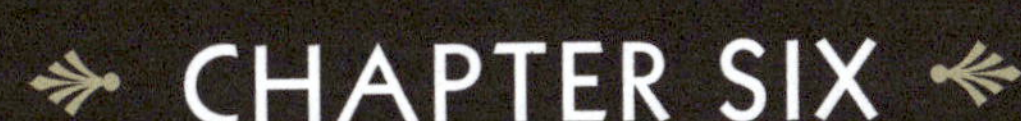

Two Truths and a Lie

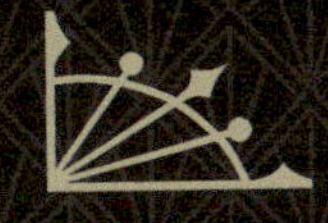
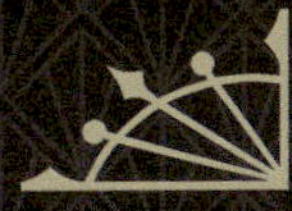

A.

Merceedees Walton was a dynamic singer and all-around entertainer from Chicago who settled in Seattle after World War II. She took the city by storm with her rousing concerts and stunning good looks. In the early fifties, Seattle had two separate (but not equal) unions for musicians. Merceedees belong to AFM Local 493, the union for Musicians of color. As things (slooooowly) changed in Seattle and the hints of what would become the Civil Rights Movement began to appear, Merceedees was there leading the way. She had her own popular local TV and radio shows and in 1953 decided to run for City Council, telling local papers, "If elected, I would like to help in every way to make Seattle a better city. I am interested in my race and feel we should have representation on the City Council." She eventually pulled out of the race for unknown reasons.

B.

On the morning of March 29, 1968, an African American student at Belltown High School (closed down in the early 1970s) called the Black Student Union at the University of Washington for help. The student said two young girls wearing Afros had been sent home to straighten their hair. The African American students were pissed off! The members of the Black Student Union soon met the students, organized a protest, and stormed the principal's office. The principal was seen running down the hall to make his escape.

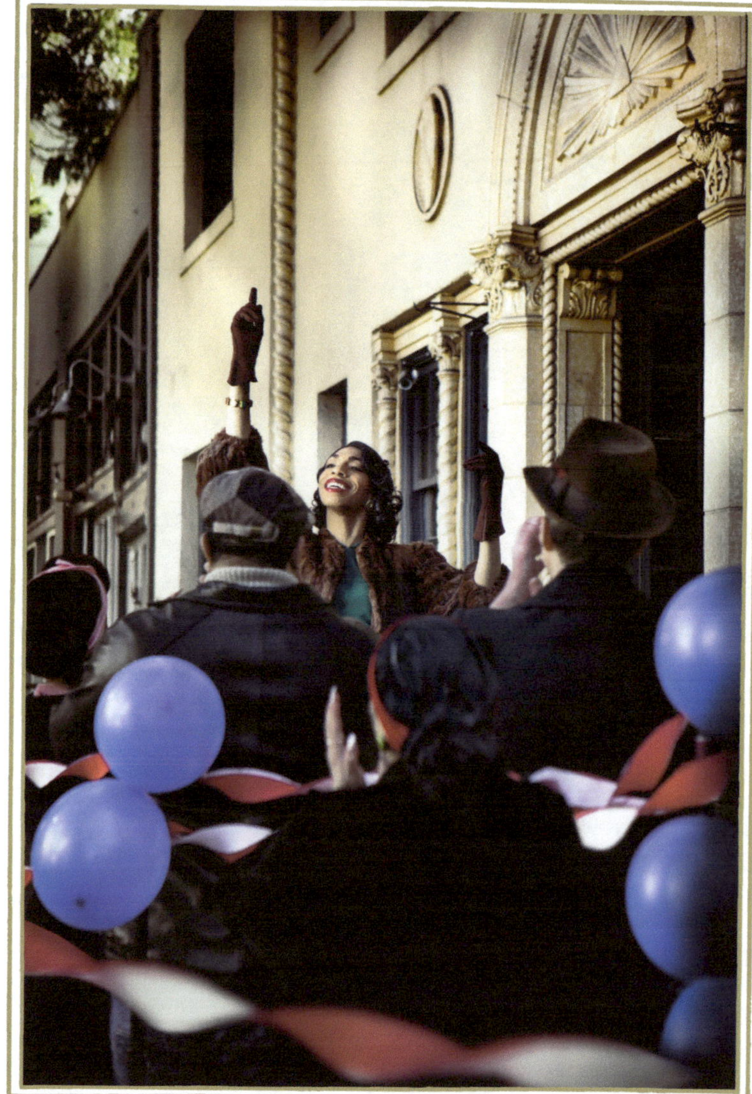

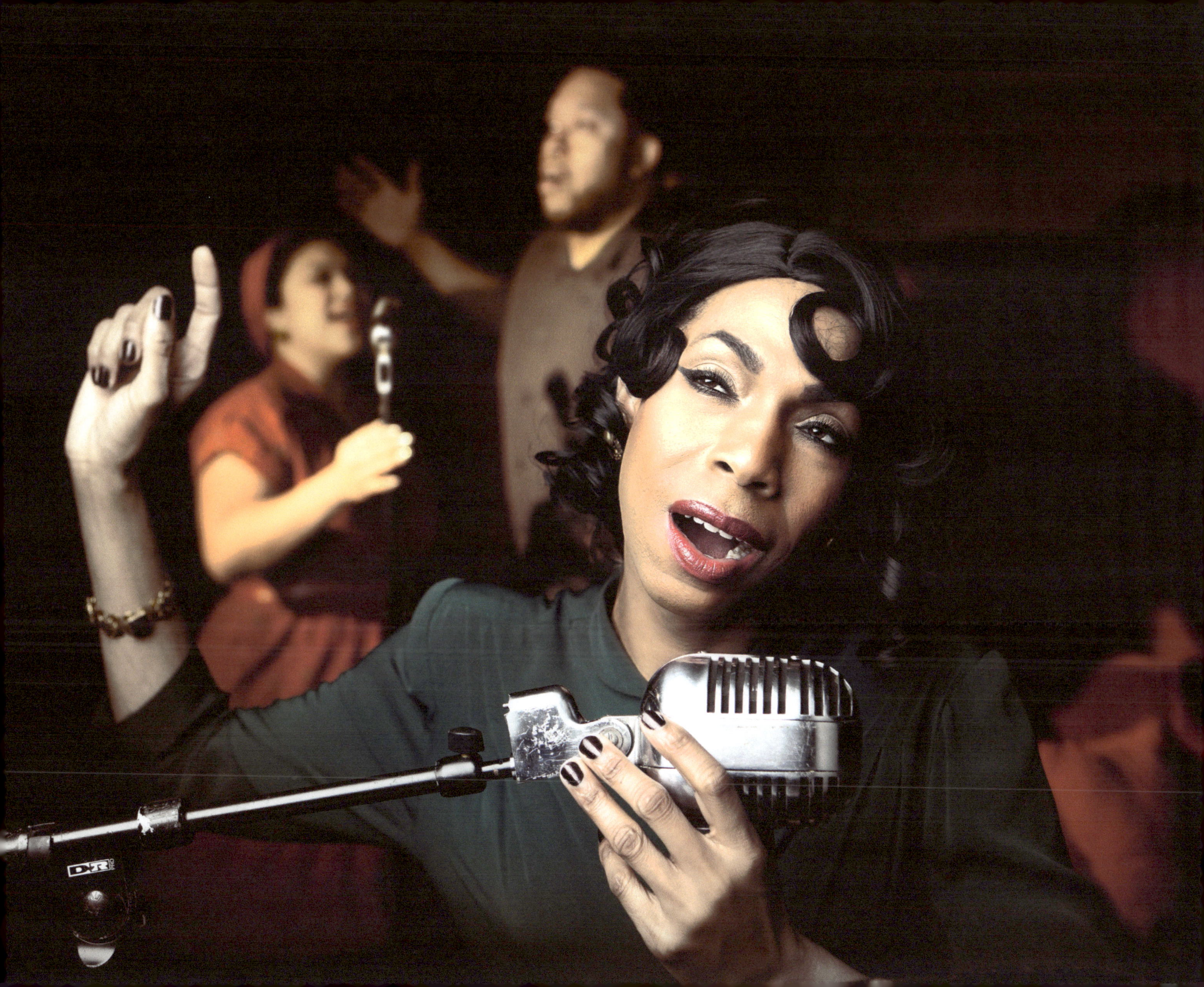

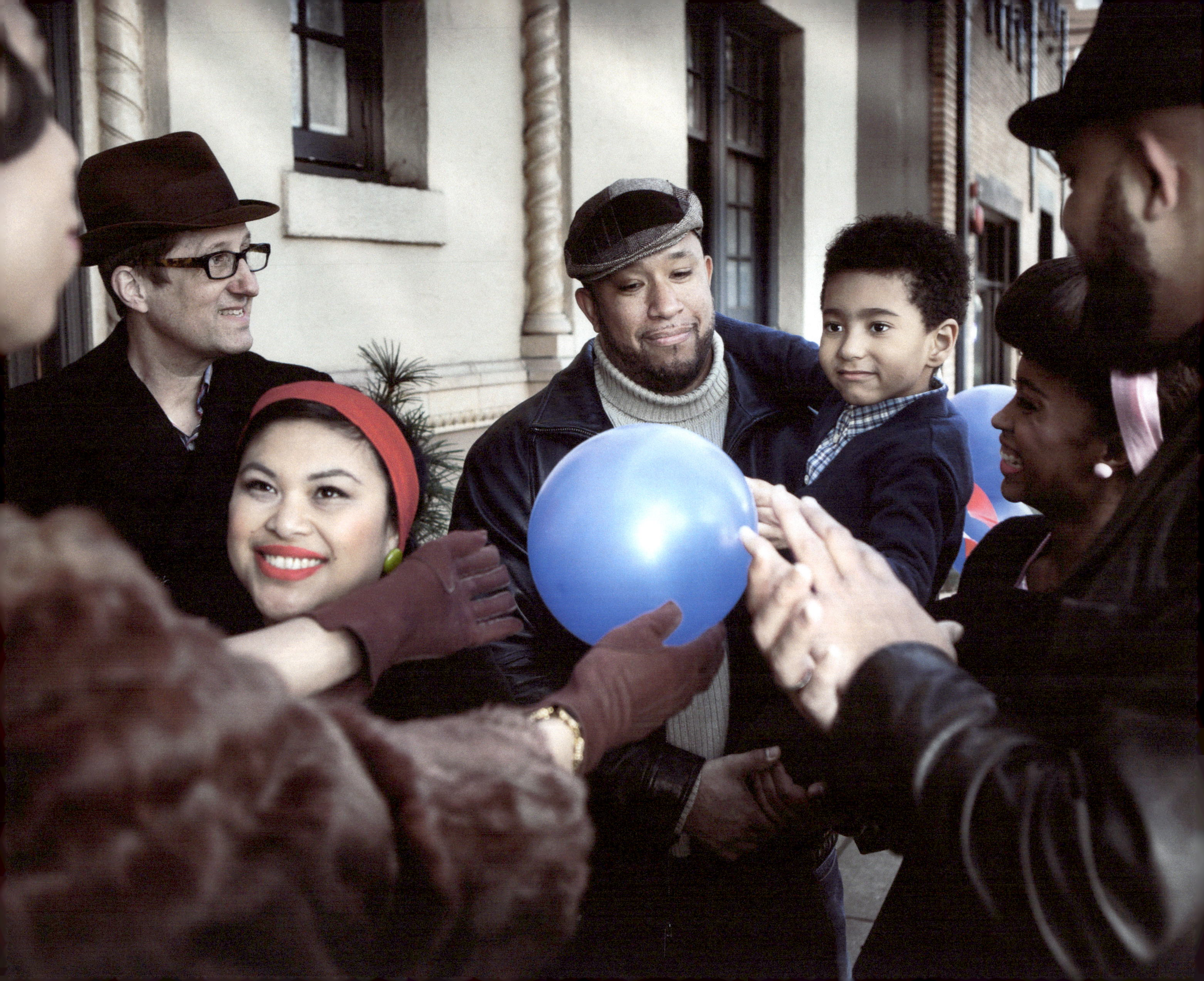

C.

The Civil Rights Movement could not come to Belltown soon enough. The neighborhood suffered deep prejudice roots dating back to the mid-nineteenth century. In the 1920s, the Ku Klux Klan even had its local headquarters here. One of their leaders, Major Luther I. Powell, adopted the title "King Kleagle." Damn! Those racists loved the letter K. Their newspaper's motto was "The Klan, The Konstitution and the Kross Shall Be Our Faith, Our Hope, Our Law, Our Creed of Liberty." It's a mystery as to why Creed got to keep its C. Turns out, Powell was hated everywhere he went. When he spent time in Canada (Not Kanada), the Vancouver chapter expelled him, and Victoria asked the local authorities to deport him.

TWO *are true.*
Which one is a **LIE**?

[ANSWER KEY ON PAGE 86]

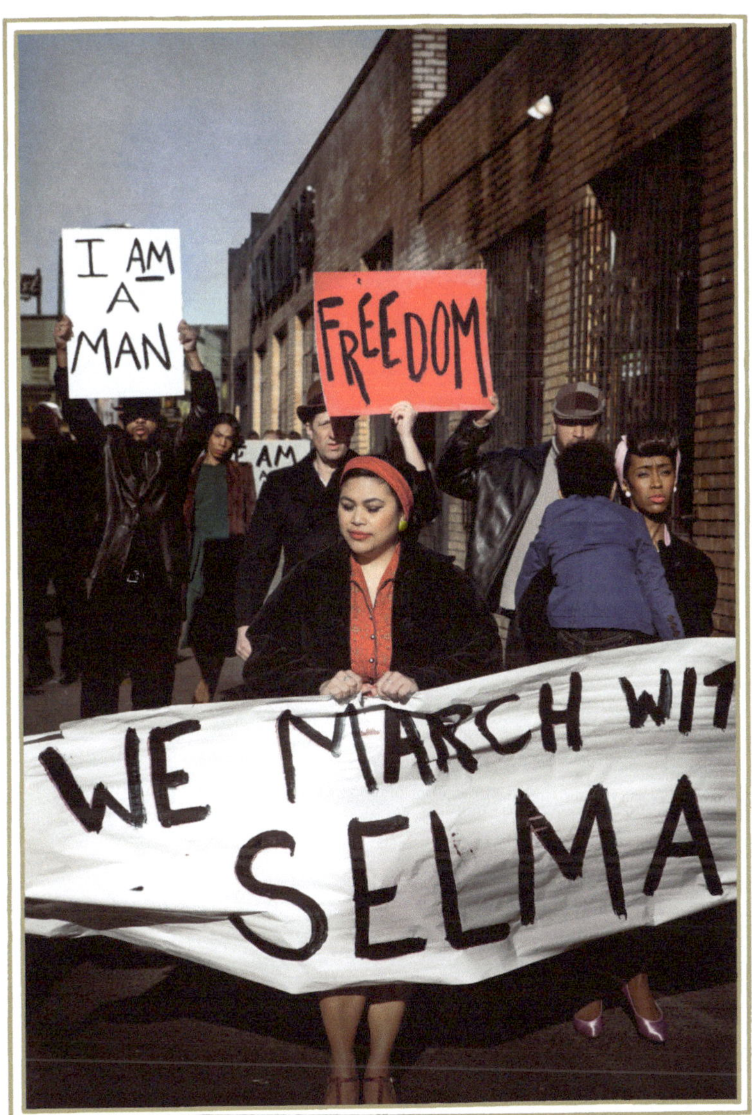

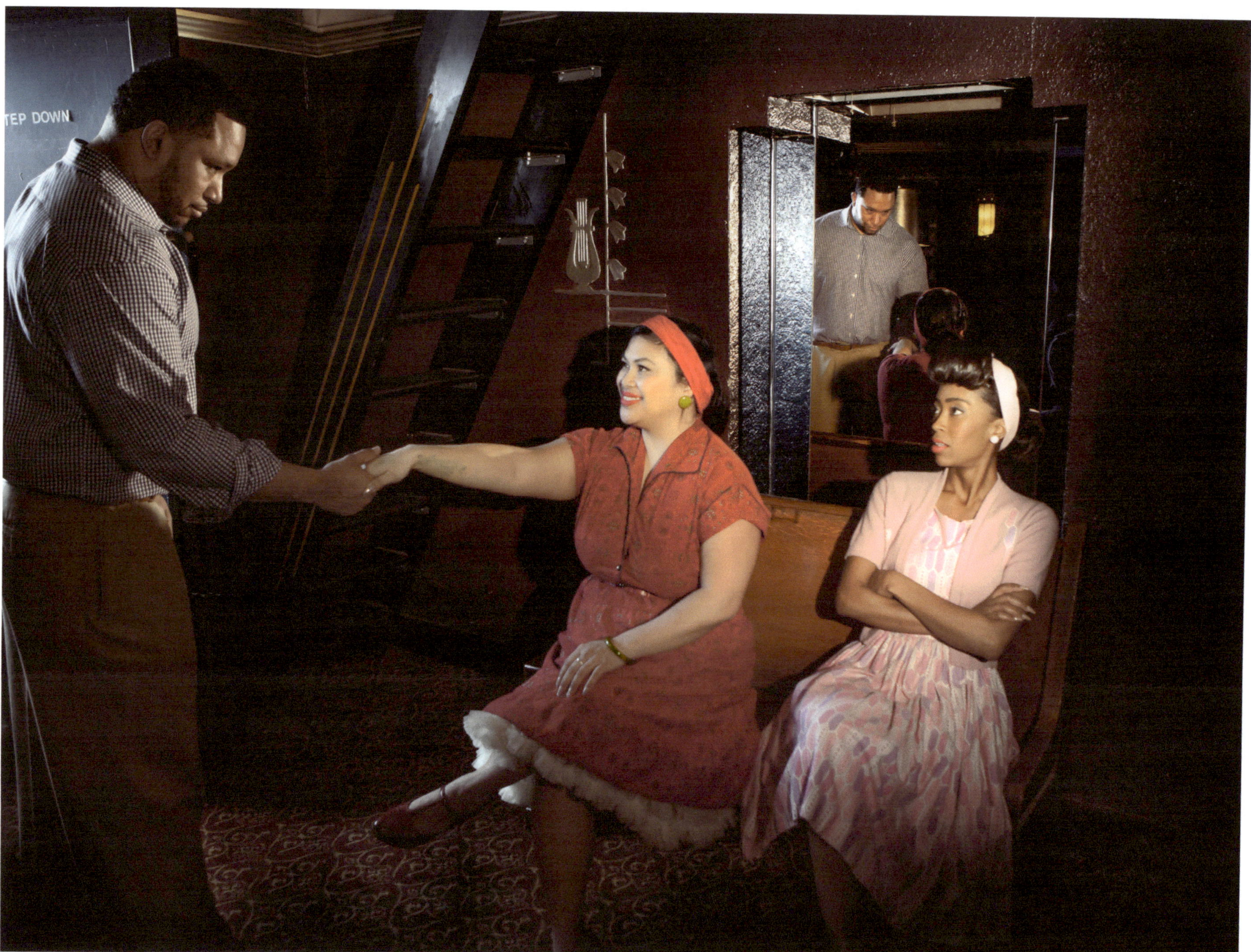

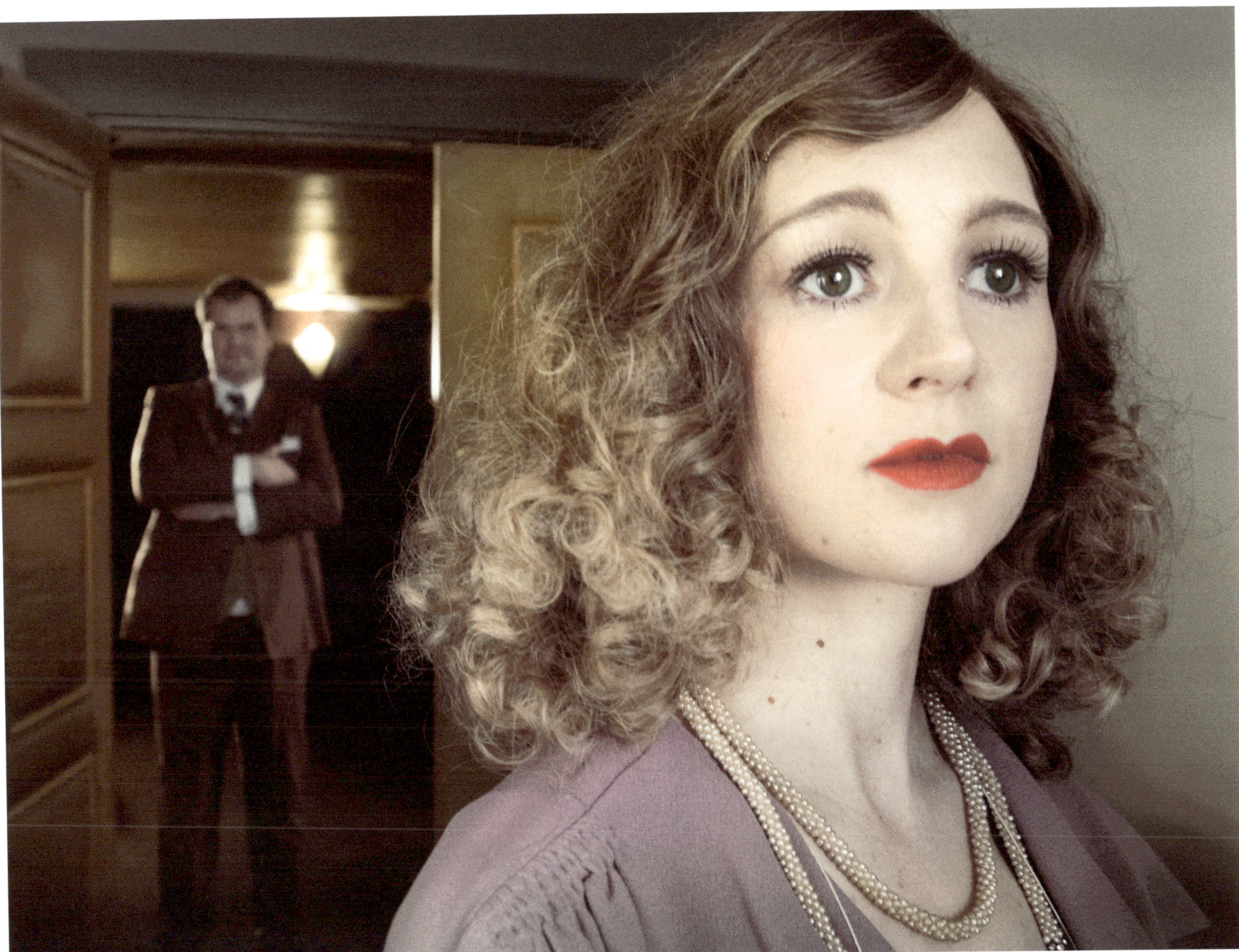

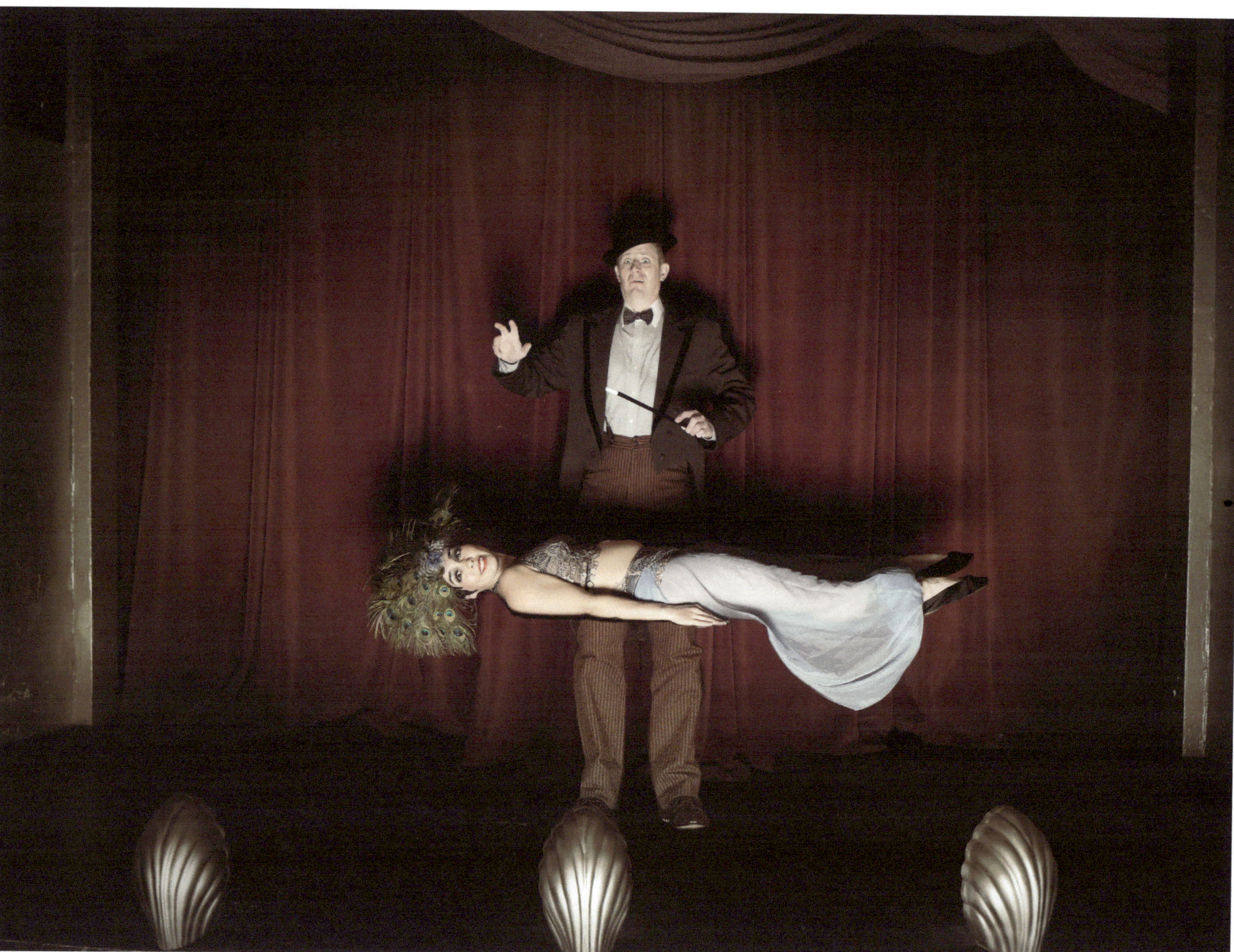

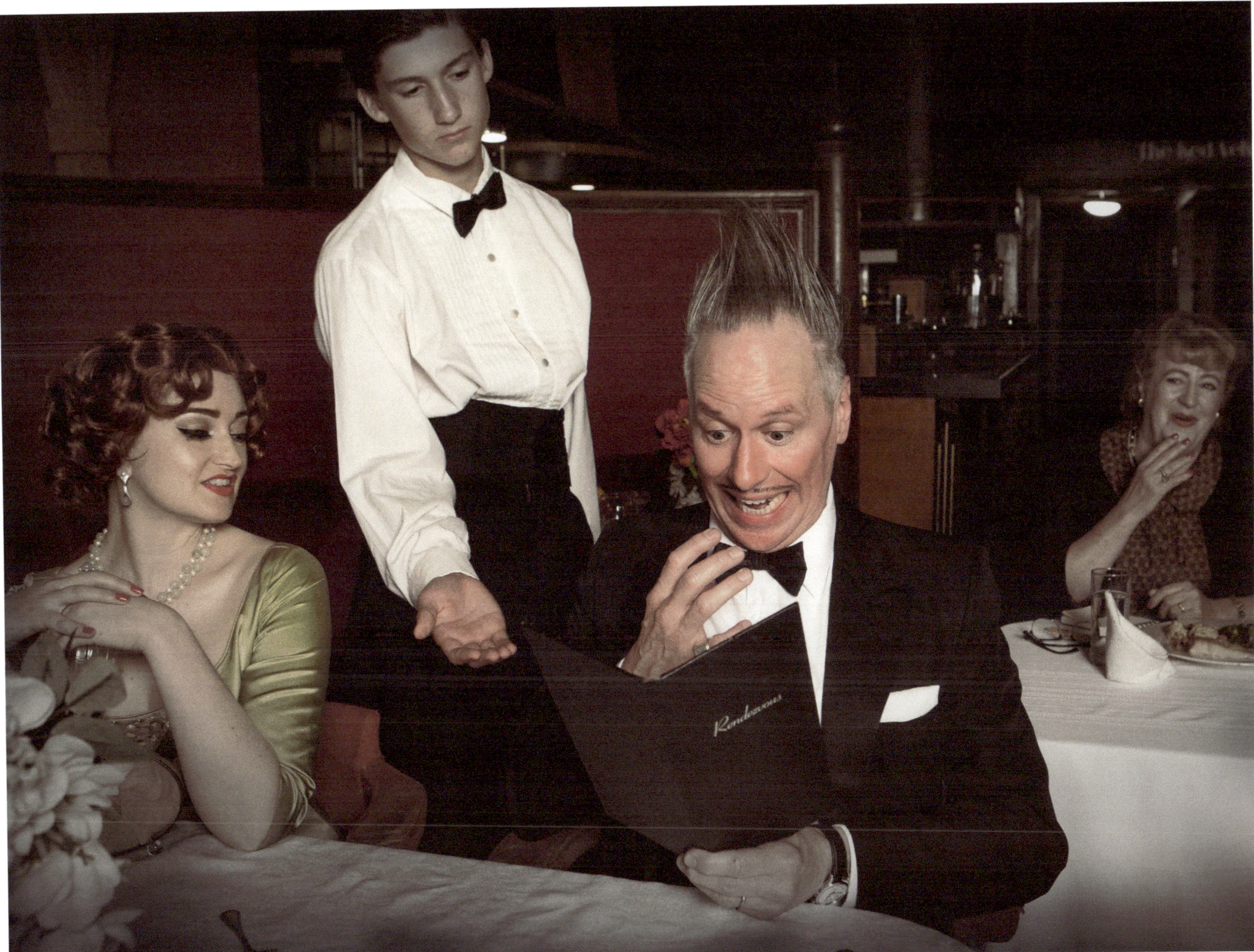
Rendezvous

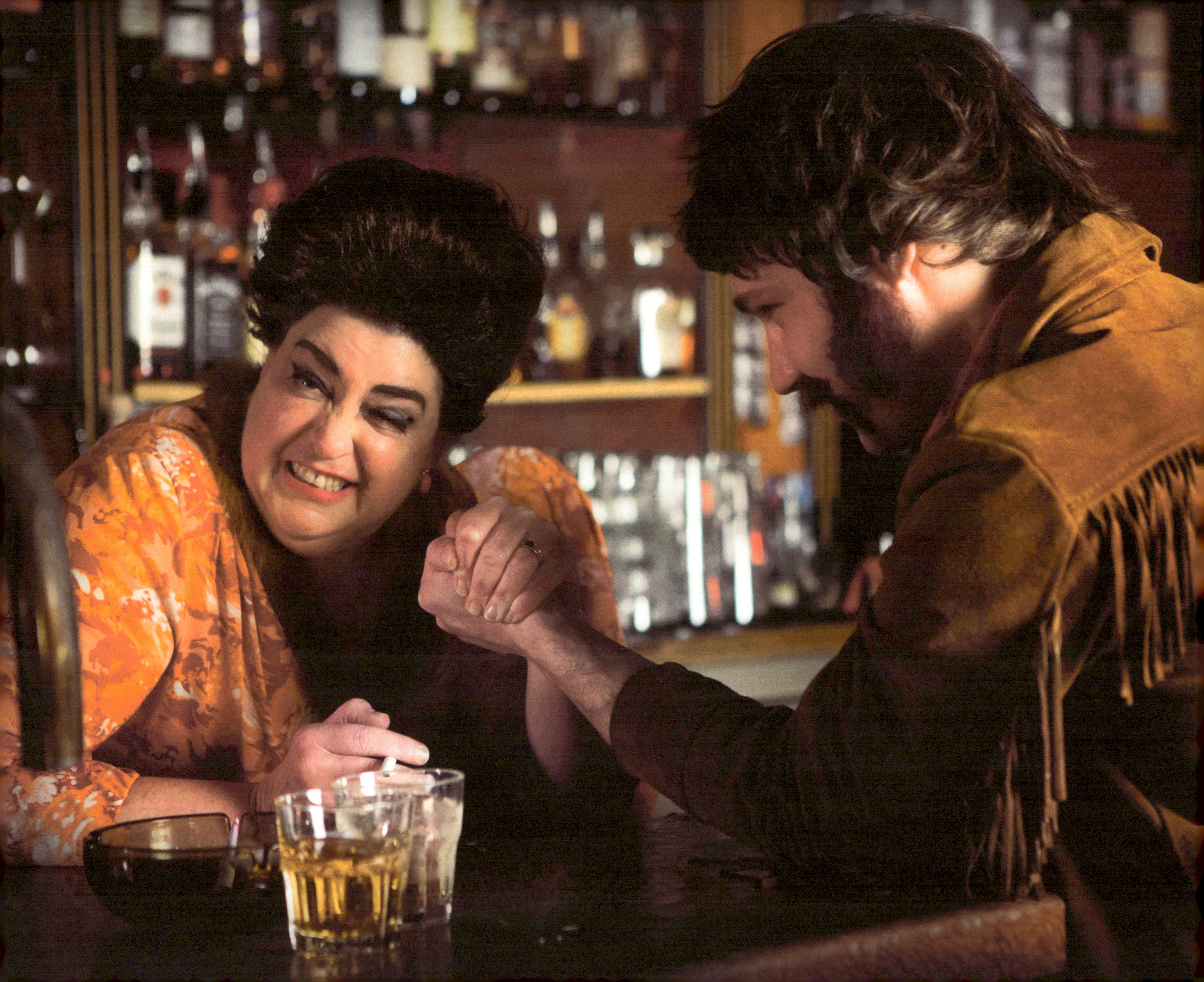

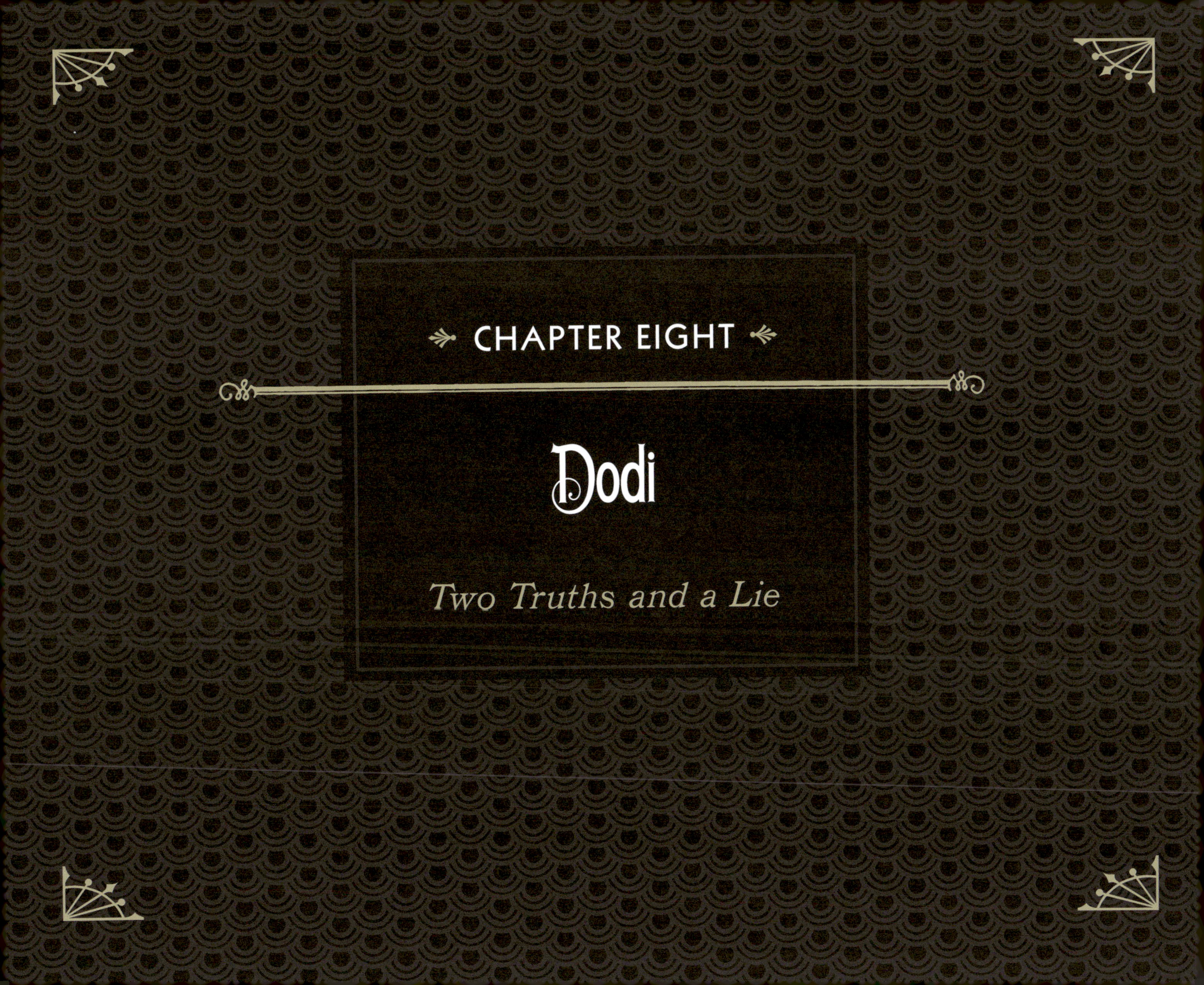
CHAPTER EIGHT
Dodi
Two Truths and a Lie

A.

Before becoming a bartender at the Rendezvous, Dodi drove Chain Demo Derby cars in California. She also raced motorcycles.

B.

Dodi was well-endowed and knew how to use her large chest to her advantage. On one occasion, she used it to bump a diminutive drunken troublemaker right out the front door.

C.

Dodi ran a tight ship at the Rendezvous and was tough as nails, but her musical taste didn't really match her personality. She would often play Spandau Ballet and The Smiths on the sound system, much to the chagrin of the Grunge-hungry crowds.

TWO *are true.*
Which one is a **LIE**?

[ANSWER KEY ON PAGE 86]

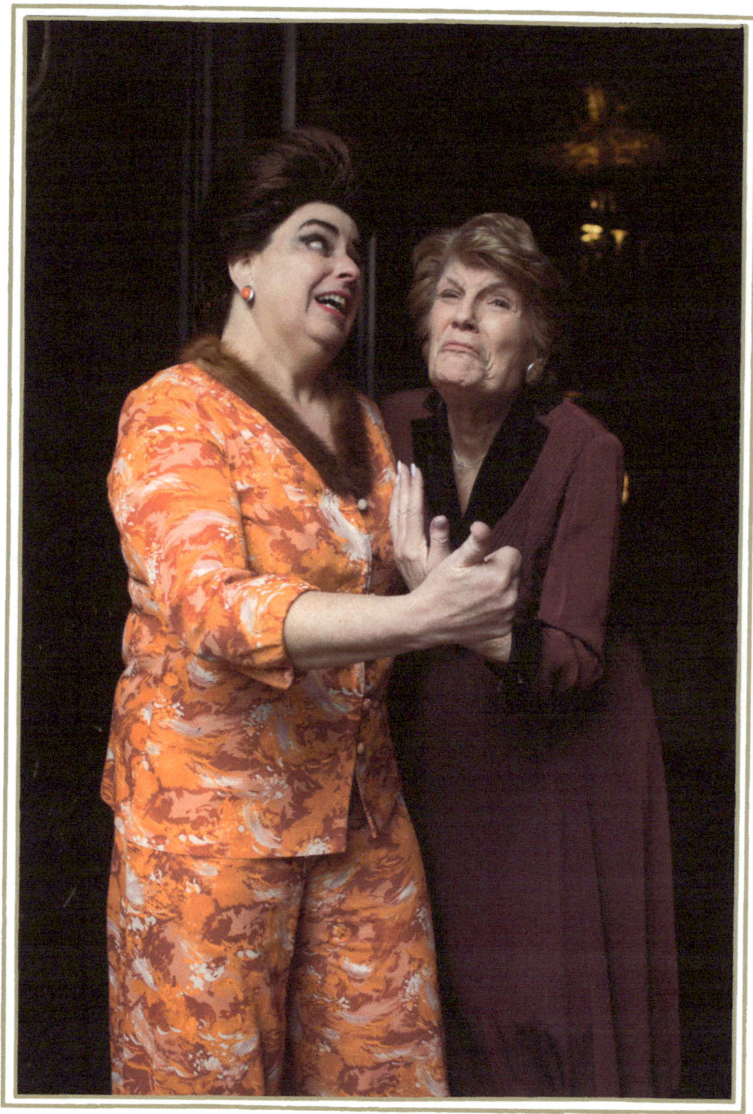

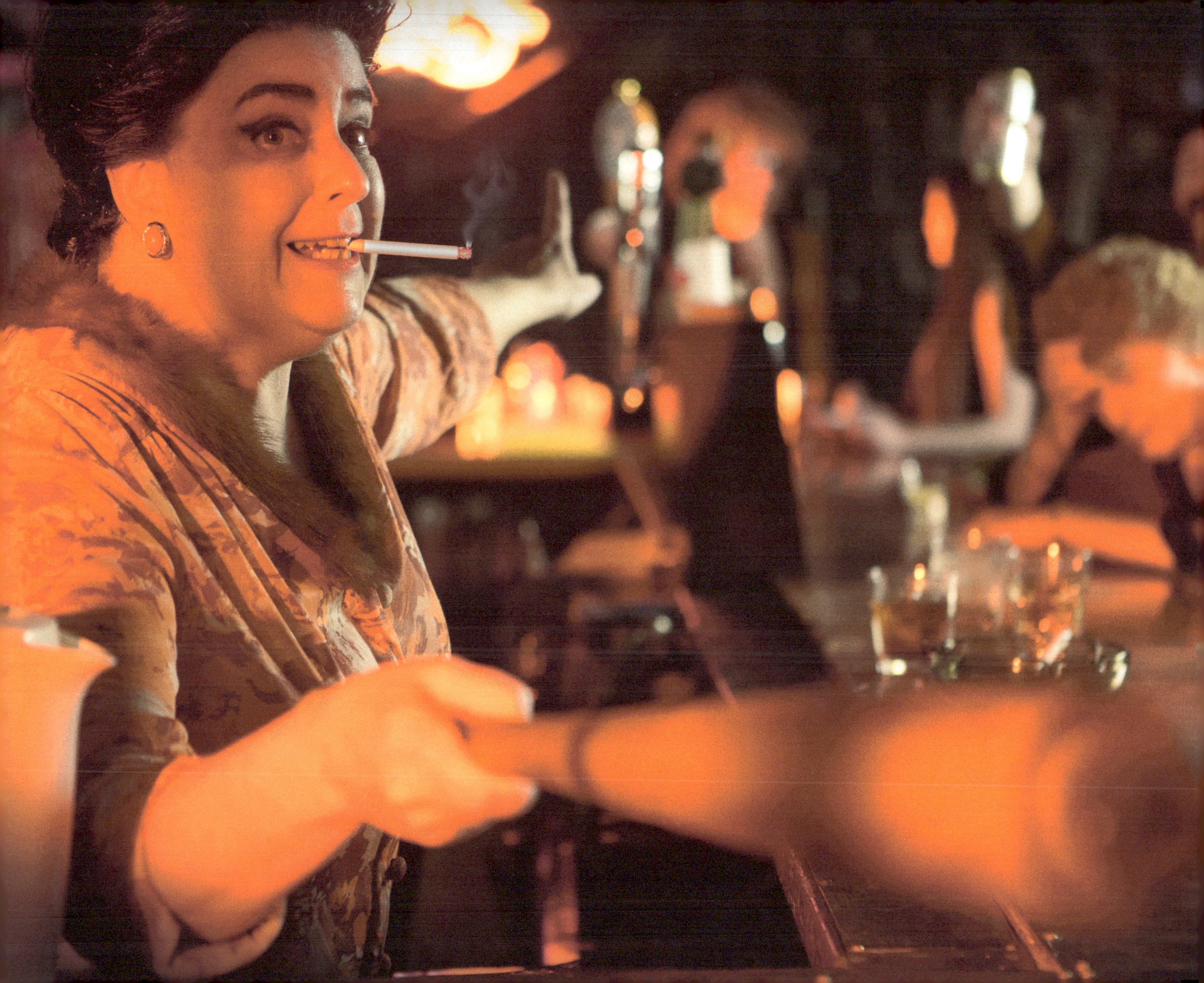

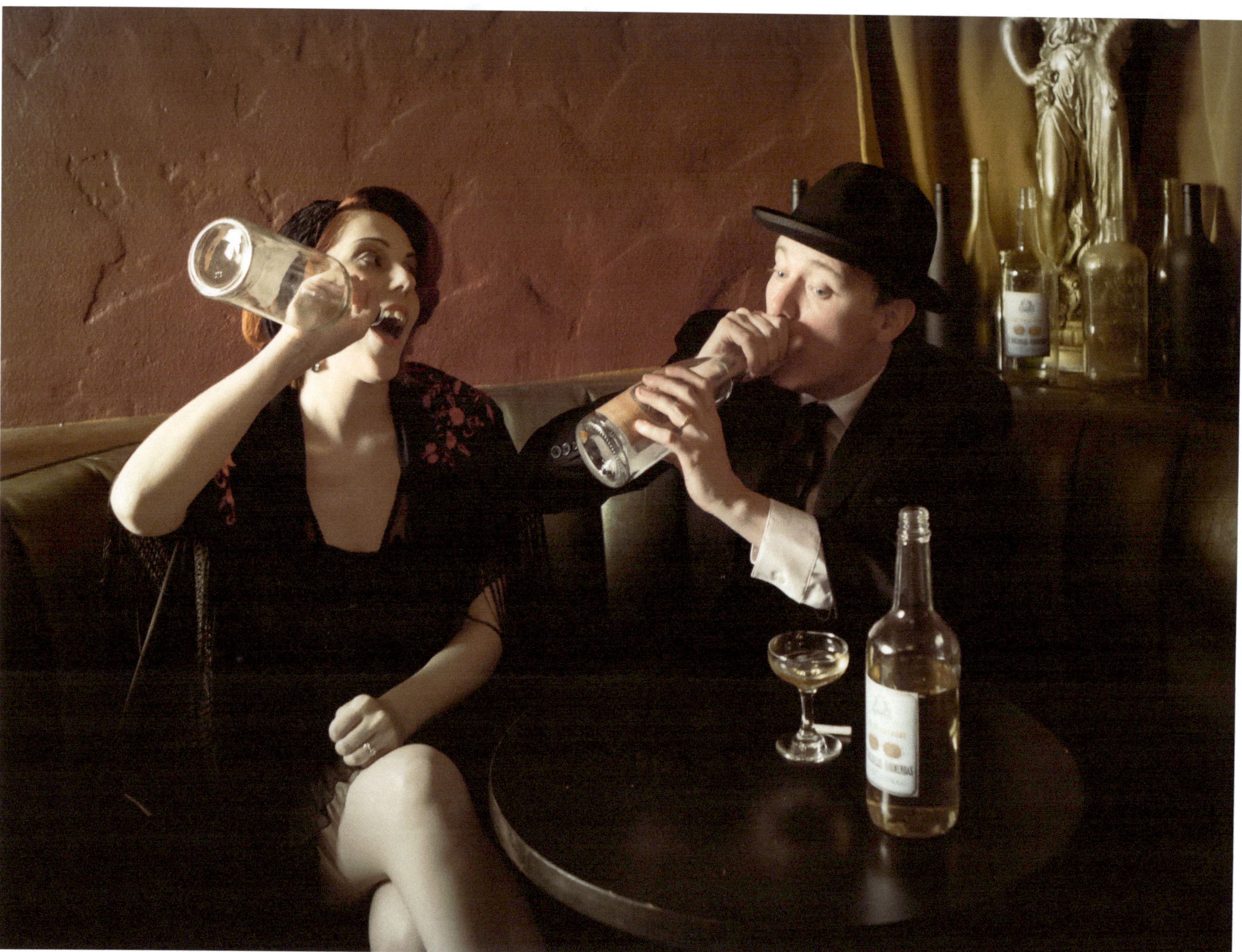

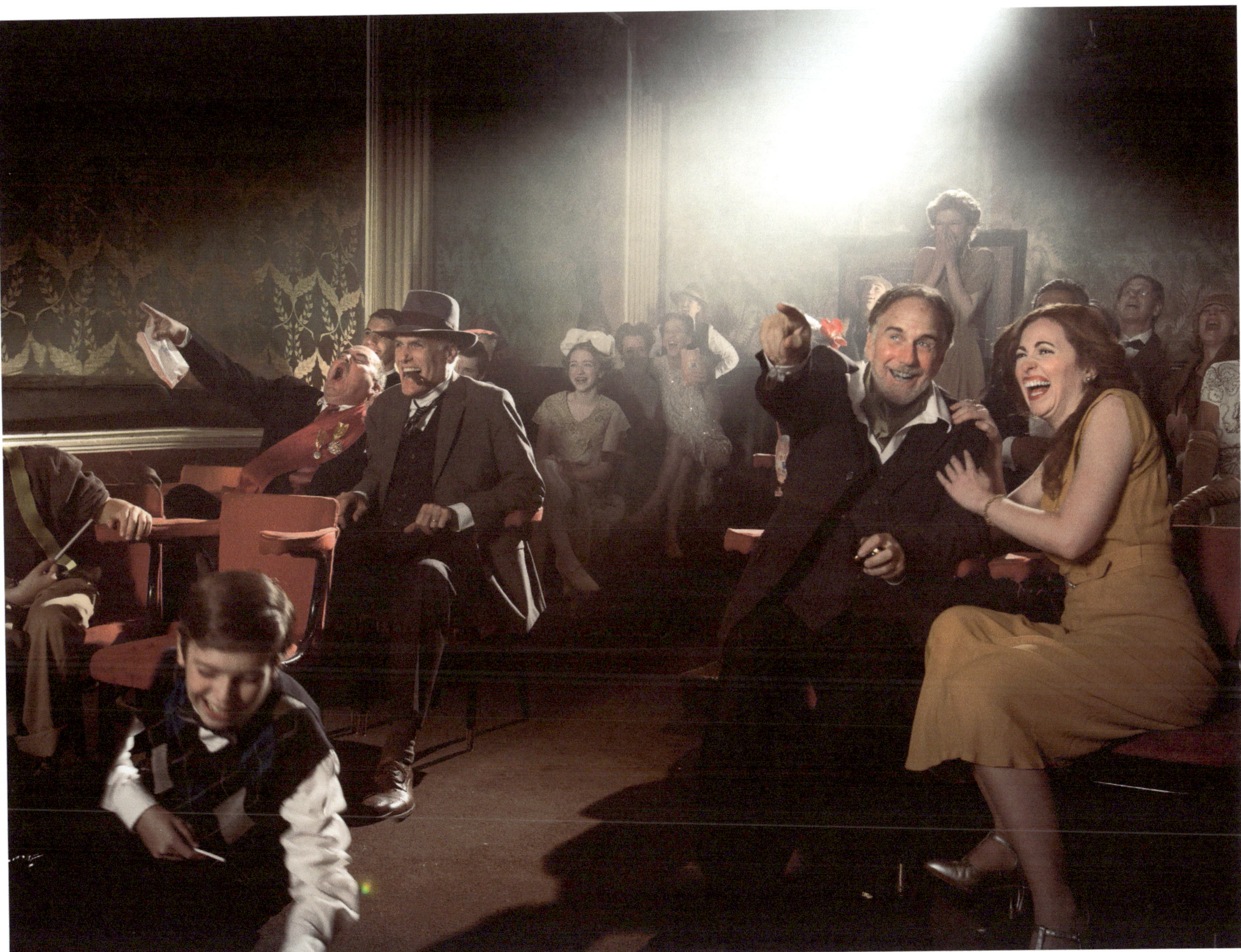

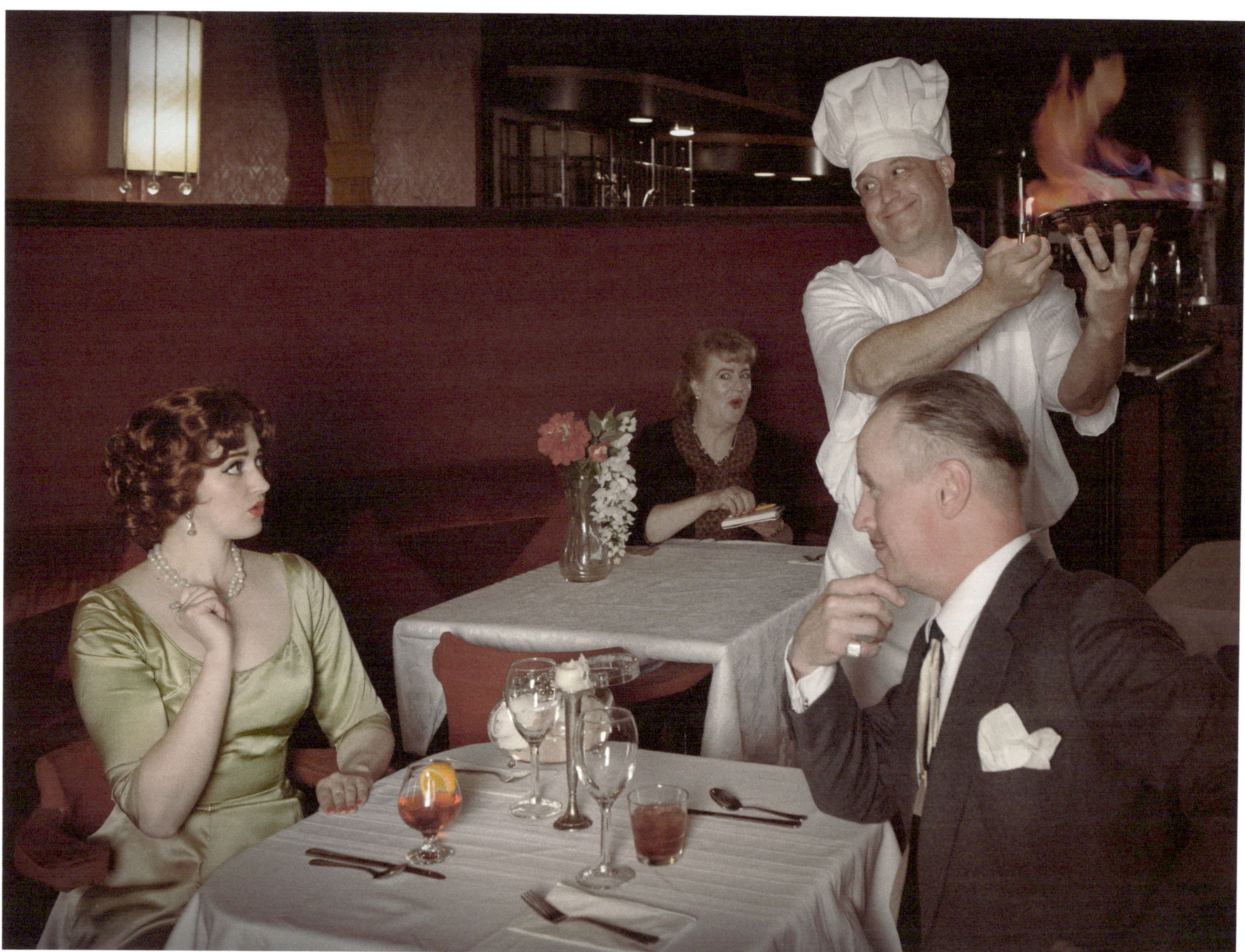

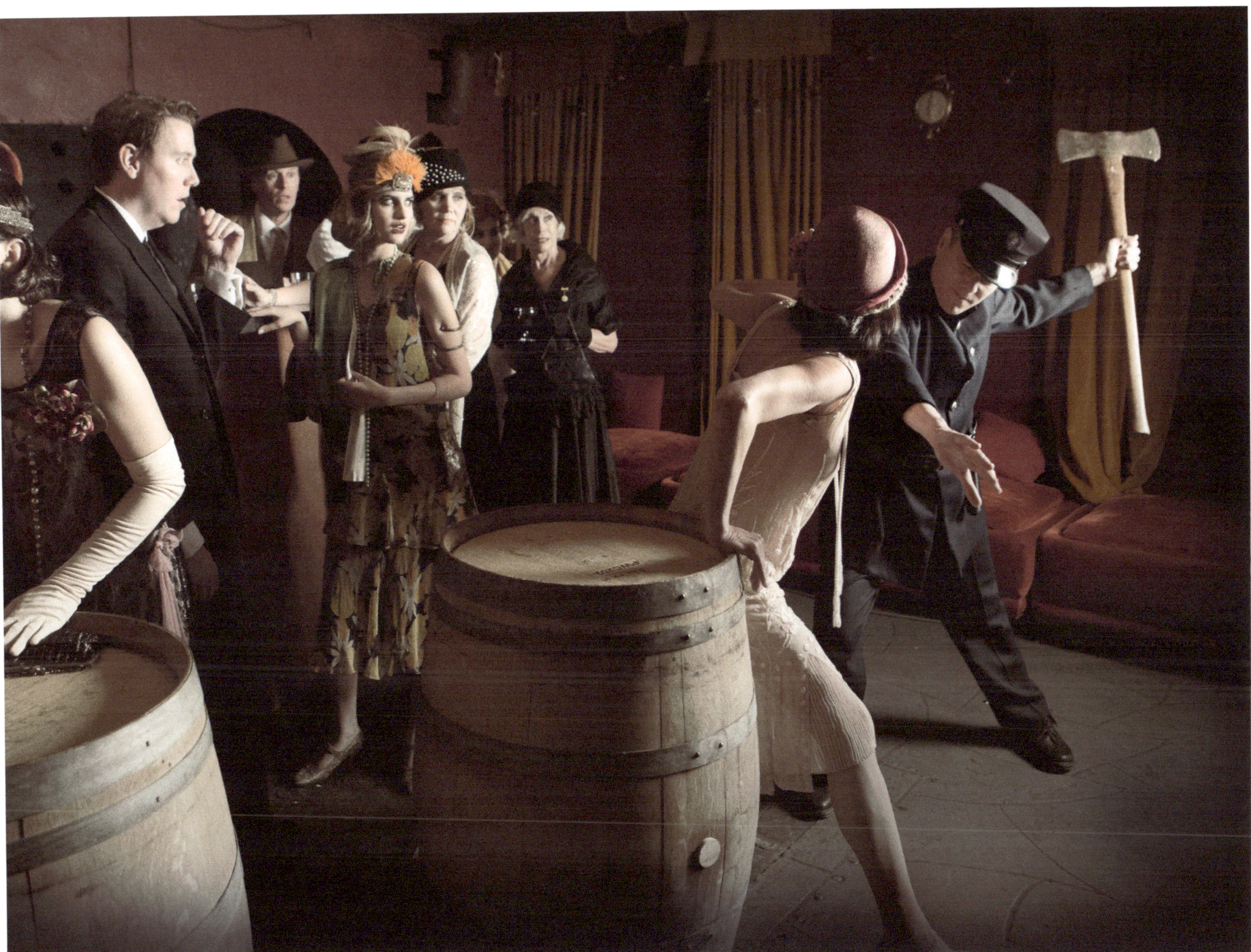

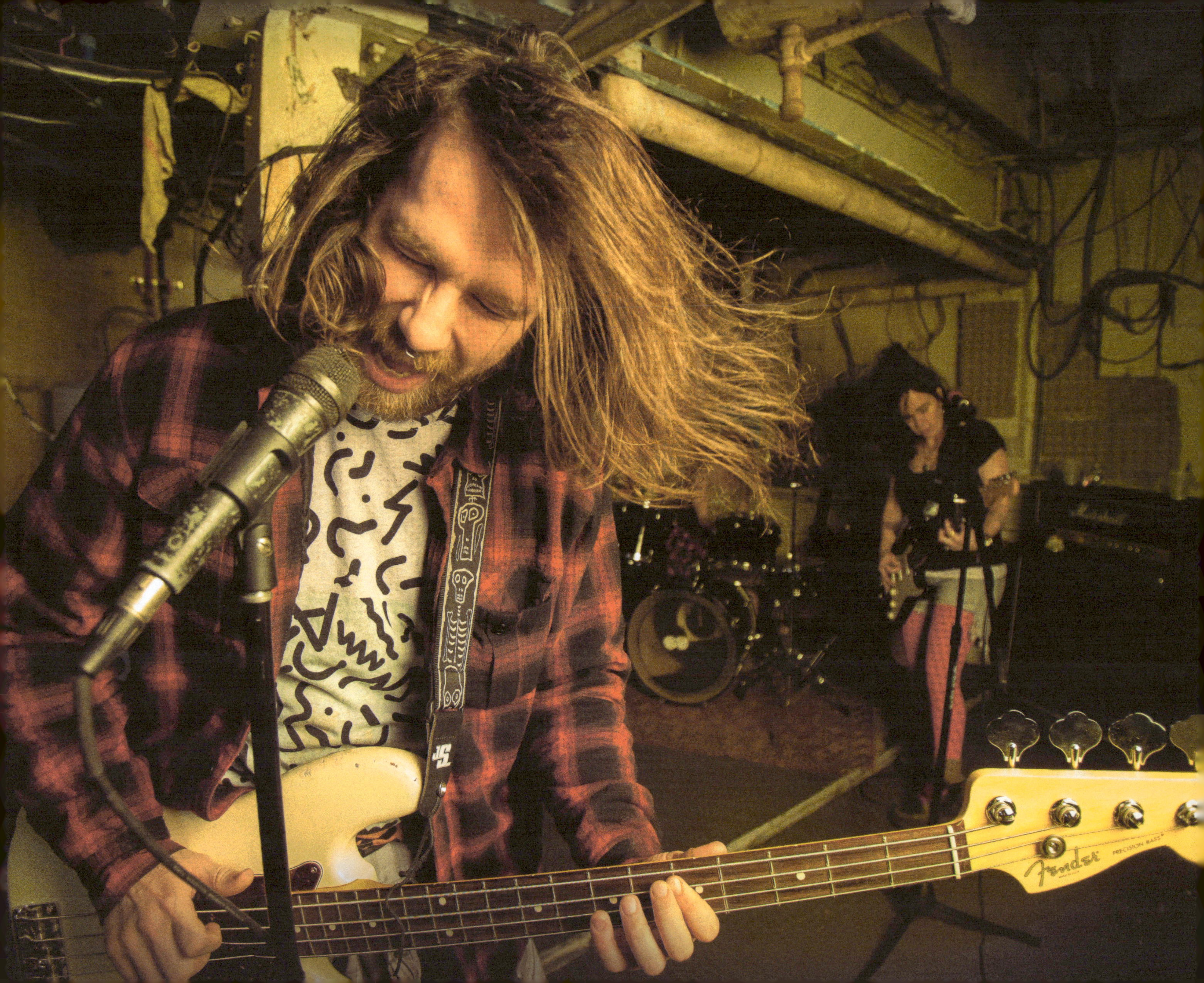

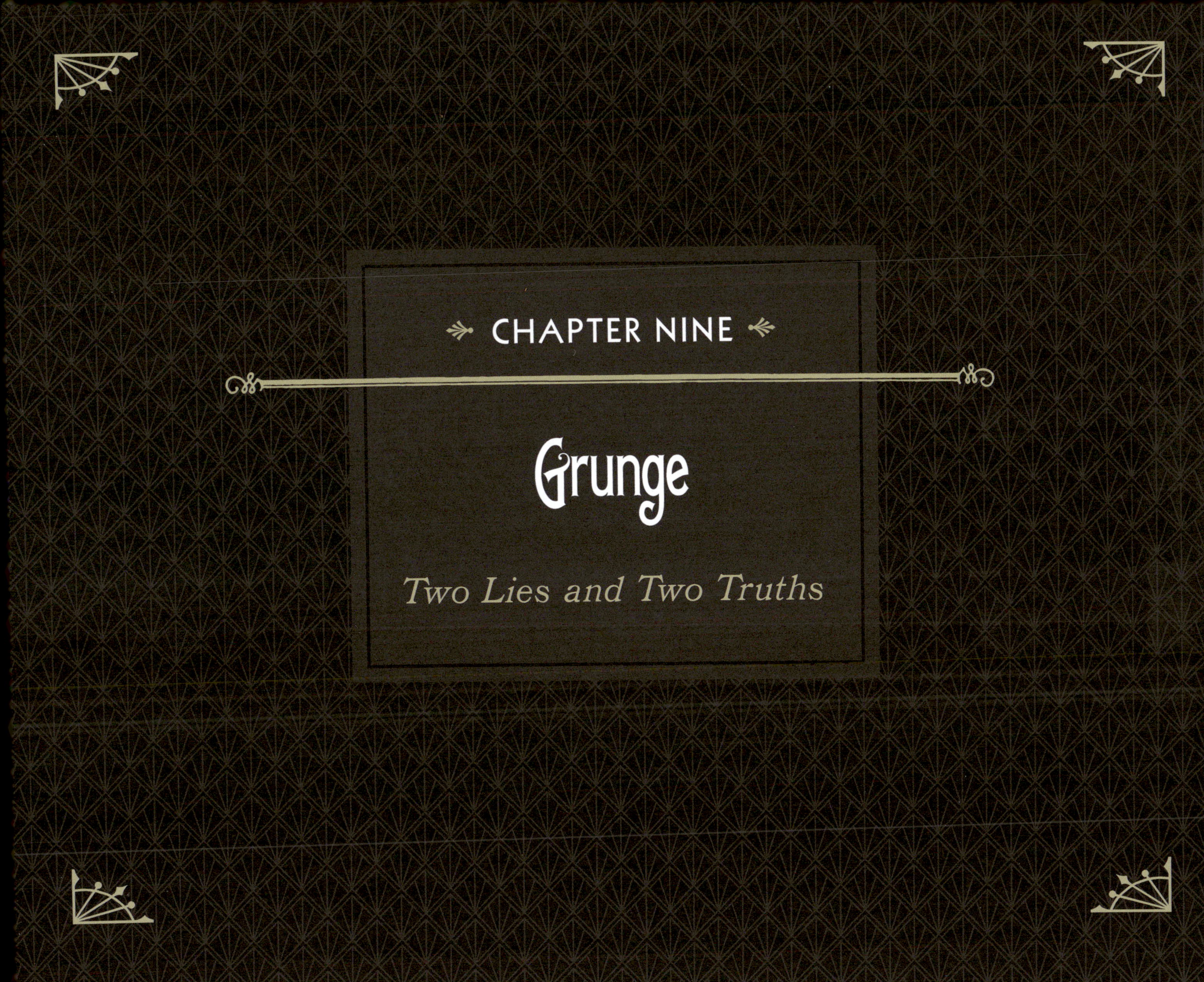

Grunge

Two Lies and Two Truths

A.

Back in the late Eighties, when Grunge was first emerging from the bowels of the earth to foist itself on an unsuspecting world, Seattle had some pretty tight-ass laws on the books that kept restaurants from playing live music. But a handful of entrepreneurial lawyer friends found a loophole. Seems a restaurant could acquire the innocent sounding "Additional Activities License." The AAL was drafted to allow a bit of light piano or a strolling violin serenading diners. Well, this group of sharp shysters bought the (soon to be legendary) Crocodile. The "additional activities" ended up being not the tickling of ivories but Nirvana smashing their instruments and setting the world on fire.

When Nirvana ended up on Saturday Night Live, the Crocodile was packed watching their hometown band on the bar's TV. After the group performed "Territorial Pissing," drummer Dave Grohl threw his drums from the stage and Kurt Cobain attacked the speakers with his guitar. This inspired one of the Crocodile's owners to shove the television from the bar smashing it onto the floor. The crowd went wild.

B.

Some respectable Belltown businesses allowed Grunge bands to rehearse for free after hours in their basements as a crime deterrent. One furniture shop owner was quoted as saying, "Yeah, that god awful racket keeps the burglars at bay!"

C.

If you look at the early account books of some of the Grunge bands, you'll see some curious abbreviations:

PIB
(Paid in Beer)

BSU
(Bastards Stiffed Us)

BPBT
(Balance Paid By Theft)

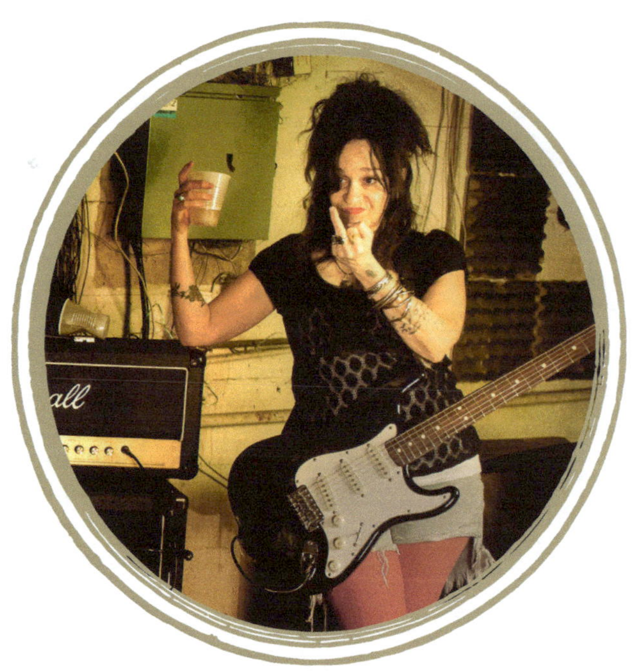

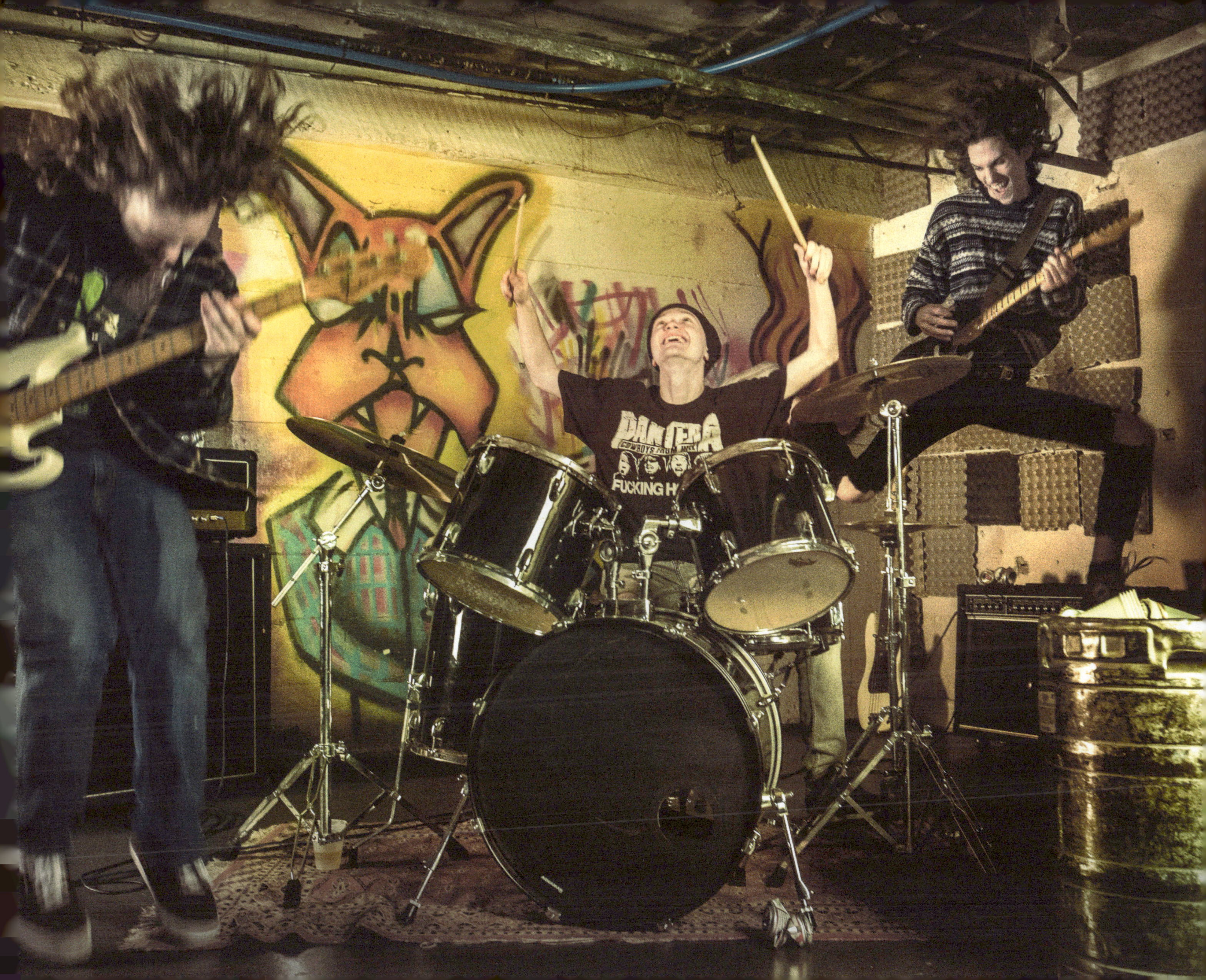
PANTERA
COWBOYS FROM HELL
FUCKING H

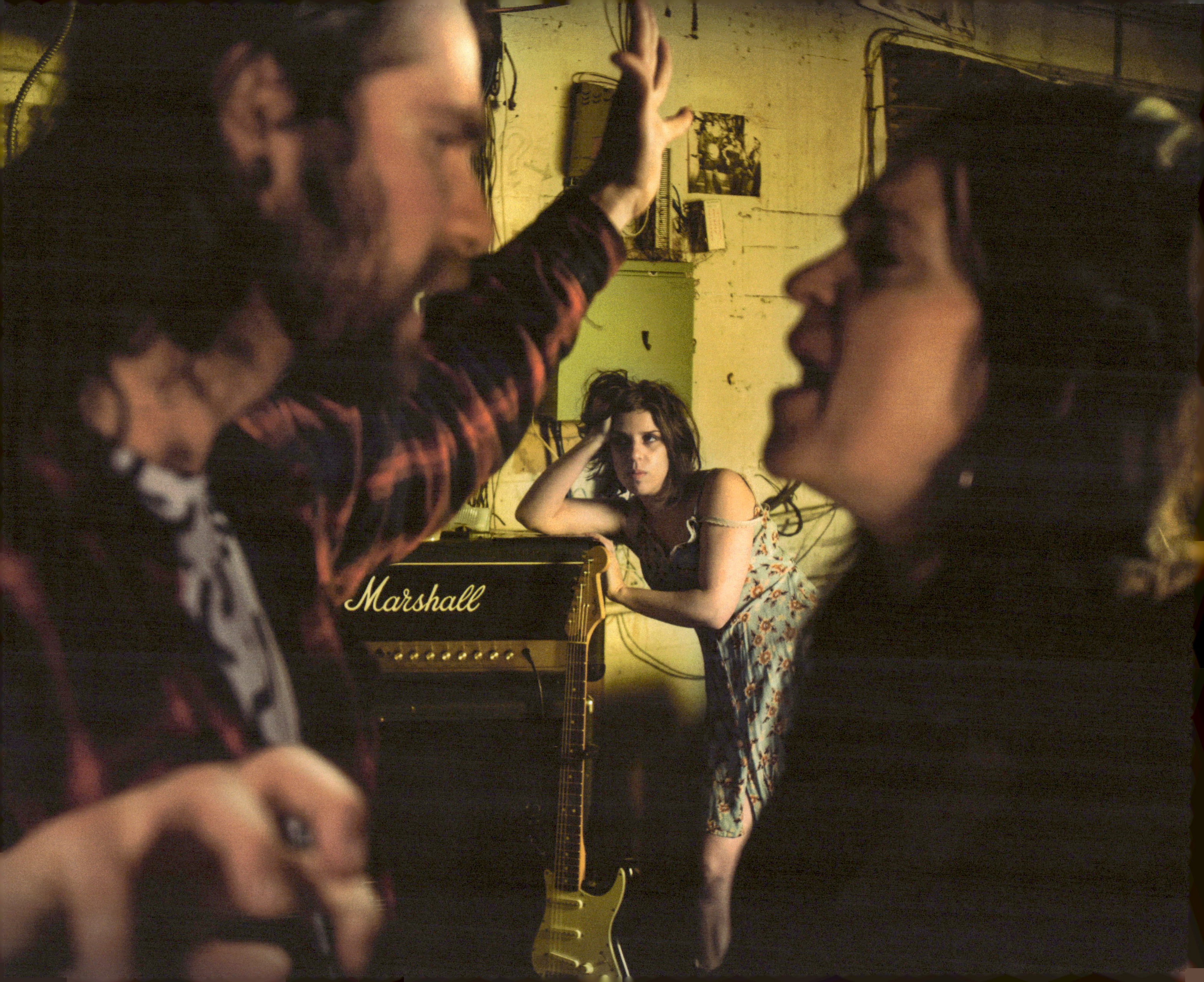

D.

The Rendezvous, once known as the place to be seen and nicknamed the Vous, had fallen on hard times in the 1990s. Grunge bands practiced in its basement; locals lined up to start drinking early in the morning when cigar-chomping bartender Dodi opened the doors. The Vous had become the Zoo, and only someone as tough-as-nails as Dodi could preside over it. She'd show unruly patrons the door without a second thought. If they were big and scruffy, all the better. All around the Zoo, Belltown was gentrifying, and the gentry in their condos would often spread rumors (hopes?) that the Zoo was going to close. One intrepid reporter went to see Dodi to find out if the rumors were true. "No, we're not closing," she told the reporter. "Maybe it's the Woodland Park Zoo that's closing. People often confuse us with them."

2 *are lies*

&

2 *are true so*

who even cares?

[ANSWER KEY ON PAGE 86]

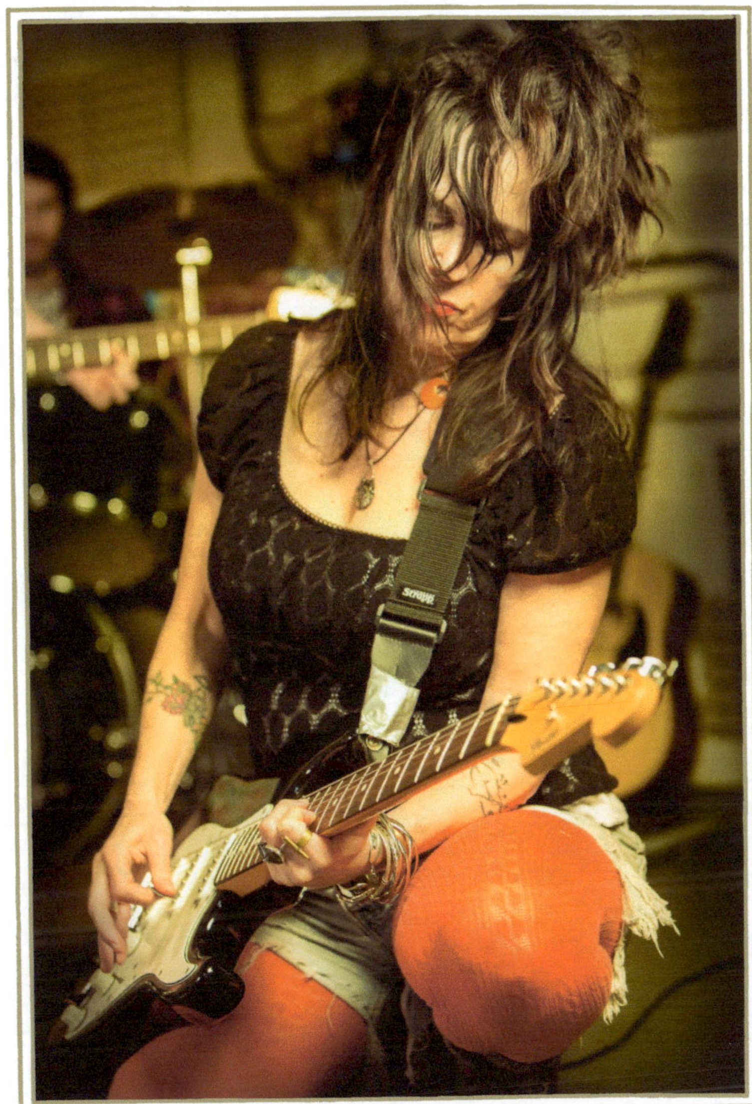

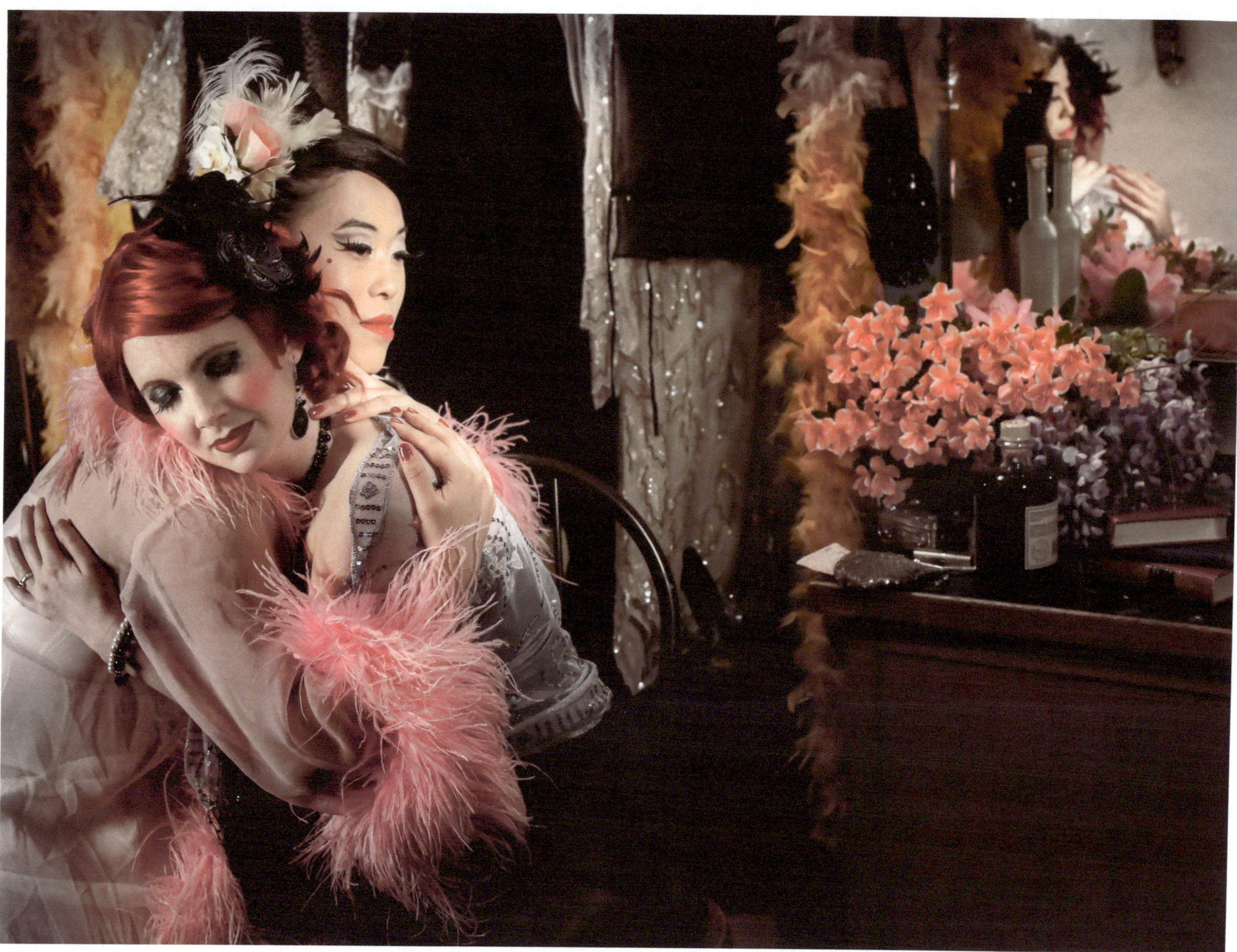

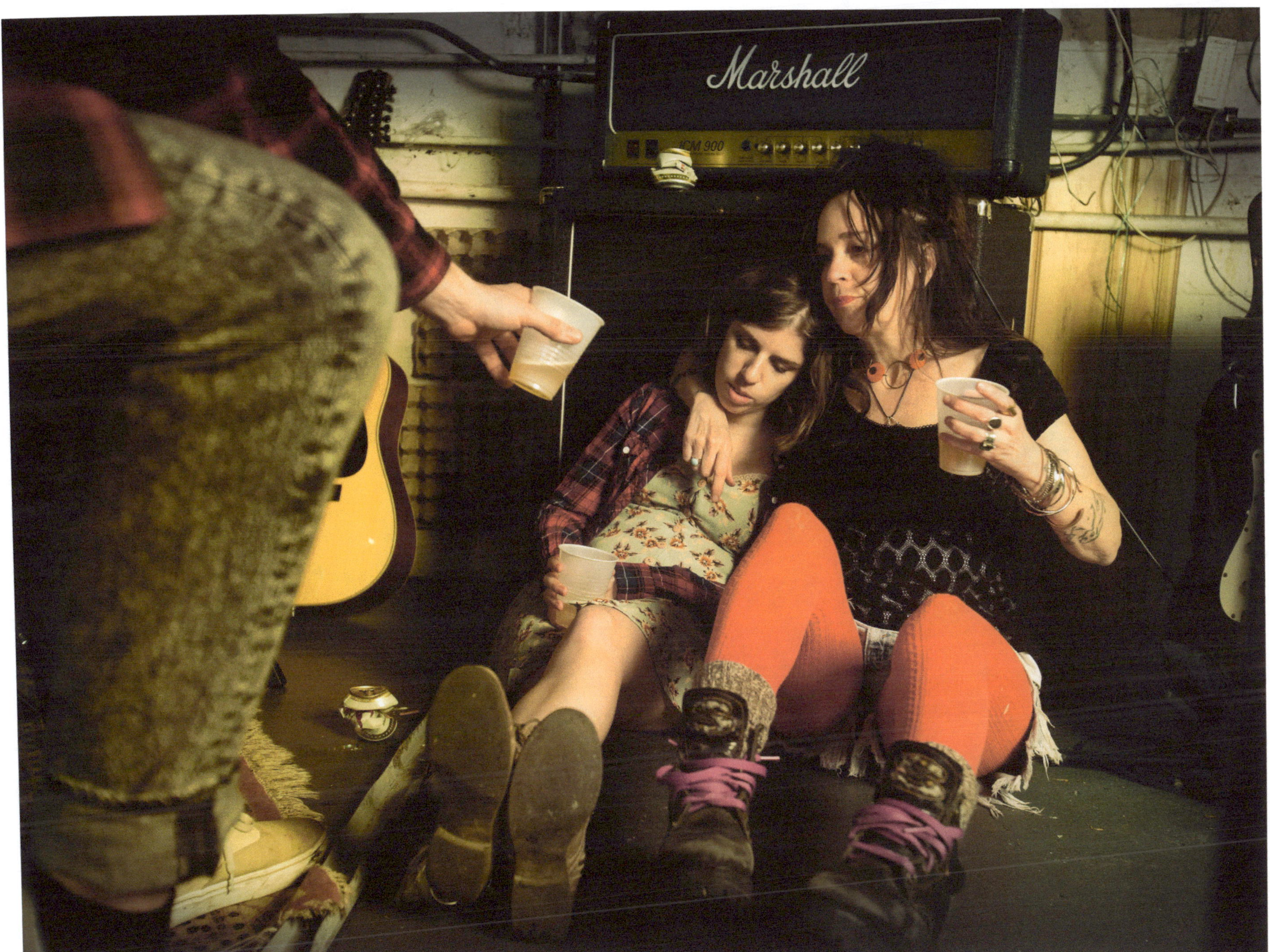
Marshall
JCM 900

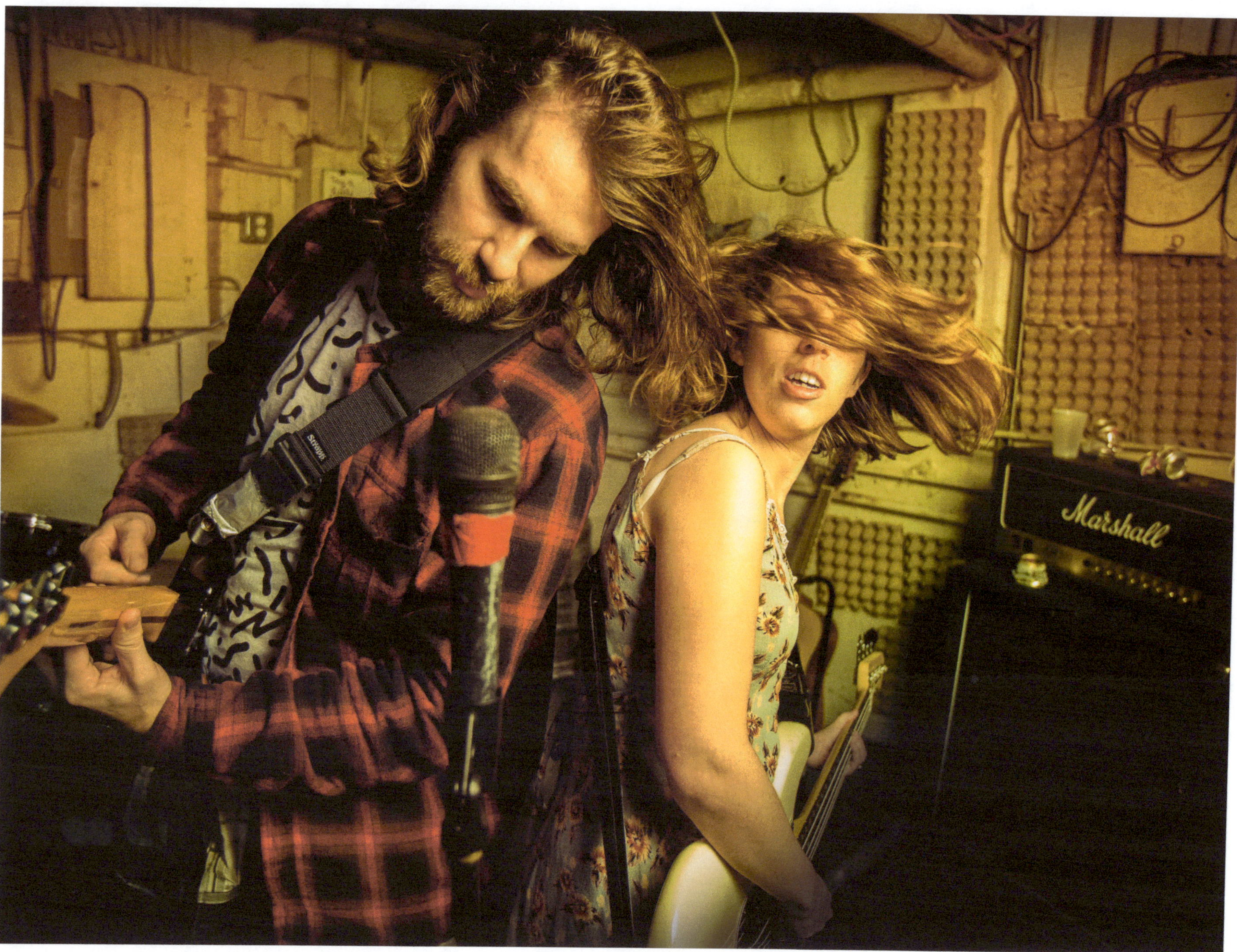

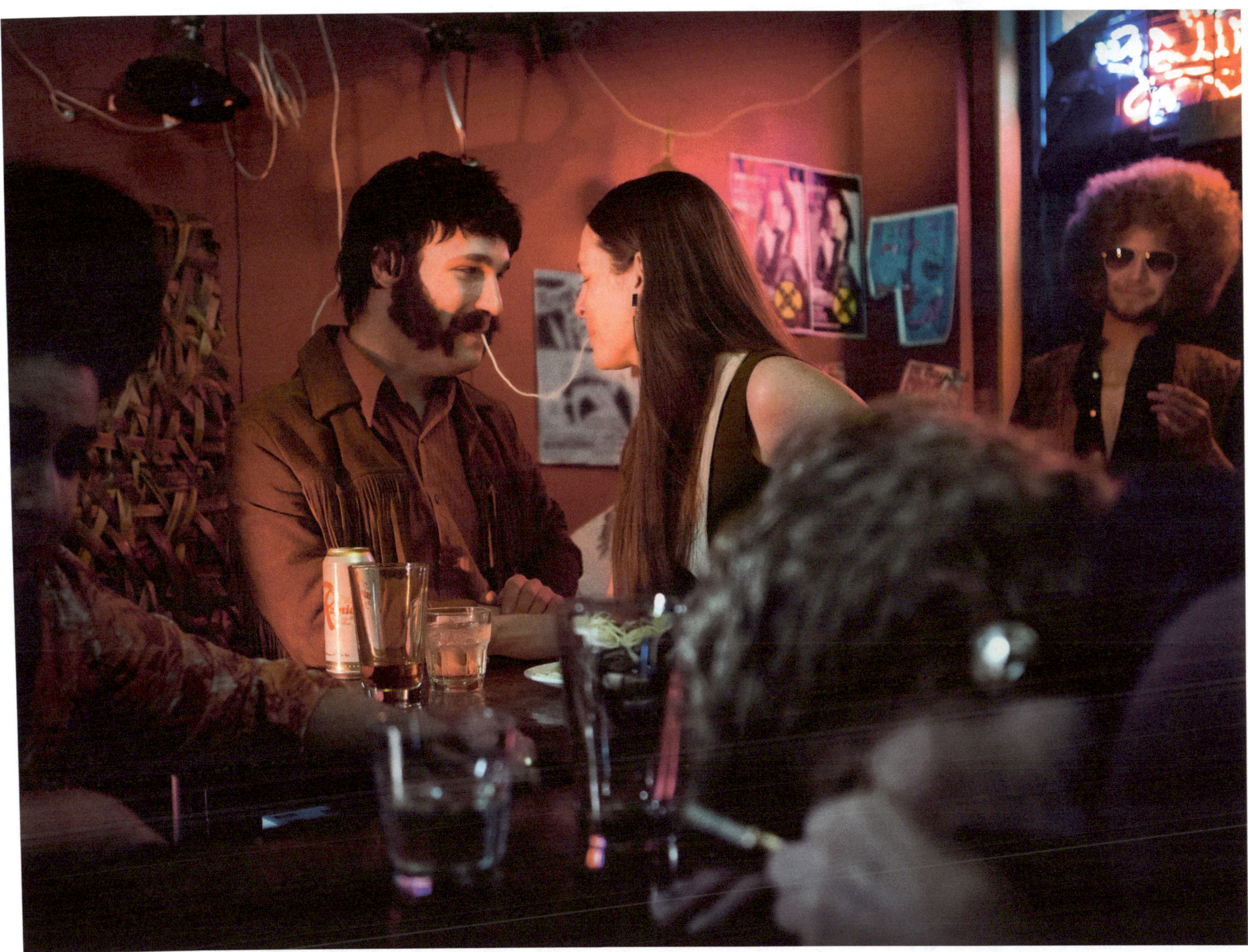

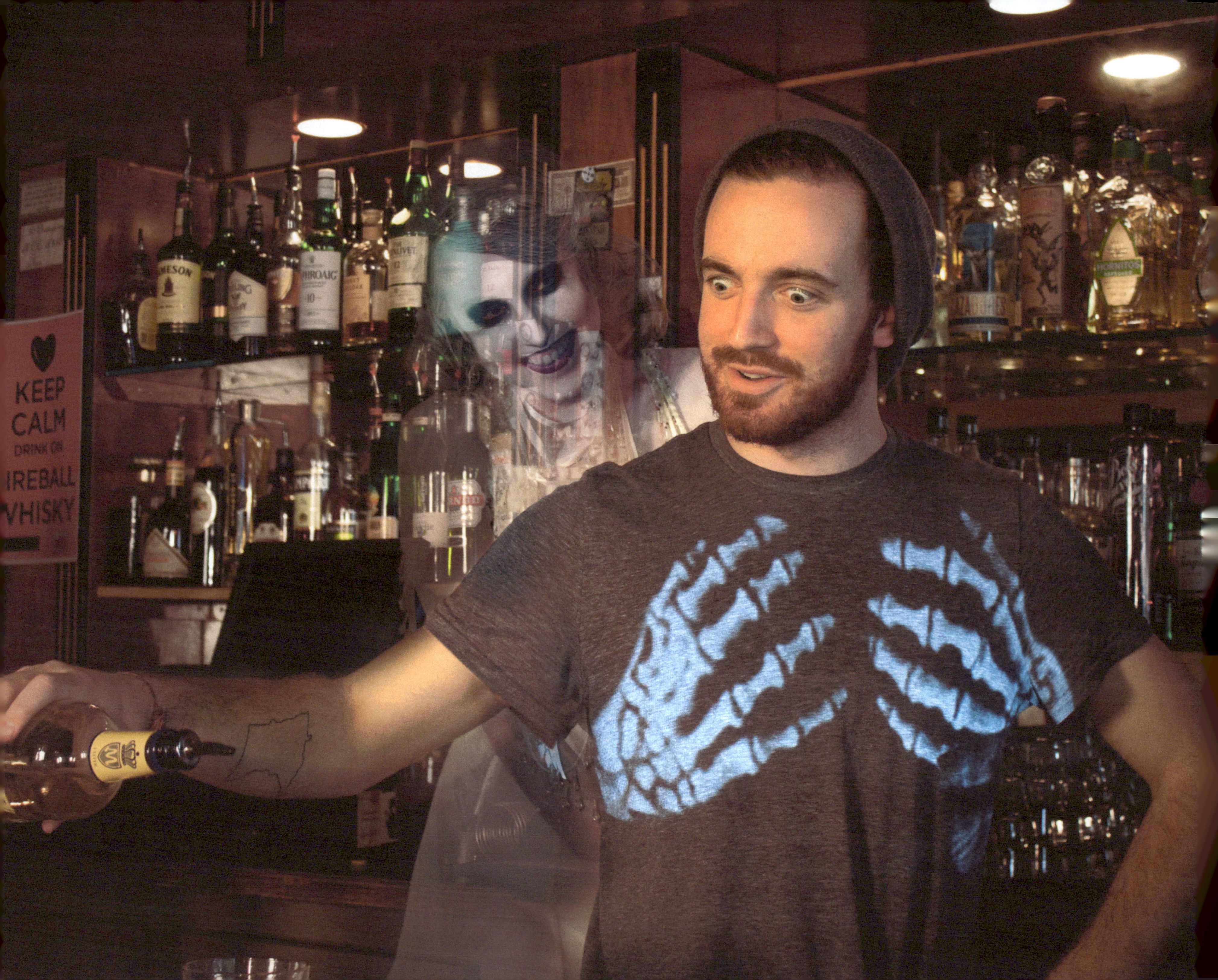

KEEP
CALM
DRINK OR
IREBALL
WHISKY

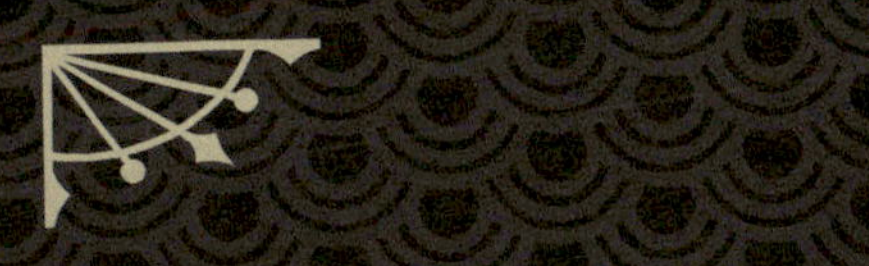
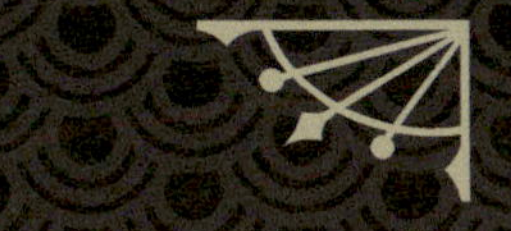

CHAPTER SEVEN

The Ghosts of Belltown

Two Lies and a Truth (maybe?)

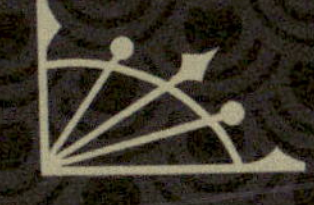
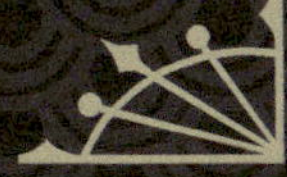

A.

In 1908 at the seedy Spraxton Hotel (where there now sits a dog park) Annie Flannigan's armed husband burst in on her and her lover (known to the historical record only as French Pete). Annie managed to wrestle the gun away and shoot her spousal intruder. She then finished up her carnal business with Pete and then shot him too. When asked at her trial why she shot the poor Frenchman, Annie winked and replied, "Mama always said, can't trust a man with gossip." Her last words on the gallows were, "Haven't seen the last of me." And it was true! She haunts the bedrooms and backrooms of Belltown to this day, whispering words of encouragement to cheating lovers.

TWO *are definitely lies.*

Which one might be **TRUE**?

[ANSWER KEY ON PAGE 86]

B.

The Rendezvous was once one of the finest dining establishments in the city. But by the late Sixties it was… well, it was a dive. As a building, it lead a full and interesting life. So, it's not surprising that it is home to (at least) three ghosts: A former projectionist who can be seen in the booth offering technical help from beyond the grave; A mysterious dark-haired man who has shown up in damn near every corner of the space; And an unsettling female specter who can be identified by her distinctive perfume. They've always been benevolent, but they are still ghosts, so treat them kindly. We don't know what they are capable of.

C.

Not all the ghosts of Belltown walk on two legs. Back in 1917 a pack of stray dogs kept chasing Della Klausen's cat (Mr McMittens) up trees. While fetching the feline from the branches of fir, Della fell and fractured her foot. Fed up, Della fed the mutts a leg of lamb laced with strychnine. On summer nights at the corner of Blanchard and Second, you can hear the ghost dogs howling along with the singers at The Crocodile.

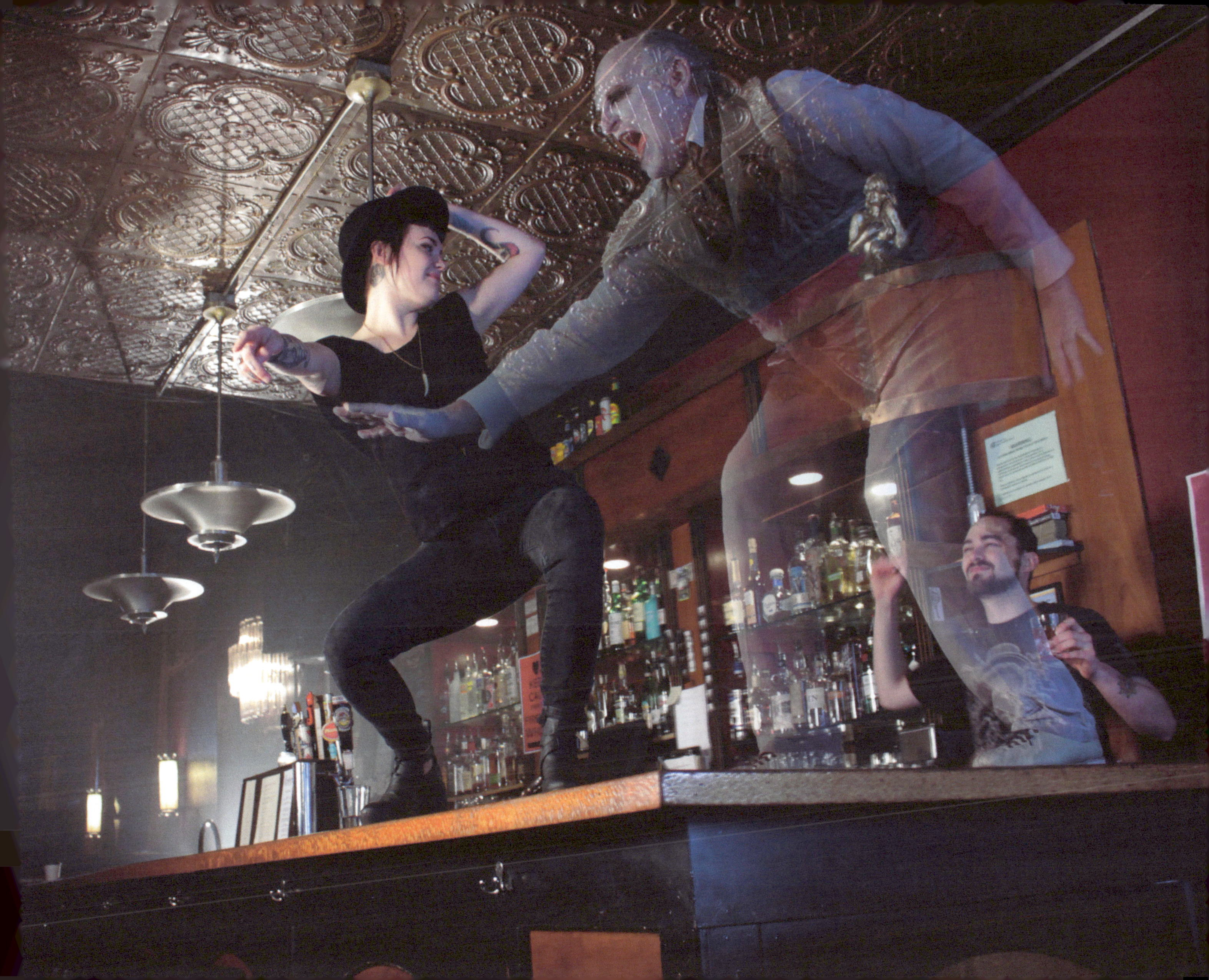

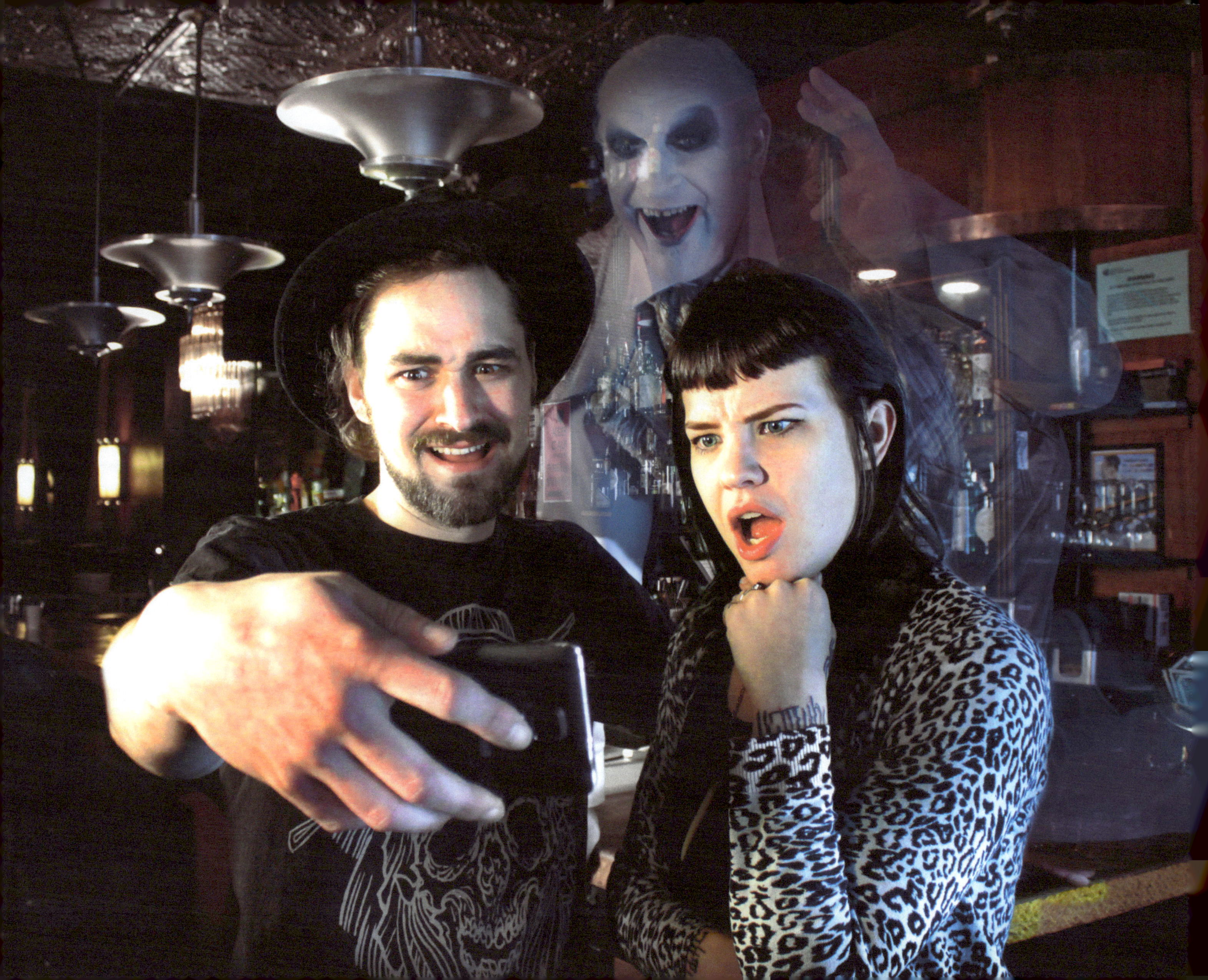

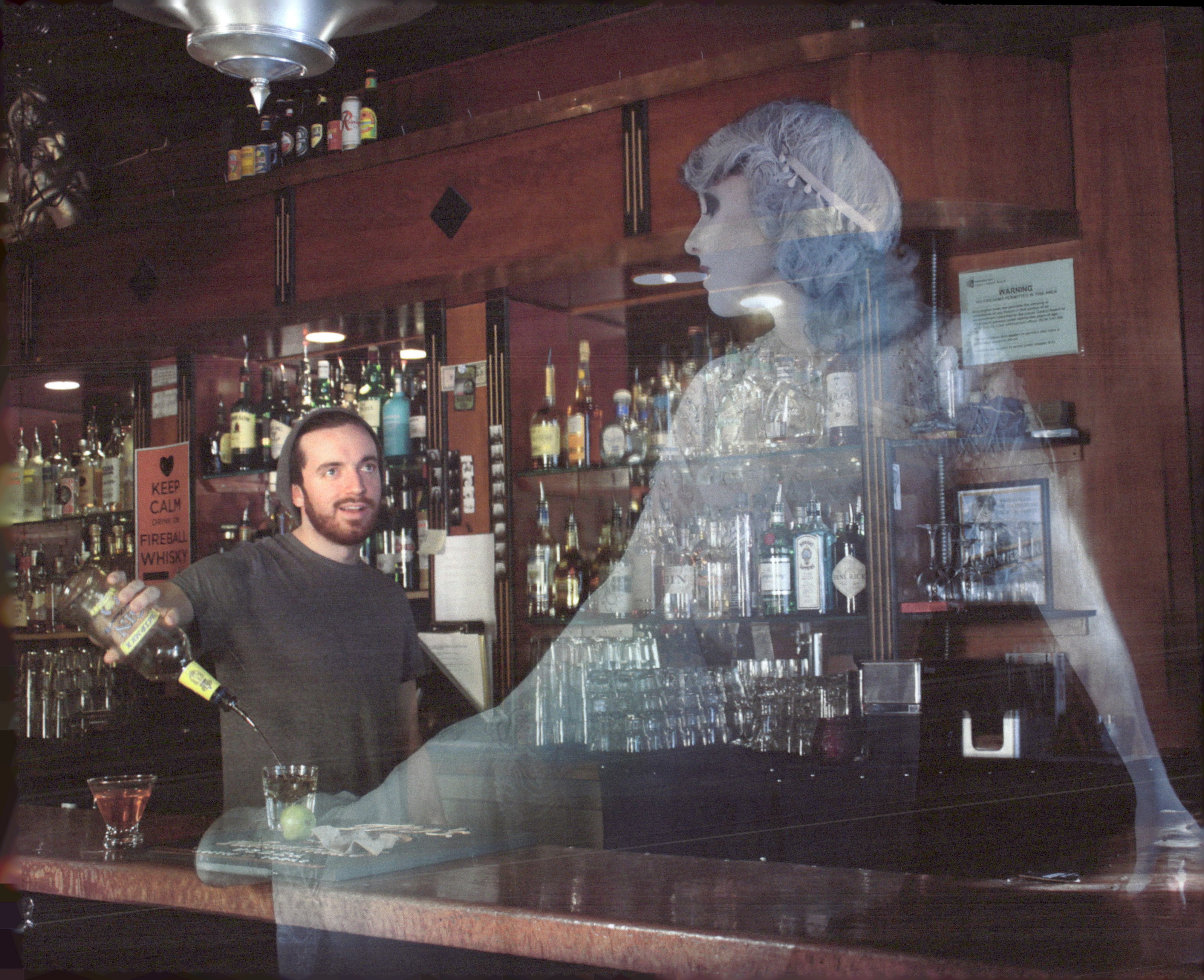

KEEP
CALM
DRINK ON
FIREBALL
WHISKY
WARNING
NO FIREARMS PERMITTED IN THIS AREA

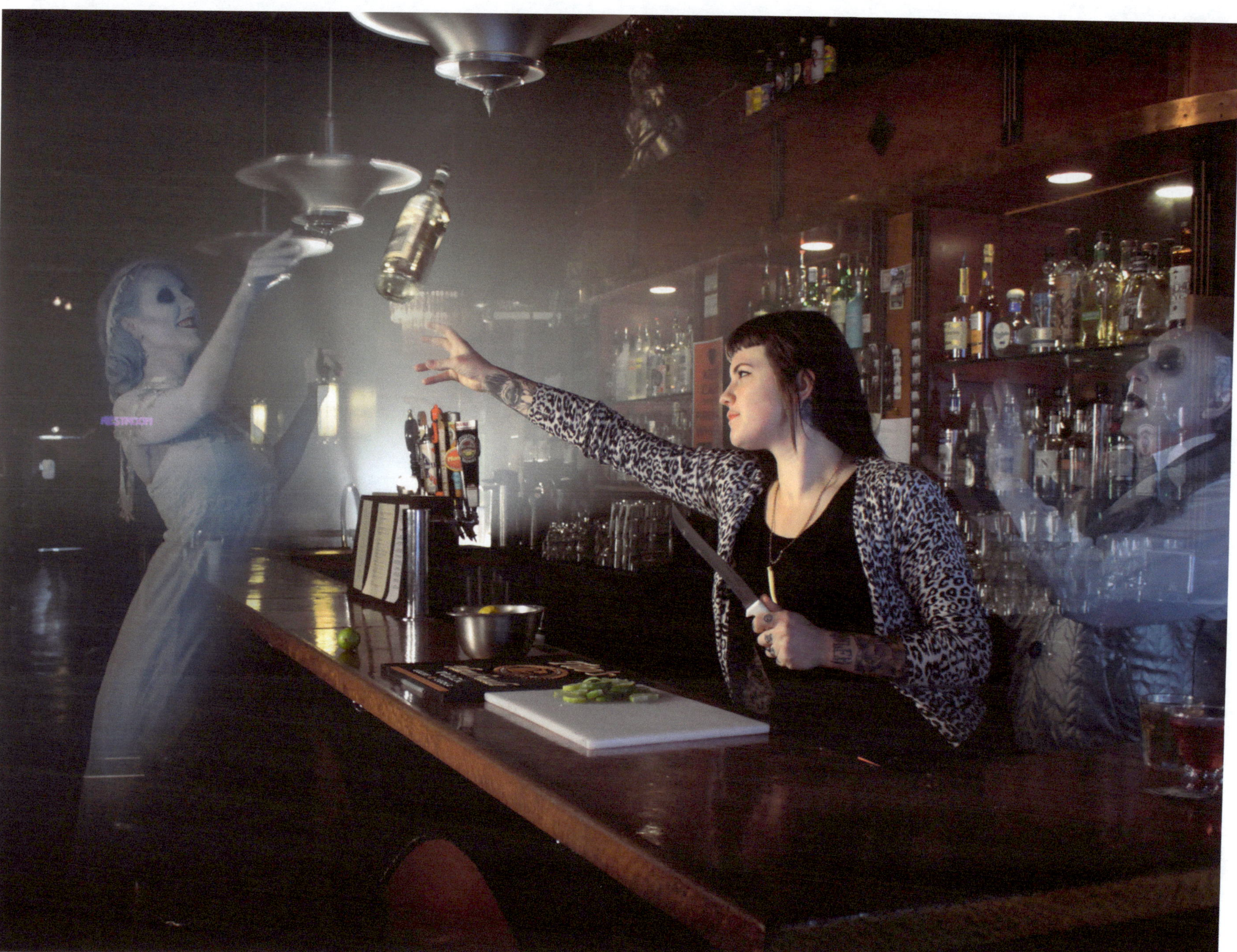

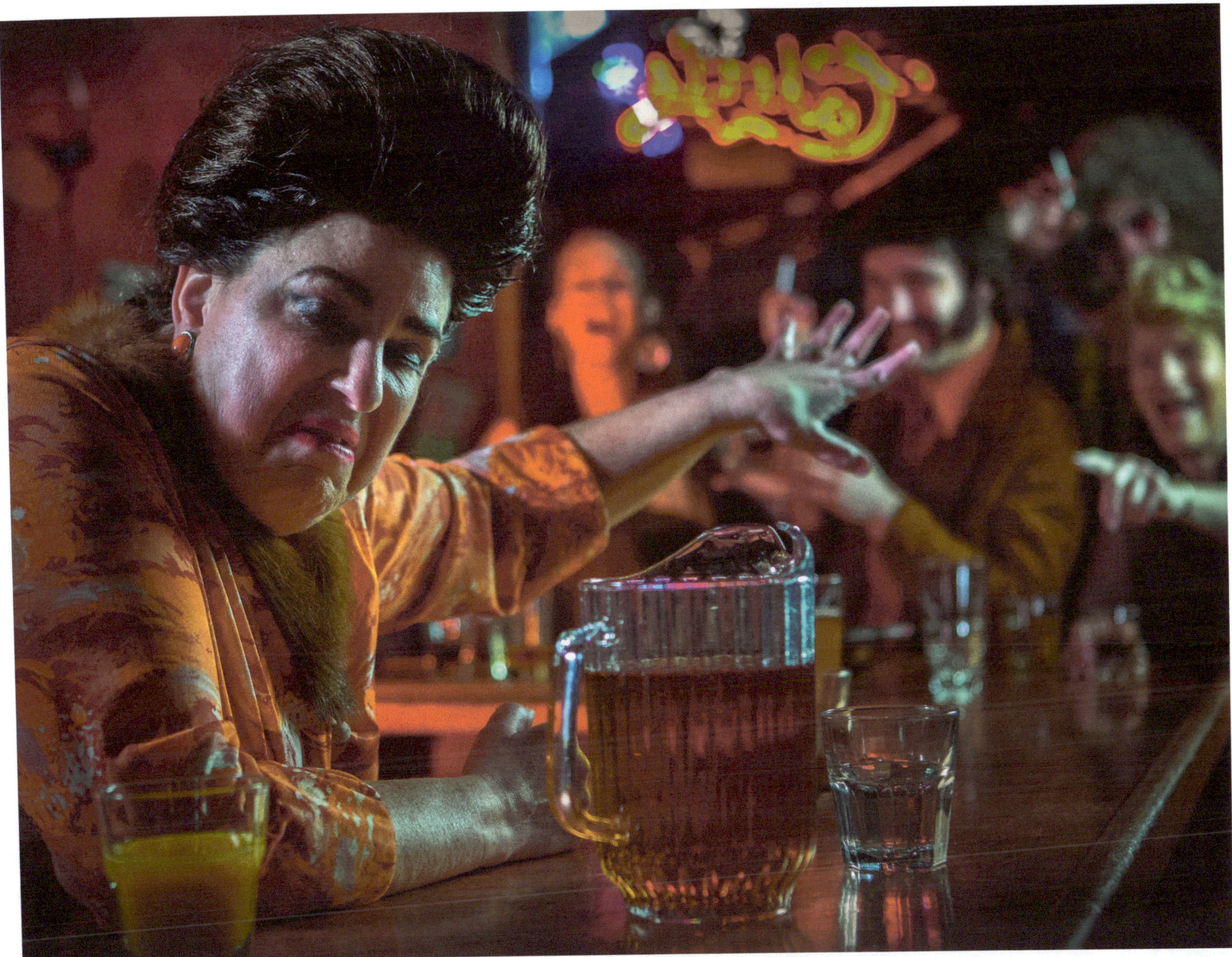

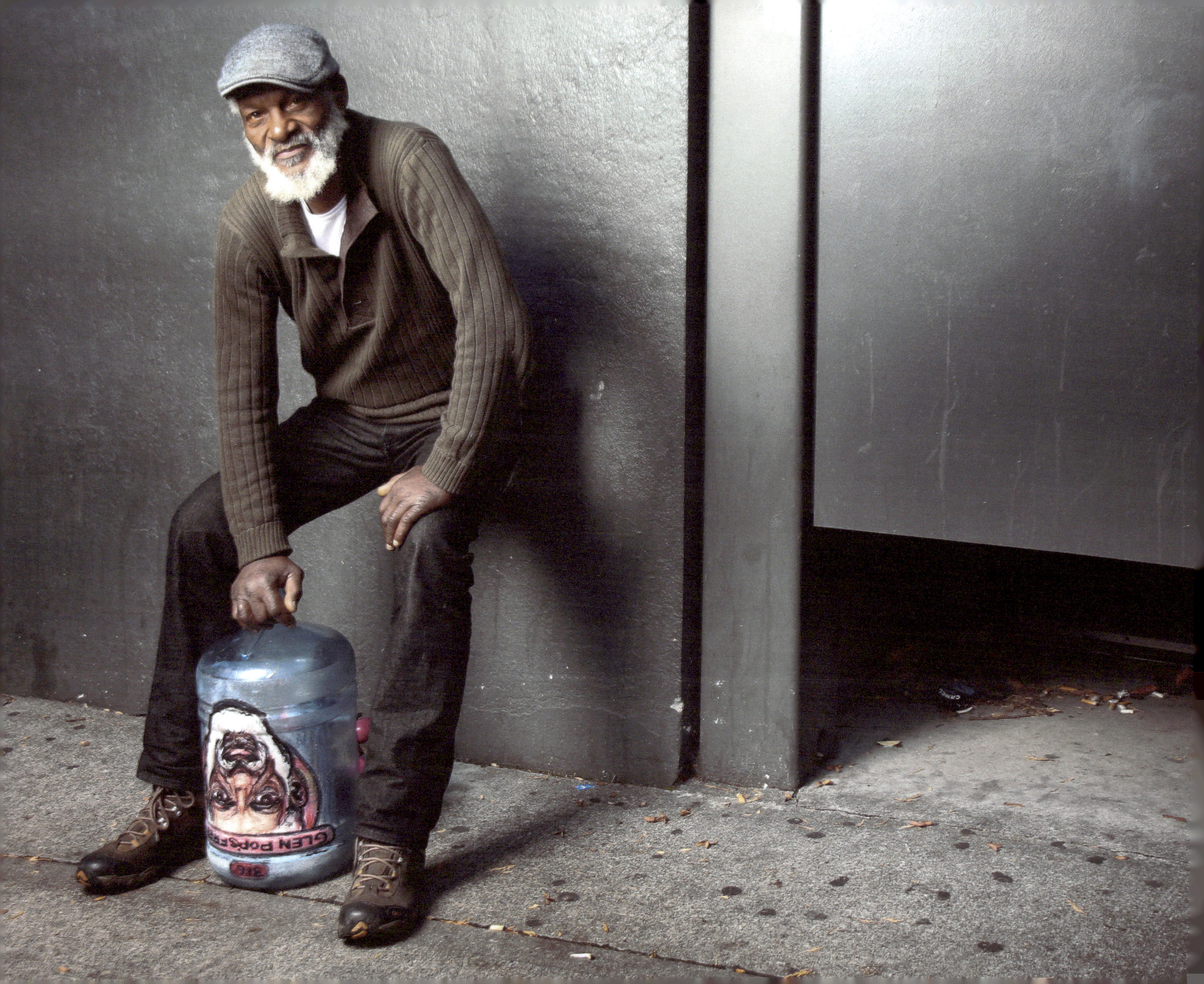

GLEN POP

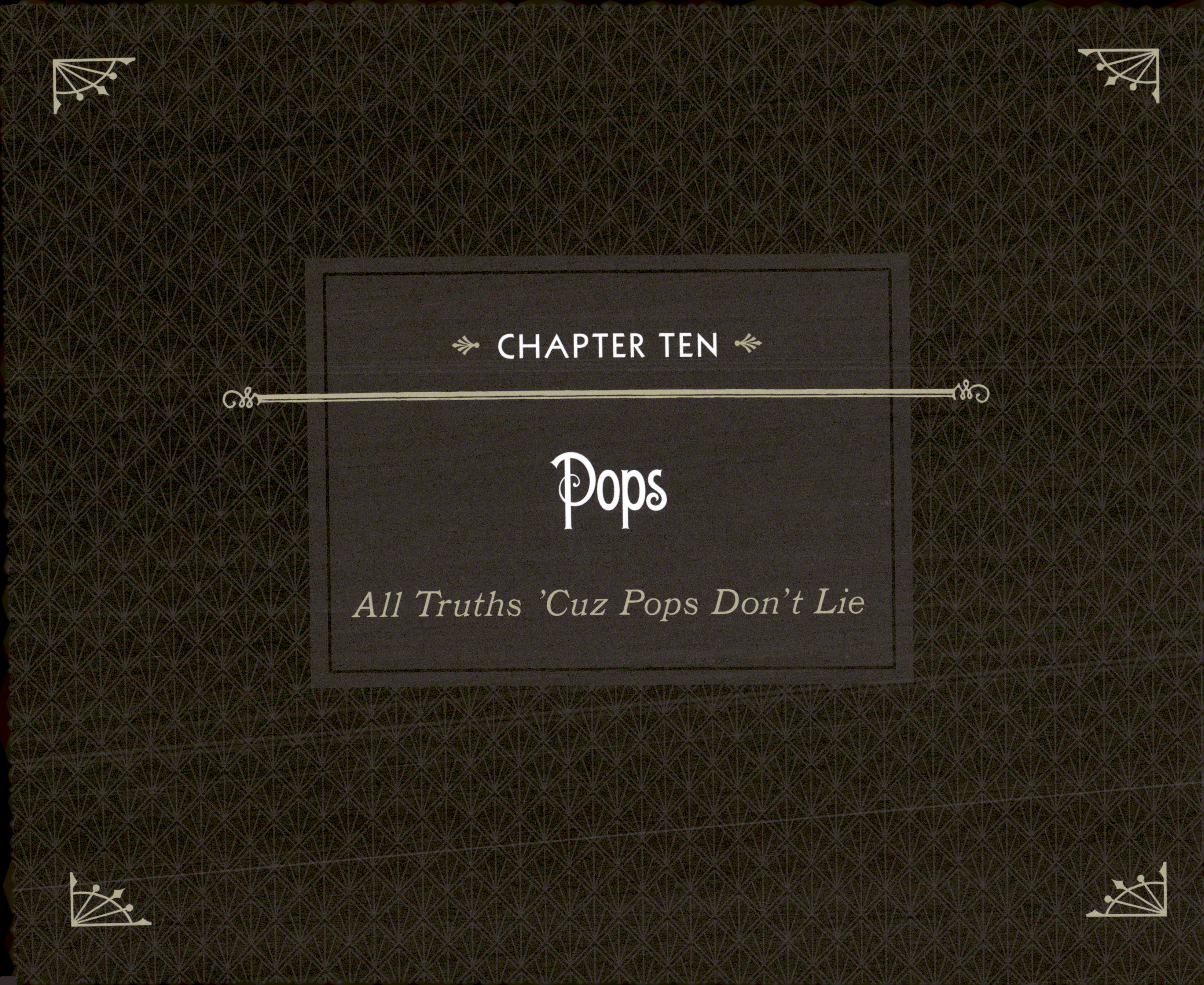

CHAPTER TEN

Pops

All Truths 'Cuz Pops Don't Lie

A.

Glen "Pops" Freeman is a street musician who frequented Belltown streets tapping percussive beats on his water bottle and singing original songs until he returned to San Diego, his hometown, before the winter of 2018. Pops, known as the unofficial mayor of Belltown, would walk up and down the Belltown streets serenading passers-by and diners with his one-minute songs. Why one minute? "That's how long it takes the light to change," he said. Pops spent 35 years in Seattle before heading back home.

B.

Pops grew up in a junkyard in San Diego with thirteen other brothers and sisters. He settled in Seattle, where he lived for more than three decades. One day, a friend on the street who was from San Diego told Pops that he had a daughter back in San Diego. Pops decided to go home and meet her. He continued to perform on the streets of San Diego but as of this writing has yet to find his daughter.

C.

In summer 2019, Pops returned to Seattle. He heard we were making a book about Belltown and offered us the following poem, which seems apropos for this book!

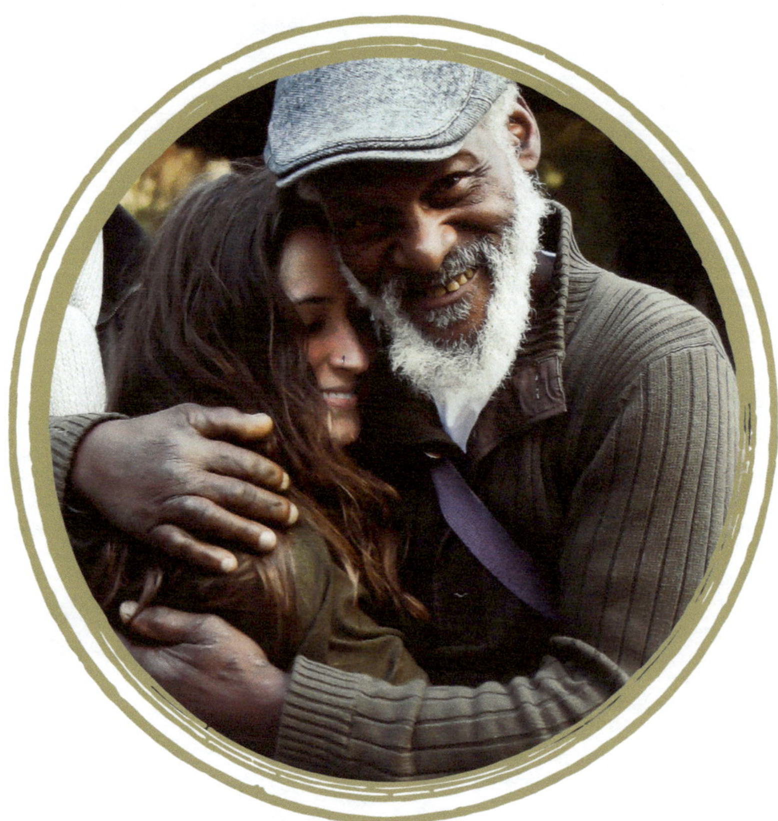

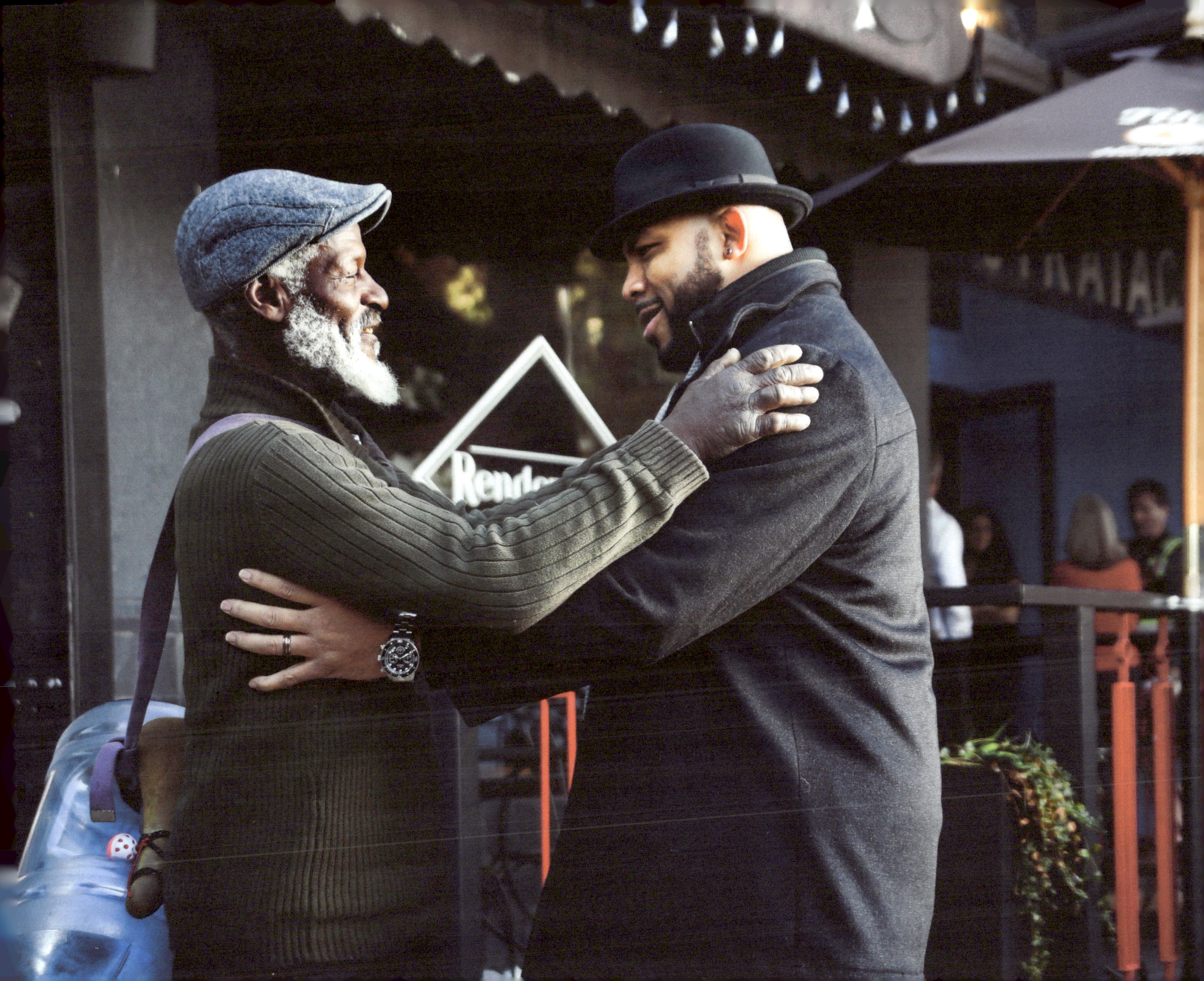

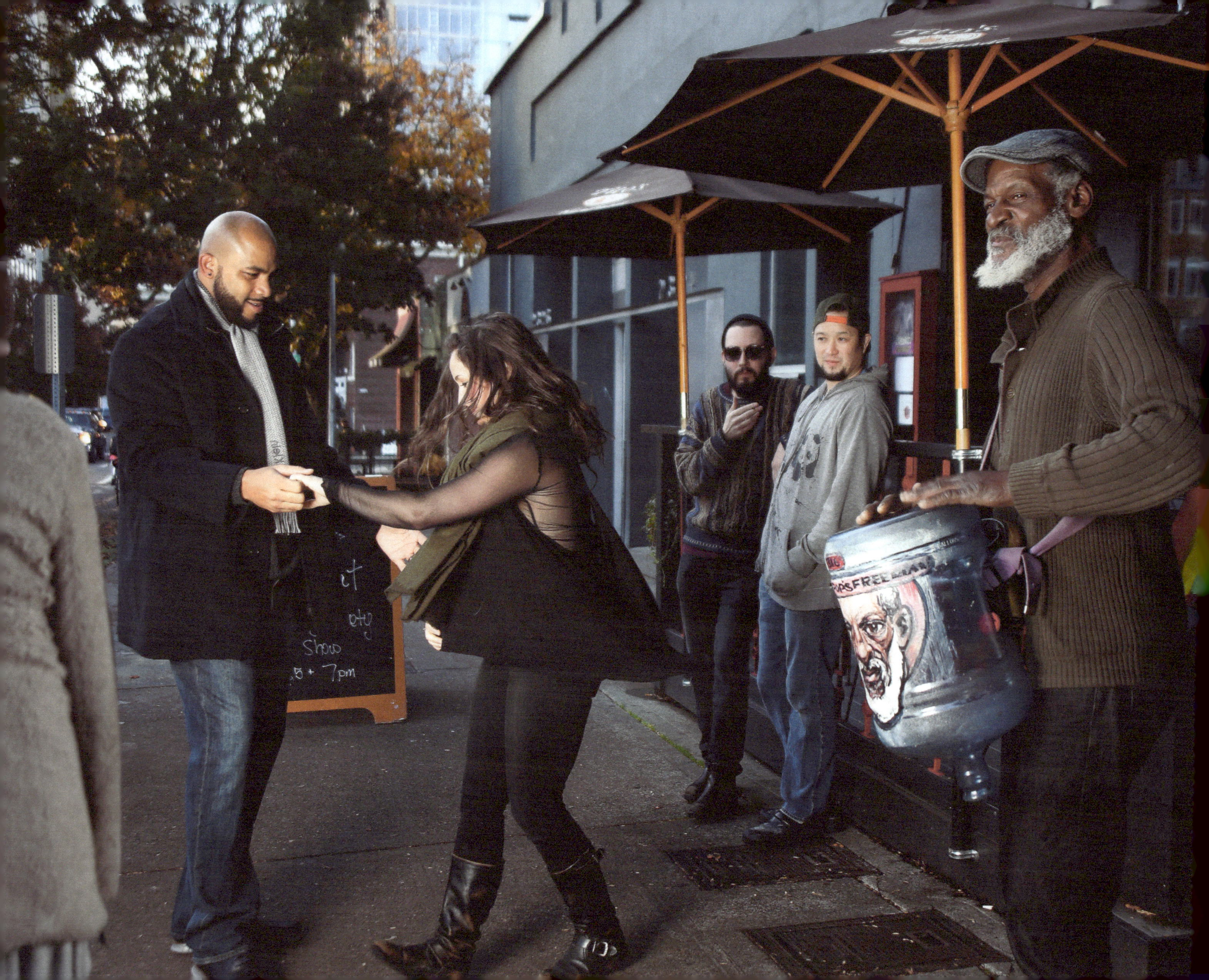
et
ete
show
5 + 7pm

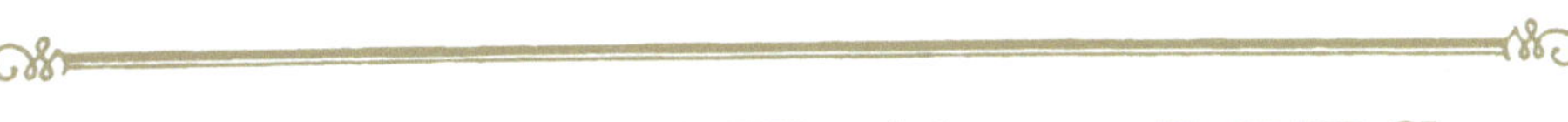

The **TRUTH** About **LIES**

Glen "Pops" Freeman, 2019

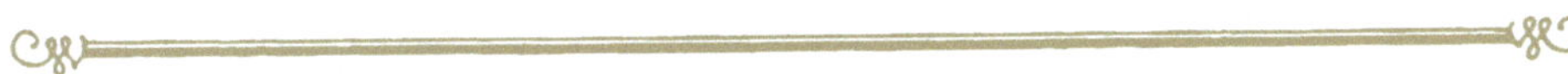

This is the truth about lies

Truth is what you must seek within yourself

But remember truth is hard to find because truth likes to hide behind lies

But it doesn't seem to mean a thing when everyone's satisfied

Its only when there's discontent that truth or lies seems to make a difference

You see one hand never knows what the other is doing but one hand will always wash the other

So one may be open to receive, but the other may be closed to deliver a blow

Its for protection or for profit, to reveal or to conceal, to acquit or to accuse

Truth or lies are what people use but it depends on who they are talking to and why

Because truth seems to be a confession and you'll never get it without proof

So sometimes the truth will have to do if a good damn lie don't get you through

But if the truth is spoken once and a lie a thousand times, yet we know the truth will always come out

Be careful of your mouth because your tongue is like a well sharpened knife and we all know sometimes truth can hurt more than lies

So that's why you have to find within yourself where your own truth lies

That's the truth about lies

To your own self, be true.

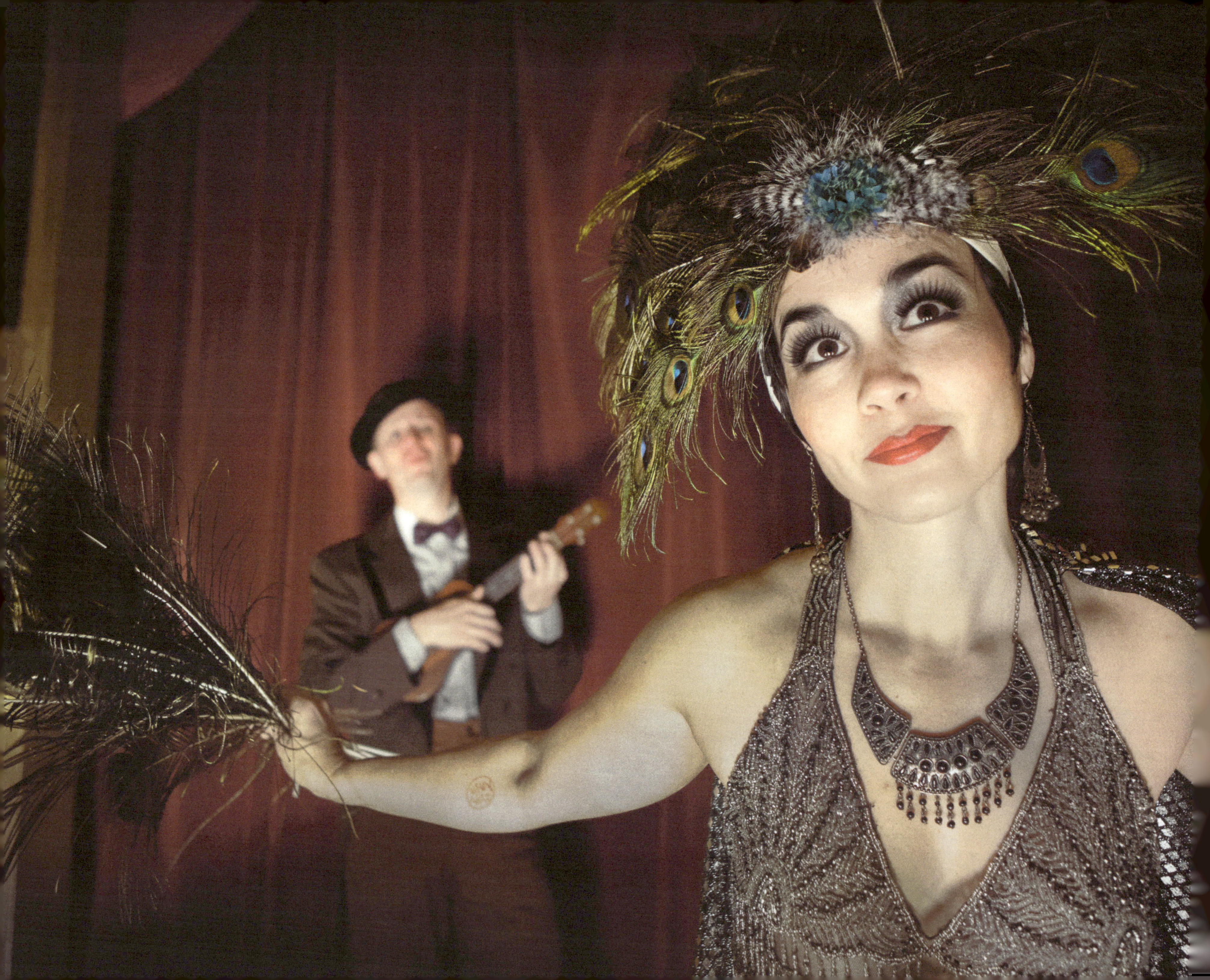

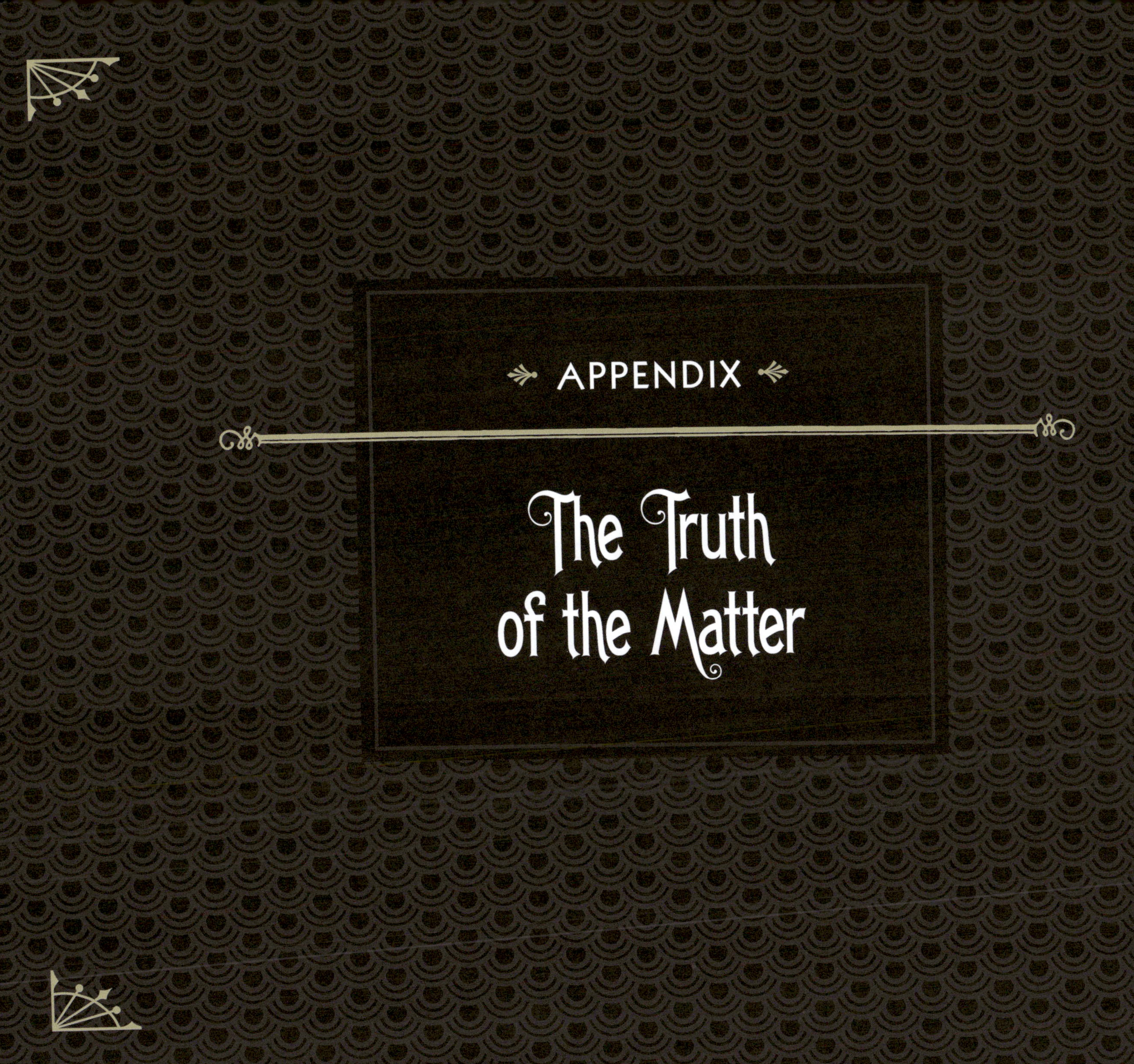

APPENDIX

The Truth
of the Matter

ANSWER KEY

Vaudeville Days

C is true. We're not sure Gustav actually lost thirty pounds, but that's what the papers reported!

The Alleyways

D is true. Our source is not exactly impeccable, but we believe him. Those alleyways were crazy!

The Speakeasies

A is true. Drop in the Rendezvous and you can still see the Jewelbox and the Grotto and imagine that staircase up to the execs' office.

Film Row

A is true.

Fine Dining

B and **E** are true.

The Fight for Civil Rights

A and **C** are true, except the Klan Bakes were called Klan Frolics. Also **B** is mostly true, except it all happened at Seattle's Franklin High School, nowhere near Belltown.

Dodi

A and **B** are true.
Dodi's favorite band was Kiss. She also had a locally famous grunge band named after her.

Grunge

A and **D** are true.

The Ghosts of Belltown

B is true. At least, that's what the folks at the Rendezvous say.

RATE YOURSELF

7–8 CORRECT	Mayor of Belltown	**1–3 CORRECT**	Back to school for you!
4–6 CORRECT	Amateur Historian	**0 CORRECT**	Um, really?

Now that we've had some fun, here are some well-researched and documented articles on Belltown from our friends at HistoryLink. Please visit HistoryLink.org for the full library of articles about Washington state history.

THE MOORE THEATRE, Seattle's oldest existing entertainment venue, stood as one of the finest houses on all the West Coast when it opened in December 1907. Located on 2nd Avenue and Virginia Street, the new venue (with its attached hotel) was built by local developer James A. Moore (1861–1929) after his plans to expand and add a theater to his Washington Hotel (the former Denny Hotel) were derailed by the Denny Regrade project. Instead, he built the Moore and turned its management over to John Cort (1861–1929), who later became a prominent New York impresario. Now more than a hundred years old, the Moore Theatre's stage has seen everything from vaudeville to symphony to religious revivals to hard rock and, as the Moore Egyptian, was the original home of the Seattle International Film Festival. It today retains much of its historic ambience and hosts musical artists and touring stage productions from around the world.

A Visionary Developer

JAMES A. MOORE was born in Nova Scotia and arrived in Seattle around 1886. Shortly thereafter he teamed with William D. Wood (1858–1917), who later became Seattle's mayor, to develop property in and around the city. Together they developed almost a thousand acres in the Green Lake area, as well as another eight hundred acres in what is now West Seattle.

After the Wood/Moore partnership ended, Moore continued his efforts to "tame the wilds" of early Seattle, developing portions of northern Lake Union, as well as the Rainier Beach area. He was also busy leaving his mark on Seattle's downtown—the Estabrook, Whitcomb, Chilberg, and Curtiss blocks all bore his stamp. Moore was also active in a group that backed the controversial idea of constructing a waterway that would link Lake Washington to Lake Union and perhaps even to Puget Sound ("New Playhouse One of Moore's Great Triumphs"). This idea became reality when the Lake Washington Ship Canal opened in 1917.

James Moore's Plan A

MOORE HAD BEEN PLANNING a new entertainment venue in the city for some time, and he first announced his intentions in September 1903. He told John Cort, who was to manage the new theater, that he wanted it to be "the best in America" ("Proposed Theater Rivals Any In America") and promised publicly that it would be opened within fifteen months.

Earlier that year, Moore bought the Denny Hotel, which straddled 3rd Avenue between Stewart and Virginia streets on the south summit of Denny Hill. Started shortly after the Great Fire of 1889, the hotel fell victim to partnership disputes and the financial panic of 1893, and it sat vacant and unfinished for over ten years. Moore completed the project, renamed it the Washington Hotel, and managed to run it at a profit for a short time. His original plan was to extend the hotel and add the theater. As John Cort, explained:

"At first Mr. Moore thought of putting a theater in his Arcade Building, but as soon as he completed his purchase of the Washington and began to figure on its extension we came to an agreement that a modern theater was to be the principal feature of the Second Avenue Building" ("Proposed Theater Rivals Any In America").

But Seattle's massive Denny Regrade project, which ultimately included the leveling of Denny Hill just north of the city's downtown core, would scotch Moore's original plans. Not immediately, however—he fought to save his beloved Washington Hotel and apparently had some temporary success. In April 1905 it was announced that "In connection with his hotel addition and theatre ..." excavation had started and "the erection of the retaining wall against the big hill on which stands the Washington will be begun ..." ("Dirt is Being Taken From the Site of The Moore Theatre"). Clearly, at this point, Moore still had hopes for his original plan to make his new theater part of an expanded Washington Hotel.

It was not to be. The city's regrade plan ultimately led to the complete leveling of Denny Hill, and this of course meant the demise of the luxurious hotel that sat on its summit. Moore's original plan was doomed to be, quite literally, undercut by larger civic considerations.

James Moore's Plan B

WHEN IT BECAME CLEAR that the Washington Hotel would soon not have a hill to stand on, Moore made new plans. He still wanted a theater, he still wanted a hotel, and he still owned the land at 2nd Avenue and Virginia Street. He would have his Moore Theater, and he would also have a hotel to go along with it. It just wouldn't be the Washington Hotel.

Nearly eighteen months before breaking ground on the new project, Moore commissioned architect E. W. Houghton (1856–1927) to do the design. Houghton was one of the Northwest's premier architects. Among the more than 375 buildings he had a hand in were Moore's Arcade Building on 2nd Avenue and the *Post-Intelligencer*'s headquarters. Seattle-based architect B. Marcus Priteca (1889–1971), who would later become one of America's foremost theater designers, began his career as a draftsman for E. W. Houghton.

Houghton also had considerable experience in theater design and had worked on venues in Bellingham, Spokane, Tacoma, Aberdeen, and Walla Walla, as well as theaters in British Columbia and Montana ("Architect Houghton Has Designed Many Theaters"). He had arrived in Seattle just before the fire of 1889 wiped out virtually all of the city's main entertainment houses, and this gave him ample opportunity to practice his architectural skills.

Houghton's plans for the Moore Theatre were both elaborate and revolutionary. He incorporated several innovative features into the interior design, none more impressive than the vast openness created by the complete absence of support posts for the theater's large balcony. Such vertical supports, which inevitably obscured the view to the stage from certain seats, were a typical if unfortunate feature of theaters of the period. In Houghton's design for the Moore, the balcony immediately above the main floor was entirely supported by massive steel girders, the largest of which weighed almost twenty-two tons, that spanned the width of the house. This technique, a relatively new and untested idea in the realm of theater construction, prompted much admiring comment when the Moore finally opened for business:

"One of the most impressive features of the theater is the absence of any supports whatsoever from the floors, to either the balcony or gallery, the former being supported on an immense steel girder, five feet four inches deep and seventy-five feet long, carried in the steel construction of the side walls, the latter hung from the roof" ("New Theater is Very Beautiful").

Moore built much more than just a new theater at his 2nd and Virginia site. The theater occupied the northwest corner of the first floor, but the remainder of the building extending south along 2nd Avenue was home to the six-story Moore Hotel, which is still operating today.

The Lap of Luxury

THE PHYSICAL CONSTRUCTION of the Moore was impressive, and the theater sported other unique features and luxurious interior trappings. There were no stairs from the lobby to the balcony level; instead there were sloping inclines that rose from the 2nd Avenue foyer. The Moore proudly boasted in the opening night program that these inclines were so wide and so gradual as "to permit an automobile to be driven into the balcony from the street" ("Program, Moore Theatre"). There is no indication, however, than anyone actually tried this. The only stairs in the theater's public areas descended to the space directly under the foyer, where the men's smoking room was located on one side and the women's lounge on the other.

The Moore's foyer was reputedly the largest of any theater in the country. Its wainscoting was of Mexican onyx, and the room was illuminated by lighting fixtures of solid brass. The floor was exquisite marble, set in a decorative mosaic pattern. The onyx and marble were said to have cost thirty thousand dollars, and the interior stucco work cost another twenty thousand. Adding to the look and feel of the foyer area were representations of Muses from Greek mythology, done in the Moore's general color scheme of ivory, gold, olive, and old rose. Although the house was described in the opening night program as being Gothic in nature, more than a few journalists were struck by the Pompeian influences visible in the foyer.

The carpeted areas of the house were done primarily in a rose or crimson velour (reports vary on this detail) and matched the color of the drop curtain, which was embroidered in gold. There were twenty-six large private boxes high along the sides of the main auditorium, plus three smaller ones near floor level. The latter arrangement was unusual in that the lower boxes were simply sectioned off from the remainder of the floor seating and not cantilevered above them. Seats in both the auditorium and balcony levels were upholstered in leather.

With an official seating capacity of 2,436, the Moore was claimed by its management to be the third largest theater in the United States at the time, and the builders were careful to consider the safety needs of such a large crowd. An asbestos curtain (this was decades before the dangers of asbestos were recognized) was installed directly behind the formal drop curtain, and exits were arranged in such a manner that management made the Titanic-like boast that "the house may be cleared of people within two minutes in case of fire" ("Last Touches on Moore Theater"). Fortunately, this claim has never been put to the test.

The View from Backstage

THE MOORE WAS AS impressive from a staging perspective as it was from the audience's point of view. In addition to providing the largest stage area of any theater in Seattle, the venue boasted substantial space in the wings and fly areas where props and backdrops could be stored. This allowed increased maneuverability for stagehands and made for faster scene changes. Actors, too, were spoiled when working at the Moore—there were four large "star" dressing rooms on the main floor and an additional sixteen smaller ones both in back of and underneath the stage.

The theater's electrical system was state-of-the-art for the time and was run from a single switchboard. Touting its safety, the Moore claimed that every electrical wire was "protected against cross circuiting or other pranks which electricity sometimes plays" ("New Theater is Very Beautiful").

A Grand Spectacle

WHEN A FINAL accounting was made, building the Moore had cost in the neighborhood of $350,000, although estimates put the value of the land and the theater at approximately $500,000. The house was leased and managed by John Cort, who moved his first-run attractions out of the Grand Opera House on Cherry Street and directly into the Moore. Cort's son Harry served as the Moore's assistant manager.

The theater's debut was a big event for the city. A local paper, commenting on its significance, said:

"Henceforth Seattle is to be a metropolis in things theatrical, with a metropolitan theater and metropolitan attractions ... . [I]t marks the passing of the old provincial order of things and the ushering in of a regime which will make this city the Western home of drama" ("Moore Theater to Open Tomorrow Night").

On December 28, 1907, crowds swarmed the corner of 2nd and Virginia awaiting admittance to see *The Alaskan,* a Yukon-themed operetta that was opening for a week's run at the sparkling new theater. With a large number of "standing-room-onlies" on hand, the Moore's capacity jumped from 2,400 to somewhere near 3,000 for opening night.

The dedication in the Moore's opening program was somewhat grandiose in placing the new theater into the larger context of Seattle's history:

"The close of the year 1907 witnesses the most artistic expression of the 'Seattle Spirit' ever given since the phrase was coined ... Today Seattle is possessed of the finest and most modern theater in the great domain west of the Mississippi river."

Calling the house the "epitome of architectural elegance," the program went on to note that "Seattle is one of the emphatic theater-going communities of the United States and it is fitting that the best the country affords in the way of entertainment should find a housing in every way adequate and up-to-date" (*Program,* Moore Theatre).

The *Seattle Daily Times* was no less enthusiastic, going as far as to class the venue among the great theaters of Paris, Vienna, and Milan ("Moore Theater is Opened to Public").

Early Attractions

FOLLOWING ITS OPENING with *The Alaskan,* the Moore for the next ten years put on varied fare. Among the entertainments appearing on its stage between 1908 and 1918 were:

- **1908** The Seattle Symphony, which called the Moore home from 1908 to 1911

- **1909** Ethel Barrymore (1879–1959) and George M. Cohan (1878–1942)

- **1910** A staging of *Madame Butterfly*

- **1911** Ruth St. Denis (1879–1968), a pioneer of modern dance

- **1912** Presentations of Shakespeare's *Julius Caesar* and *Othello*

- **1914** Anna Pavlova (1881–1931) and deaf-blind lecturer Helen Keller (1880–1968)

- **1917** Ballet dancer Vaslav Najinski (1889–1950) and *Ballet Russes*

- **1918** The Marx Brothers and actress Sarah Bernhardt (1844–1923)

Separate and Not Equal

WHILE HOUGHTON'S DESIGN for the Moore stressed innovation, it also bowed to an odious tradition that was reflected in its architecture. Above the formal balcony there was constructed a smaller section, called the gallery, which could be accessed only from the street via an outside stairway, totally bypassing the lobby area. This had a most unfortunate purpose.

Although Seattle was a more welcoming place for African Americans than many other cities of that era, meaningful integration was still a very long way off. As did many other cities, Seattle had a vaudeville group called "The Negro Ensemble," made up of "colored" vaudevillians, which was a popular attraction for both white and black theatergoers. The isolated gallery at the Moore—with its separate entrance and its seats separated from the rest of the house and farthest away from the stage -- was reserved for Seattle's black audiences. Attitudes would change for the better, however, and the discriminatory use of this special-purpose gallery was eventually abandoned.

The Orpheum Vaudeville Circuit

SHORTLY AFTER THE END of World War I the Moore Theatre was purchased by the Orpheum Vaudeville Circuit, the largest and most successful of several similar operations that toured famous vaudeville acts across the nation. These larger circuits generally owned their own theaters, and the top acts of the day would tour from one city to another. For nearly a decade, the Orpheum circuit treated Seattle audiences to some of the most famous names in entertainment, including, among many others, Jack Benny (1894–1974), Harry Houdini (1874–1926), Sophie Tucker (1886–1966), and Marie Dressler (1868–1934).

With its ornate and luxurious trappings and seating for nearly 2,500, the Moore was considered one of the finest theaters on the circuit. But its prominence ended in the summer of 1927, when the Orpheum Vaudeville Circuit built a

new Orpheum Theatre in Seattle at 5th Avenue and Stewart Street. It was the largest venue for films and vaudeville in the Pacific Northwest, and it became the city's new home for the circuit. With its opening, the Moore, although owned by the same company, was relegated to second-class status, and the physical plant was intentionally downgraded so as to not draw audiences away from the Orpheum. Among other insults, the portions of the luxurious private boxes that jutted into the air above the main seating area were removed. But someone was thinking ahead—plaster casts were made of all the removed sections, and these remain in storage at the Moore to this day should anyone wish to recreate the theater's original look. The Orpheum Theatre fell to the wrecking ball in 1967.

Vaudeville's days as America's favorite live entertainment were ebbing by 1927, but the Orpheum's theft of the Moore's thunder, along with much of its audience, still hurt. Without the sure draw of famous national variety acts, the Moore was forced to return to its former and less lucrative role as a playhouse for road shows and stock-theater troupes. Just two years later, Wall Street crashed, and the Great Depression set in. There seemed little hope for venues like the Moore, but it managed to struggle along until 1935 when, thanks almost entirely to the efforts of a formidable female impresario, it enjoyed a rare mid-Depression renaissance that would last for years.

Cecilia Schultz Takes the Reins

CECILIA AUGSPURGER SCHULTZ (1878–1971) was a pioneer promoter of the arts in Seattle who had headed the Seattle Symphony for two years and brought a series of popular matinee

performances to the Olympic Hotel's Spanish Ballroom. When she first leased the Moore Theatre for one year in 1935, she explained her intentions to *The Seattle Times*:

"I have had the Moore Theatre in mind for over two years as an ideal home for music. It has very fine acoustics, and an atmosphere of dignity and simplicity that give the theatre rare charm and offer one the opportunity of making a fitting home for music" ("Moore Theatre Leased by Woman Impresario").

After some remodeling and refurbishment, Schultz reopened the Moore on July 29, 1935, calling her program "Cecilia Schultz Attractions." It started with a three-day run of a "dance extravaganza," which included performances of the *Coppelia Ballets* and the *Midsummer Night's Ballets* ("Extravaganza to Add to Potlatch Week"). This first season also saw performances by famed violinist Jascha Heifetz (1901–1987) and the equally famous English pianist, Myra Hess (1890–1965), among other attractions.

Schultz later would start a "Greater Artist Series" at the Moore, bringing to Seattle audiences accomplished and noted actors, musicians, and dancers from both Europe and America. But her tastes were nothing if not varied, and her time of booking the Moore saw shows ranging from the well-known dancer Martha Graham (1894–1991) to the lesser-known Trudi Shoop (1904–1999) and her comic ballet; from the Shakespearean "Old Globe Theatre Players" to a black-face presentation of Stephen Foster (1826–1864) songs and a lecture by Robert Ripley (1890–1949) of "Ripley's Believe It or Not" fame.

Cecilia Schultz had a long run at the Moore, renewing her lease every year from the premier season until finally retiring in 1949 (she would live another twenty-two years). The end of her reign as one of the leading impresarios the city had seen was marked by considerable sadness. As *The Seattle Times* reported:

"Seattle music and theatre enthusiasts note with regret the passing of the Moore Theatre as a center of cultural entertainment. It will be closed as a theatre on June 1 with the expiration of a lease. For fourteen years under the management of Mrs. Cecilia Schultz, and before that under other auspices, it has been the scene of many of the best productions in the fields of the concert, ballet and drama that have been available in the West. Seattle audiences will miss the friendly atmosphere of this community landmark, which through the years has provided so much genuine enjoyment for old and young alike" ("A Landmark's Passing").

Fittingly, the last concert Schultz staged at the Moore featured one of the most famed classical musicians of the twentieth century, the pianist Artur Rubinstein (1887–1982).

What Now?

CECILIA SCHULTZ WAS A tough act to follow. Both the entertainment industry and the public's theatrical tastes had changed during her long tenure at the Moore, and the theater was a bit rudderless after her departure. A review of the advertising for the next several years indicates that the Moore paid its bills mostly by renting itself out for religious revivals, often featuring the preaching of pioneer radio evangelist Brother Ralph J. Sanders, with musical interludes provided by such Christian entertainers as "Billie Opie and His Singing Saxophone" (*The Seattle Times*, September 30, 1950). While these drew in the faithful and kept the doors open, it seemed a rather sad comedown

from the theater's glory days under the hand of the indomitable Cecilia Schultz.

But the resilient old showbox had yet another renaissance when, in December 1954, Seattle's Metropolitan Theatre closed its doors, and that venue's longtime manager, Hugh Becket (1922–1986), took over the Moore. He did some minor refurbishment and cleaning, and he hung a new marquee from the front façade that read "Hugh Becket's Moore Theatre." On May 24, 1955, Becket opened his run at the Moore with the Broadway musical hit *The Pajama Game*, and for the next few years he would bring an eclectic mix of entertainment to the theater, including more Broadway productions, well-known individual artists—including locally produced Japanese Kabuki dance drama. During Becket's time the theater's mezzanine was converted to an art gallery and put on display works by such famous Northwest artists as Mark Tobey (1890–1976), George Tsutakawa (1910–1997), Guy Anderson (1906–1998), June Nye (1916–2003), and Kenneth Callahan (1905–1986).

Becket's tenure was to prove but a brief respite from the theater's slow decline, and after he left, the Moore was reduced to eking out a rather shabby existence as a pure rental house, with various promoters bringing in a somewhat low-brow mix of everything from travel films to boxing matches. The theater's physical plant deteriorated, maintenance was deferred, and by 1974, despite being placed on the National Register of Historic Places that year, the Moore Theater was struggling to survive. One employee from that era recalled those sometimes-challenging days:

"It was boasted that the theater was the only one west of Chicago that had a manually operated stage curtain. Hardly something to brag about. One evening, when several members

of the staff did not show up for work, I found myself selling tickets, closing the booth to sell candy and soda, then running down to the stage and pulling the curtains, then running back to the booth to sell more tickets to impatient patrons" (Bruce Paddock).

The Moore Egyptian

IT TOOK THE EFFORTS of two young men from north of the border to rescue the Moore from its long decline. In 1975 Darryl MacDonald, an expatriate Canadian, and Dan Ireland, an American who had been living in Vancouver BC for several years, leased the theater, spent several months giving it a thorough cleaning, remodeled the lobby, installed a new screen and sound system, and reopened it as The Moore Egyptian. Their plan was to provide the public with a mixture of classic-movie revivals and foreign films. In an interview with *The Seattle Times* they explained the new name and format:

"It's called the Egyptian because a lot of theaters built in the 1930s were called the Egyptian—like the one in Los Angeles and the one that used to be in the University District—and we'd like to suggest that era ...We'd like to show a mixture of different kinds of films, and do a good job of it ... Everything will be shown in the proper screen ratios, so that in the older films you won't see heads and feet being chopped off to accommodate wide screens" (What Is a Moore Egyptian?).

The theater's reopening was preceded by a multi-day series of teaser ads in the local newspapers, all featuring a dramatic shot of Yul Brynner (1920–1985) in his role as the pharaoh Rameses in Cecil B. DeMille's (1881–1959) epic *The Ten Commandments*, slouched on a throne and holding, of all things, a bunch of bananas. Each day's ad had a new line of dialogue in a cartoon "bubble" emerging from Brynner's trademark shiny dome. On one day he posed the query, "Moore Egyptian than what?" (*The Seattle Times,* December 5, 1975). The answer came the next day: "Moore Egyptian than Cleo's snake, that's what" (*The Seattle Times,* December 6, 1975). Later ads promised "Moore Egyptian than you bargained for" (*The Seattle Times,* December 8, 1975) and "There's a hot banana for you at the Moore Egyptian" (*The Seattle Times,* December 9, 1975).

Despite the somewhat hokey advertising campaign, Ireland and MacDonald were true film aficionados, and they brought to their Moore Egyptian a broad range of fare, from early Hollywood extravaganzas to first-run foreign films. Seattle got a taste of what was in store on opening night, December 14, 1975, when the feature was Busby Berkeley's (1895–1976) musical camp classic from 1943, *The Gang's All Here,* featuring Carmen Miranda (1909–1955) and her famous fruit hat (this may explain the otherwise inexplicable addition of bananas to the Rameses photo). This was followed over the Christmas holiday by a double bill of Humphrey Bogart (1899–1957) in *Casablanca* and Cary Grant (1904–1986) in *Arsenic and Old Lace,* and these would be followed in turn by a retrospective of Federico Fellini's (1920–1993) best films and restored 35mm classics from the MGM vaults.

The Seattle International Film Festival

IRELAND AND MACDONALD were to have a huge impact on Seattle's status in the world of film buffs when, in 1976, their Stage Fright Incorporated kicked off the first annual Seattle International Film Festival (SIFF), which ran at the Moore that year from May 14 to May 31. The first season's lineup featured eighteen movies, with entries from Germany, France, Italy, Britain, Switzerland, Australia, The Netherlands—even one from Egypt. Thrown into the mix was one American production, horror-meister George Romero's (b. 1940) *The Crazies,* which went on to become a cult classic and was remade in 2010. During the festival the Moore Egyptian also put on weekend midnight showings of such movies as the seminal rock-festival documentary *Woodstock,* which could be seen for a mere ninety-nine cents. The Moore was also the first venue in Seattle to feature midnight presentations of an enduring cult favorite, *The Rocky Horror Picture Show.*

The film festival was an immediate success and would steadily expand its offerings in subsequent years. In 1979 no fewer than 120 films were shown, and the festival lasted more than a month. The following year, 1980, saw the first post-screening audience discussions with filmmakers, a feature that helped move SIFF into the major league of film festivals.

After the 1980 season, SIFF moved to the former Masonic Temple on Capitol Hill, which was renamed The Egyptian. In 2011, festival headquarters were relocated to the SIFF Film Center, which was opened that year on the grounds of Seattle Center. Now running an average of twenty-five days each year, the Seattle International Film Festival is the largest, most highly attended film festival in America, and in 2011 it drew over 150,000 movie lovers to its presentations. Currently (2012) festival screenings take place at the film center, the Egyptian, and the Uptown Theater on lower Queen Anne, which has now become a dedicated venue for the Film Center.

Saved Yet Again

AFTER IRELAND AND MacDonald lost the lease to the venue in 1985, it reverted back to its original name of The Moore Theatre and again became an event-by-event rental house for a wide variety of entertainment, from dance troupes and alternative rock to classic movies and stage productions. As in some of its earlier periods, the quality of the presentations offered was spotty, and the historic old venue again seemed somewhat bereft of any overarching purpose. But once again, help was on the way, and once more it was a woman who would lead the way.

In 1992 Microsoft alumna Ida Cole had purchased the also-historic Paramount Theatre, rescuing it from near-certain doom and spearheading an expensive and extensive restoration. Shortly thereafter, the nonprofit Seattle Landmark Association that Cole headed (and which, in 1999, was reorganized as the Seattle Theatre Group) leased the Moore Theatre from George Toulouse (1917–1998), a Seattle attorney and real-estate investor who had purchased the theater and hotel many years earlier. His family now (2012) owns the property, which is still under lease to STG.

Toulouse is an unsung hero of the Moore's survival as a largely intact example of early-twentieth-century theater architecture. He endured many long years of low return on his investment in both the theater and the hotel, but consistently balked at allowing any ventures that would have threatened the venue's historic ambience. He delighted in his ownership of the theater, as revealed by an anecdote from his obituary:

"Once, when giving a local reporter a tour of the Moore Theatre, Mr. Toulouse hopped on stage and began singing 'The Impossible

Dream.' In later years, he enjoyed watching musicals from the first balcony of the theater" ("George Toulouse; Lawyer With Passion For Education").

The Seattle Theatre Group, which now also owns the Paramount and also leases the Neptune Theatre in the University District, was the perfect vehicle to both honor the Toulouse family's dedication to the Moore and maintain its reputation as a venue for diverse, high-quality entertainment. From September through early December of 2007, the group celebrated the centennial of "Seattle's Oldest Operating Theatre ("The Moore Centennial") with a series of events, including a tribute to various entertainments that had graced its stage over the years. Among the celebratory events were:

- The Martha Graham Dance Company, which Cecilia Schultz first brought to the Moore in 1936;

- Performances by the Seattle Symphony Orchestra, which called the theater home in the early 1900s;

- A Hundredth Anniversary Improv Comedy night on October 15, 2007;

- A screening of Land of the Headhunters, Edward Curtis's 1914 feature film that was the first dramatic movie to use an all-Native cast (members of British Columbia's Kwakwaka'wakw linguistic group). Descendants of the original players also performed at this screening;

- A grand open-house celebration on December 10, 2007, that featuring theater tours and local performing artists paying tribute to its long history.

Under ongoing management by the Seattle Theatre Group, the Moore today offers a wide variety of entertainment, from dance troupes and alternative rock to classic movies and stage productions. Virtually every musical genre, from the most hard-core punk to flashy funk, has had a place on the Moore stage in recent years. Although its historic character remains largely intact, various remodeling efforts over the years have changed some of the features of the original theater, and it now seats approximately fourteen hundred, about on thousand fewer than it did when first opened.

Seattle is fortunate to have organizations, government agencies, and private citizens willing to put time and money into preserving the city's theatrical heritage. The continued vitality of the Moore Theatre is just one example of what that dedication and hard work has achieved.

THIS ESSAY MADE POSSIBLE BY: NW Arts Encyclopedia: Nesholm Family Foundation and Seattle Office of Arts & Cultural Affairs

SOURCES: "Last Touches on Moore Theater," *Seattle Post-Intelligencer*, December 18, 1907, p. 3; "The Alaskan," *Seattle Post-Intelligencer*, December 22, 1907, Magazine Section II, p. 7; "Opening of the Moore Theater," *Ibid.*, December 28, 1907, p. 7; "Theater Opening Brilliant Affair," *Ibid.*, December 29, 1907, Second Section, p. 4; "Architect Houghton Has Designed Many Theaters," *Ibid.*, December 29, 1907, Second Section, p. 4; "New Playhouse One of Moore's Great Triumphs," *Ibid.*, December 29, 1907, Second Section, p. 4; "New Theater is Very Beautiful," *Ibid.*, December 29, 1907, Second Section, p. 5; "Moore Theater to Open Tomorrow Night," *Seattle Star*, December 27, 1907, p. 6; "Moore Theater Opens With The Alaskan," *Ibid.*, December 30, 1907, p. 8; "Moore Theater Opens Tonight," *Seattle Star*, December 28, 1907, p. 3; "Proposed Theater Rivals Any In America," *The Seattle Daily Times.*, September 23, 1903, p. 1); "Dirt is Being Taken From the Site of The Moore Theatre," *Ibid.*, April 7, 1905, p. 1; "Moore Theater is Opened to Public," *Ibid.*, December 29, 1907, p. 1, 3; M. McV. S., "Alaskan Warmly Welcomed," *Ibid.*, December 29, 1907, p. 3; "Extravaganze to Add to Potlatch Week," *Ibid.*, June 30, 1935, p. 38; "Mrs. Schultz Will Present Fine Artists," *Ibid.*, August 11, 1935, p. 35; "Frontier Comedy, 'Roadside,' Offers Laughs Galore," *Ibid.*, September 20, 1935, p. 30; "A Landmark's Passing," *Ibid.*, April 12, 1949, p. 6; "Billie Opie" (advertisement), *Ibid.*, September 30, 1950, p. 5; Virginia Boren, "Moore Theatre Leased by Woman Impresario," *The Seattle Sunday Times*, March 3, 1935, p. 9; John Hartl, "First Seattle Film Festival Starts May 14 at the Moore," *The Seattle Times*, April 25, 1976, p. A–20; Jim Simon, "George Toulouse; Lawyer With Passion For Education," *Ibid.*, May 11, 1998 (http://community.seattletimes.nwsource.com); *HistoryLink.org Online Encyclopedia of Washington State History*, "Schultz, Cecilia Augspurger (1878–1971)" (by James R. Warren), and "New Orpheum Theatre opens in Seattle on August 28, 1927" (by Eric L. Flom), and "Denny/Washington Hotel (Seattle)," (by Paul Dorpat) http://www.historylink.org/ (accessed April 9-12, 2012); Misha Berson, "Off-Stage News," *The Seattle Times*, October 7, 1999 (http://community.seattle-times.nwsource.com/); Bruce Paddock, "Moore Theatre," Silent Era website accessed April 9, 2012 (http://www.silentera.com/theaters/USA/washington/seattle/moore.html); "The Moore Centennial," (Program), Seattle Theatre Group, 2007; "Program, Moore Theatre," December 28, 1907, J. Willis Sayre Papers, University of Washington Libraries Special Collections; Sean McIntyre, "History of The Moore," Seattle Theatre Group website accessed April 2012 (http://www.theparamount.com/about/moore/history.html); Jeffrey Karl Ochsner and Dennis A. Andersen, "Edwin W. Houghton," in *Shaping Seattle Architecture: A Historical Guide to the Architects* ed. by Jeffrey Karl Ochsner (Seattle: University of Washington Press, 1994), 46-51; Lawrence Kriesman, *Made to Last: Historic Preservation in Seattle and King County* (Seattle: University of Washington Press, 1999), 36.

NOTE: This essay, originally written in June 2002, was greatly expanded in April 2012.

FILM ROW

SEATTLE'S BELLTOWN NEIGHBORHOOD just north of downtown was home to the Northwest's Film Row even before the dawn of "talkies" in the late 1920s. Hollywood's major movie studios based regional distribution outposts there and several historic sites survive. Among them are the Rendezvous Cafe and the adjacent Jewel Box—the former *the* place where movie-biz bigwigs met to eat, drink, and strike deals; the latter one of the row's private screening rooms where theater owners previewed new Hollywood films. Both are located in a building that also housed the factory of the B. F. Shearer Company, a provider of theater seating, curtains, and lights, which it supplied to theaters including the 5th Avenue, the Embassy, the Orpheum, and the Paramount. The film industry eventually vacated Belltown and by the 1970s the Jewel Box was being used for more diverse programming, including foreign films and indie-theater groups. In the 1980s rock bands began performing there, and the building provided rehearsal spots. By the 1990s the Rendezvous was a dive treasured by the grunge-rock crowd, and today the cafe is a popular touchstone of bygone days, while the theater presents films, music, comedy, and burlesque shows.

Bell's Town

ON NOVEMBER 13, 1851, the Denny Party of pioneers arrived from Portland, Oregon, by ship at Alki in what is now West Seattle. Among that group of settlers was William Nathaniel Bell (1817–1887). Toward the end of the following winter, a few of the men decided to scout out other spots across Elliot Bay to make their land claims. Carson D. Boren (1824–1912) and Arthur Denny (1822–1899) grabbed sections bordering what would develop into Seattle's old-town Pioneer Square neighborhood—Bell went northward. Bell's claim was on a narrow bayside shelf that backed up to one of Seattle's steepest hills, Denny Hill, which would be flattened beginning in 1897 in the Denny regrade project initiated by city engineer R. H. Thomson (1856–1949).

Relatively isolated because of this terrain, Bell's property didn't enjoy the rapid and profitable development that saw a central business district arise on Boren and Denny's land to the south, and Bell left for California in 1855, returning in 1870 to a much-grown Seattle. Indeed, the low demand for real estate in "Bell's Town" caused it to remain a modest semi-industrial area for the following century. In between, it garnered a reputation as a rather sketchy area. Indeed, in a 1902 article about curfew laws sub-headlined "Young Girls and Boys Roam About Streets," *The Seattle Times* noted that "North Seattle, particularly the district known as Belltown, seems to be the rendezvous of all the young thieves in the city" ("Curfew Law ..."). In later decades the low-rent area was favored by seamen and dockworkers, the struggling elderly, and artists and musicians, but it also eventually became the scene of open-air drug markets for a time. By the second decade of the twenty-first century, however, the Belltown neighborhood, by then the most densely populated in Seattle, was crowded with upscale condos. But a lot occurred in the years between.

Film Row (1)

IT WAS SEATTLE'S NEW land-use zoning rules in 1923 that caused Belltown to become the Pacific Northwest's center of the film industry. Due to the extreme flammability of the nitrocellulose film then in use, its storage was restricted to the under-populated Belltown area and Seattle's first "Film Row" began to be established along 3rd Avenue at Virginia Street (named for Bell's daughter). At the time the silent-film industry used distribution centers—called film exchanges—where the region's theater owners could visit and preview new movies to select those they wanted to screen back in their towns. Prints of the chosen films would then be shipped by rail from Hollywood and delivered to local theaters.

It seems that this all began with the arrival of the French firm Pathé, then the largest film-equipment and movie-production company in the world, which opened the Pathe Theatre at 717 1st Avenue around 1910, and established the Pathe Exchange Inc. at 2113 3rd Avenue. Then in August 1916 the Mutual Exchange opened in a building with an auditorium at 3rd and Virginia. In 1922, Pathé moved into the handsome new Pathe Building at 2025 3rd Avenue (which was razed in 2016–2017). "The Pathe Building included office, clerical, inspection and shipping spaces as well as two fireproof and well-ventilated storage vaults, a viewing booth, a rotation room and a large poster storage space" ("Summary for 2025 3rd Ave"). The following year's Polk *Seattle City Directory* listed 26 firms under the "Motion Picture Machines and Supplies" category—all clustered near Mutual and Pathé.

Film Row (2)

THE LATE 1920S SAW the emergence of movies with soundtracks and the arrival of additional film exchanges in Seattle, where the locus of the biz drifted over to 2nd Avenue between Battery and Wall Street. Among the film studios that saw the benefit of having a shop in Seattle to service the fifty-plus theaters in town and the more than 420 commercial movie theaters across Washington, Alaska, Idaho, and Montana were Columbia Pictures, De Luxe Feature Film Company, Metro Goldwyn Mayer, Paramount Pictures, RKO, 20th Century Fox, United Artists, Universal, Vitagraph, and Warner Brothers.

In 1928, Columbia opened an exchange at 1st Avenue and Battery (as of 2017 the location of the Belltown Court Condominiums). Also in 1928, the block-long art-deco Film Exchange Building (aka the Canterbury Building), designed by Seattle architect Earl W. Morrison, was built on the west side of 2nd Avenue. Its "offices, storage vaults, editing suites, and screening rooms" were used by "major studios, along with independent distributors and publicity firms" (Humphrey, 40). MGM/Loews was based in the ca. 1930 McGraw-Kittenger-Case building at 2331 2nd Avenue, in the space occupied in 2017 by Buckley's Restaurant.

Next door to MGM was the Lorraine Hotel at 2327 2nd Avenue, built in 1925 by noted modernist architect J. Lister Holmes (1891–1986). The hotel's location made it the film industry's favorite. "Managers, studio representatives and movie stars on publicity tours all reportedly stayed at the Lorraine" (Pryne), Jimmy Stewart reputedly among them. (Later renamed the William Tell Hotel, the building became low-income housing for a time; in 2017 it was being operated as the City Hostel.)

Directly across the street from the Lorraine was Film Row's most popular restaurant, the Rendezvous Cafe at 2320 2nd Avenue. Just south of the cafe was the 1928 RKO Distributing Company building at 2312 2nd Avenue, described in a 2010 report on potential historic-landmark designation:

"[Its] film storage vaults and the film examination room (for quality control) were at the rear of the first story, with the film exhibition room (to screen films for theater representatives) above the second floor. The middle section of the first floor was the poster room, where the film advertising posters were stored and packed for distribution. The basement, under the rear third of the building, had storage areas and two darkrooms next to the alley" (Gordon, 2-3).

The final exchange to be built, Paramount's 1937 building at 2332 1st Avenue, became the Catholic Seaman's Club in 1955 and as of 2017 the ground floor was the Sarajevo Restaurant. Surrounding all these firms on Film Row were a galaxy of additional film- or theater-related companies, including poster companies, theater-equipment dealers, and theater-furnishing suppliers. Most notable was the firm founded in 1926 by Benjamin F. Shearer (ca. 1890–1972).

B.F. Shearer Company

B.F. SHEARER WAS born in Decatur, Illinois, around 1890. In his teens he moved to a Billings, Montana, wheat ranch and began working at the Luna and Regent motion-picture theaters in Billings. In 1919 he met a redhead from Idaho named Florence "Reddy" Shannon (ca. 1898–1990). They married and he worked as a salesman for a theater-equipment company in Minneapolis and then selling theater chairs in Montana. While serving in World War I he was stationed at Camp Lewis in Pierce County, where he attended Officers Training School and was in the 75th Infantry there at war's end. He returned to Montana and began his own business, but in 1924 the couple moved to Seattle. Shearer initially took a job as a factory rep for Seattle's Heywood-Wakefield Company at 210 Virginia Street, and in 1926 he cut a deal for the company to supply one thousand opera chairs to Seattle's newest grand movie theater, the Embassy at 216 Union Street (in the twenty-first century that space would become home to The Triple Door dinner theater).

Simultaneously Shearer and his brother Tom founded B.F. Shearer Company Inc., which scored the contract to install the Embassy's projection-room equipment. The "firm also provided the carpets, drapes, the motion-picture booth and stage equipment, stage curtains and drops. This firm specializes in complete theatre equipment and is in a position to install virtually everything in the house" ("Shearer Co. Provides ..."). Shearer also supplied the swanky 5th Avenue Theater that opened in August 1926.

Shearer opened an impressive factory in the 2300 block of 2nd Avenue, with his main office at 2318 2nd. The building had been designed by local architect Earl W. Morrison (d. 1955) in 1925 for Edmond N. Canedy (1867–1950), a former shingle-mill owner and then a general contractor and real-estate investor. Morrison and Canedy also built the adjacent RKO building. Shearer quickly found success by supplying theaters with everything from seats to carpets, curtains, and lighting fixtures. His factory boasted a complete woodshop, electrical shop, research library, and a multistory tower for manufacturing stage curtains. The plant's motto highlighted the ability to provide it all: "From the basement to the roof, everything but the audience" ("How Seattle Is Becoming ...").

By 1928 Shearer's firm was touted as "the only complete theater furnishing and equipping plant in America"—one that "started from nothing, but is now recognized as one of the most important in the theatrical business in the West" ("How Seattle Is Becoming ..."). In 1928 the company handled an upgrade at the Orpheum at 506 Stewart Street and furnished the new Music Box Theater at 1414 5th Avenue. In time it would also outfit the Paramount at 911 Pine Street.

Shearer hired an entire "corps of artists, designers, cabinetmakers, scenery painters, upholsterers, architectural decorators, precision mechanics, seamstresses, drapers—skilled workers in silks, paints, wood and iron" ("How Seattle Is Becoming ..."). With a workforce that large, and a payroll to match, Film Row was thrumming with activity. "It is an industry which is annually drawing hundreds of thousands of dollars into Seattle, a large portion of which flows back through payroll channels into the stores and markets of the city" ("How Seattle Is Becoming ..."). Interestingly, at some point the Heywood-Wakefield firm's Public Seating Division was also based out of Shearer's factory at 2318 2nd Avenue.

Rendezvous Cafe and Jewel Box Theater

HAPPILY, ALSO OCCUPYING a storefront in the factory building was George Blair's Rendezvous Cafe at 2320 2nd. Blair ran his place with flair, and Hollywood studio magnates, movie stars, local entertainment luminaries, newspaper reporters—and Shearer's employees—all took to hanging out there. This was right at the midpoint of the Prohibition Era (1916–1933), so tales that an illicit speakeasy nightclub operated in the basement have some credibility. Regardless, dining at, and more importantly being *seen* at, the Rendezvous, became a thing, and the *Seattle Post-Intelligencer* took to regularly reporting on such sightings.

Beginning in 1932, the Rendezvous had yet another attraction for film-industry folks, because that year B.F. Shearer opened the Jewel Box Theater next door in his building at 2318 2nd Avenue. The Jewel Box was a private preview studio, a place where distributors could screen their films for theater managers and owners. Now they could enjoy a dinner, cigars—and perhaps some cocktails in the basement—and then step into the Art Deco-styled Jewel Box to preview the new-movie options. The cozy den's interior was designed for Shearer by local architect Bjorn Moe with seating for seventy, a projection booth, and a quality sound system. Moe subsequently made some modifications to the venue, and the Northwest Film Club was based in the Jewel Box by 1936.

Interestingly, during this period the film industry was consolidating, and Film Row could now only boast about eighteen film exchanges. Conversely, Shearer's company was excelling and eventually expanded, opening branches in Portland, San Francisco, and Los Angeles.

Storms and War

IN AUGUST 1940 George Blair stepped aside and leased the Rendezvous to Harry Bender, but by 1943 Blair was back. When a storm hit Seattle that January and much of the town lost electrical power, Blair opened his cafe sans waitstaff:

"[People] living in downtown apartments, dressed in the dark in cold rooms, and made their way to The Row for breakfast. The Row was dark too, but inside the cafe that serves the majority of the workers in the film exchanges, was a glow of light cast by rows of candles on the counter, and coffee, brewed on a gas stove, was being served by George Blair ... Patrons waited on themselves and when they had eaten, carried their dishes to the kitchen. ... Instead of a breakfast check, they were told by Blair: 'You know what you had, you can pay for it as you go out'" (Hays, "Amusements Along Film Row").

With World War II under way, the Jewel Box played a role as the site for some of the Seattle Savings and Loan Bank's war-bond drives. On December 8, 1944, a public screening of *For Whom the Bell Tolls* was held at $2,500 per seat with a goal of selling $250,000 in bonds. Then on December 13, *Hollywood Canteen* was shown at two thousand dollars per seat toward a goal of $150,000.

Rendezvous Revival (1)

ON OCTOBER 16, 1947, *The Seattle Times* reported that "George Blair yesterday sold his Rendezvous Cafe on Film Row to Bill Scavotto. It has been the meeting place of film folk and the center of activities on Film Row for the past twenty-two years" (Hays, "Along Film Row," 1947). By mid-December Blair resurfaced with his own theater-brokerage office at 2312 3rd Avenue. Then, on June 9, 1949, the *Times* noted:

"Completely remodeled and beautifully decorated, Seattle's famous Film Row cafe, The Rendezvous, is being reopened tomorrow by William Scavatto. B. Marcus Priteca designed and supervised the remodeling and the decoration was done by Hal Mushkin, formerly with the B.F. Shearer Company. Scavatto has engaged Vic Schodak, as head chef. Schodak, who was trained in Vienna, is a former chef of the Palmer House and Little Jack's, in Chicago" (Hays, "Along Film Row," 1949).

Changing Times

WITH THE EMERGENCE of Seattle's first TV station, KRSC, in late 1948, the television era had arrived. And, as elsewhere, the theater industry took a hit, so the B.F. Shearer Company had to adapt its services. One way Shearer coped was to refocus his team's efforts on furnishing auditoriums for schools and other locations. By 1951 the Paramount Film Distribution Company was based in the RKO building (that structure, just south of Shearer's factory, had also at times housed 20th Century Fox, the Gaumont British Picture Corporation of America, and Eagle Lion Films, Inc.) and Paramount upgraded the manager's office and built a new film vault. But many of the other exchanges were moving out, and Film Row as a whole had lost much of its exciting vibrancy. The Jewel Box saw much less action, and in 1956 the Rendezvous was sold to the Los Angeles-based Lake Theater Company and recast as the Rendezvous Restaurant. By the late 1960s the old speakeasy basement spot was converted into a card room by co-owner Bill Rausch—the famous comedian Jimmy Durante reputedly enjoyed playing cards there.

Then Seattle experienced a major economic and cultural uplift as a result of the Century 21 World's Fair in 1962. Just building the fair's infrastructure at what subsequently became the Seattle Center campus created a lot of good business, and the B.F. Shearer Company's factory manufactured all the seating for the new Seattle Opera House. After the fair's end in October things quieted back down a bit. The Rendezvous was now being managed by Nick Demco, a businessman who was also involved in the dry-cleaning and mobile-home businesses. For a few years Seattle's Variety Club held meetings at the restaurant.

Meanwhile Shearer had built a business empire that at its peak included ownership of a chain of eleven independent theaters, including two in Seattle—the Varsity at 4329 University Way NE and the Green Lake Theater at 7107 Woodlawn Ave NE—and others ranging from Alaska to California. In addition, the B.F. Shearer Company had expanded. With offices in San Francisco and Los Angeles, Shearer and his wife bought a winter home in Palm Springs, and he counted Bing Crosby, Bob Hope, and Arnold Palmer among his golfing buddies. His last hurrah in Seattle was getting a big job in 1963 revamping the Orpheum—which, sadly, would be razed in 1967, one year prior to his retirement. Upon Shearer's death in 1972, all his businesses were sold.

Film Row's Final Days

IN THE 1970S THE Seattle City Council chose to up-zone the then-sleepy Belltown neighborhood, kicking off a decades-long process of transforming it into a high-rise residential district. In addition, a string of cafes, art galleries, and dance clubs appeared, with artists and rock bands renting old industrial lofts as apartments, studios, and rehearsal spaces. The Rendezvous won a new younger clientele who appreciated its authentic rundown atmosphere of glamorous decadence. And the Jewel Box—which had devolved into a porn theater at one point—launched a new era of screening foreign films and providing space to upstart live-performance groups including the Brass Ring Theater. In addition, legal gambling was introduced and became a significant part of the overall business.

At the same time, Seattle's dwindling Film Row was in its final days:

"Changes in transportation, technology and marketing rendered film exchanges of this type obsolete by the 1960s. Modern film did not require special handling and transportation and distribution systems were much more efficient. Universal Studios was the last film business in the Film Exchange Building, leaving in 1980" (Gordon, 4).

The Jewelbox Rocks

SLIGHTLY RENAMED, THE Jewelbox eventually began to be appreciated as the last remaining screening room from the old Film Row days, and the theater community began to hold champagne parties there. Other groups began holding meetings in the space, including the Northwest Scriptwriters' Alliance. Upstairs, B.F. Shearer's old offices also found renters, including Roger Husbands, the first manager to take on a local punk-rock band, The Enemy. Then across the hall, between 1981 and 1986, were the offices of Seattle music magazine *The Rocket*.

The Seattle Theater Project produced shows in the Jewelbox beginning in 1986. The room was also the site for the premiere of P. S. O'Neil's film *Fertilichrome Cheerleader Massacre*—which included the acting debut of Mark Lanegan, singer with Ellensburg's Screaming Trees—and screened edgy experimental films including William S. Burroughs's infamous *Towers Open Fire.*

Around 1987 the Rendezvous was purchased by Fritz Zabwa. He cleared out the basement, making room for three band-rehearsal spaces. The Blood of the Lamb was among the first bands to move in, and one member, Earl Brooks, also began booking bands to perform in the Jewelbox. In 1988 the band Wigglin' Taters began a regular run of Saturday night shows there.

Belltown Rocks

AS SEATTLE'S GRUNGE-ROCK scene arose, Belltown emerged as a locus, and the neighborhood positively hummed with creative energy. The Rendezvous became even more popular as a late-night watering hole and, along with the Jewelbox, participated in all sorts of new happenings, including First Friday Belltown Art Walks, the Belltown Film Festival, and various Northwest Film Club events. Old spaces were now filling with interesting new businesses, including the Galleria Potato Head and later the Roq la Rue art gallery, while a collective of blacksmiths operated Black Dog Forge, entered from the alley between 2nd and 3rd avenues, where the basement also provided rehearsal space to a few notable hit-making bands from the grunge era, including Pearl Jam, Soundgarden, and the Presidents of the United States of America.

The Rendezvous basement and old upstairs offices also went on to serve as practice pads for numerous bands, including Hammerbox and the Walkabouts. Along the way countless bands rocked the Jewelbox, where some also recorded live shows and/or video shoots and others held album-release parties. One of the attractions was a beloved longtime bartender named Dodi who mixed strong drinks and took no guff—she was so iconic that a local band even named itself in her honor.

But by the end of the twentieth century, both spaces were in decline.

Rendezvous Revival (2)

IN 2002 NEW OWNERS stepped in, buying the Shearer Building, and thus the Rendezvous and Jewelbox— which "had slowly sunk into a seedy pit, dirty, dank, smelling like a New Year's Day hangover"—and embarked on a new chapter in what *The Seattle Times* described as a "riches-to-rags-to-riches roller-coaster ride" (Scanlon). These owners had considerable backgrounds in the local entertainment biz. They included Jerry Everard, an original co-owner of the Crocodile Cafe (located a block away at 2200 2nd Avenue), and his theater-veteran wife Jane Kaplan, in partnership with Tia Matthies and Steve Freeborn, who had run another fabled grunge-era nightspot, the OK Hotel in Pioneer Square.

Treasuring the joint's history, they embarked on a major remodeling effort, with an eye to retaining as many vintage features as possible, including the theater's light fixtures and brocade-fabric wall treatment. Under Kaplan's leadership, programming in the Jewelbox became ever more diverse, with a stated goal of providing "a safe, inexpensive and supportive facility for artists of all disciplines to experiment" ("The Jewelbox Theater"). The beginnings of Seattle's modern burlesque revival took place there around 2002, with performances by the Rollvulvas and the Burning Hearts, and the theater also served as a site for Academy of Burlesque recitals.

In time Everard and Kaplan bought out their partners, and the revamped Rendezvous included the opening of the Grotto basement lounge in the old speakeasy spot. Meanwhile, the population of Seattle exploded, and the whole enterprise was rewoven back into the Belltown neighborhood's cultural fabric. By 2004 *The Seattle Times* wrote:

"Now, on most weekends, the Rendezvous is a crowded, busy, multitasking space, with three distinct areas (bar, lounge, theater). The Rendezvous is quite a hangout for the suave-on-a-budget crowd, with some of the most fascinating (if erratic) entertainment around" (Scanlon).

Indeed, the wide-ranging bookings would include rock bands and jazz combos, fringe-theater productions, film nights, "Cineoke" events (where patrons sang live in front of projected musical movies), regular karaoke nights, cabaret, burlesque shows, and comedy nights. In the 2010s new events were launched, including Naked Brunch (an all-improvised comedy open mic) and, down in the Grotto, Emmett Montgomery's Magic Hat nights and Danielle Gregoire's Comedy Womb (a female-focused comedy show and open mic).

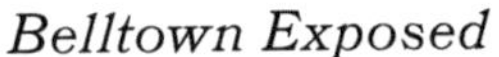

THIS ESSAY MADE POSSIBLE BY: Seattle Office of Arts & Culture and King County

SOURCES: "Washington," Motography, June 29, 1918, p. 1229; "Out in the Territory With Live Exhibitors and Exchanges," Exhibitors Trade Review, December 10, 1921, p. 115; "Summary for 2025 3rd Ave" (Pathe Building), Seattle Department of Neighborhoods Seattle Historical Sites website accessed October 20, 2017 (https://web6.seattle.gov/DPD/ HistoricalSite/QueryResult.aspx?ID=757636257); "Summary for 2327 2nd Ave" (Lorraine Hotel), Seattle Department of Neighborhoods Seattle Historical Sites website accessed October 20, 2017 (https://web6.seattle.gov/DPD/HistoricalSite/QueryResult.aspx?ID=-804031208); Karen Gordon, "Report on Designation: RKO Distribution Company Building," December 10, 2010, pp. 4-7, attachment to draft City of Seattle Council Bill 118143, Seattle City Clerk website accessed October 20, 2017 (http://clerk.seattle.gov/~public/meet- ingrecords/2014/fullcouncil20140902_8.pdf); "Curfew Law Not In Force -- Young Girls and Boys Roam About Streets," The Seattle Times, January 15, 1902, p. 7; "Embassy Theatre to Make Debut Friday," Ibid., September 16, 1926, p. 13; "Shearer Co. Provides Much of Euipment [sic]," Ibid., September 16, 1926, p. 13; "How Seattle Is Becoming the Playhouse Fashion Center of the West," Ibid., August 12, 1928, Rotogravure section, p. 6; Richard E. Hays, "No Admission Is Charged at New Theatre," Ibid., August 30, 1932, p. 16; Hays, "Amusements Along Film Row," Ibid., January 21, 1943, p. 8; Hays, "Screen -- Stage," Ibid., December 5, 1944, p. 16; Hays, "Along Film Row," Ibid., October 16, 1947, second section, p. 18; Hays, "Along Film Row," Ibid., June 9, 1949, second section, p. 25; John J. Reddin, "Showman Shearer Advises Seattle," Ibid., August 4, 1963, second sec- tion, p. 17; "B. F. Shearer, Figure in Theater Industry, Dies," Ibid., December 28, 1972, p. D-13; Charles E. Brown, "Florence Shannon Shearer; Owned Theater Business With Late Husband," Ibid., December 2, 1990, p. C-10; Tom Scanlon, "A Night on the Town in Belltown, in Two Acts," Ibid., December 10, 2004, p. H-4; Eric Pryne, "Historic Building Sold in Belltown -- William Tell Fetches $3.1 Million: Future May Be as Hotel or Hostel," November 18, 2008, Ibid., p. A–20; Clark Humphrey, Loser: The Real Seattle Music Story (Portland: Feral House, 1995), 47, 114; Clark Humphrey, Seattle's Belltown (Charleston, S.C.: Arcadia, 2007), 39-40, 89; Seattle City Directory (Seattle: R.L. Polk and Co., Inc., 1923); "From Grit to Glam: A Look at Belltown's Evolution," November 3, 2014, Curbed Seattle website accessed September 8, 2017 (https://seattle.curbed.com/2014/11/3/10031208/ belltown-grit-glam-evolution-images); Mike Lewis, "Former Pearl Jam Practice Space, Black Dog Forge Getting the Boot Out of Belltown," May 24, 2017, MYNorthwest website accessed September 17, 2017 (http://mynorthwest.com/641342/black-dog-forge-building-to-be-sold/); Jessica Price, "A Closer Look at Seattle's Unsung Hero: The Jewelbox," Burlesque Seattle Press website accessed September 10, 2017 (https://burlesqueseattle.com/2013/01/27/a-closer-look-at-seattles-unsung-hero-the-jewelbox/); Dave Lake, "Checking Back into Seattle's Legendary OK Hotel," Seattle Weekly, February 23, 2016 (http://archive.seattleweekly.com/home/963142-129/checking-back-into-seattles-legendary-ok); Jason Jensen, "We Meet Again: In Culturally Devastated Belltown, the Rendezvous Rises From the Rubble," Ibid., April 3, 2002 (http://archive.seattleweekly.com/2002-04-03/music/we-meet-again/); The Rendezvous and Jewelbox Theater website accessed September 6, 2017 (http://www.therendezvous.rocks/); "The Jewelbox Theater," Seattle Foundation GiveBIG website accessed September 6, 2017 (https://www.givebigseattle.org/jewelboxtheater).

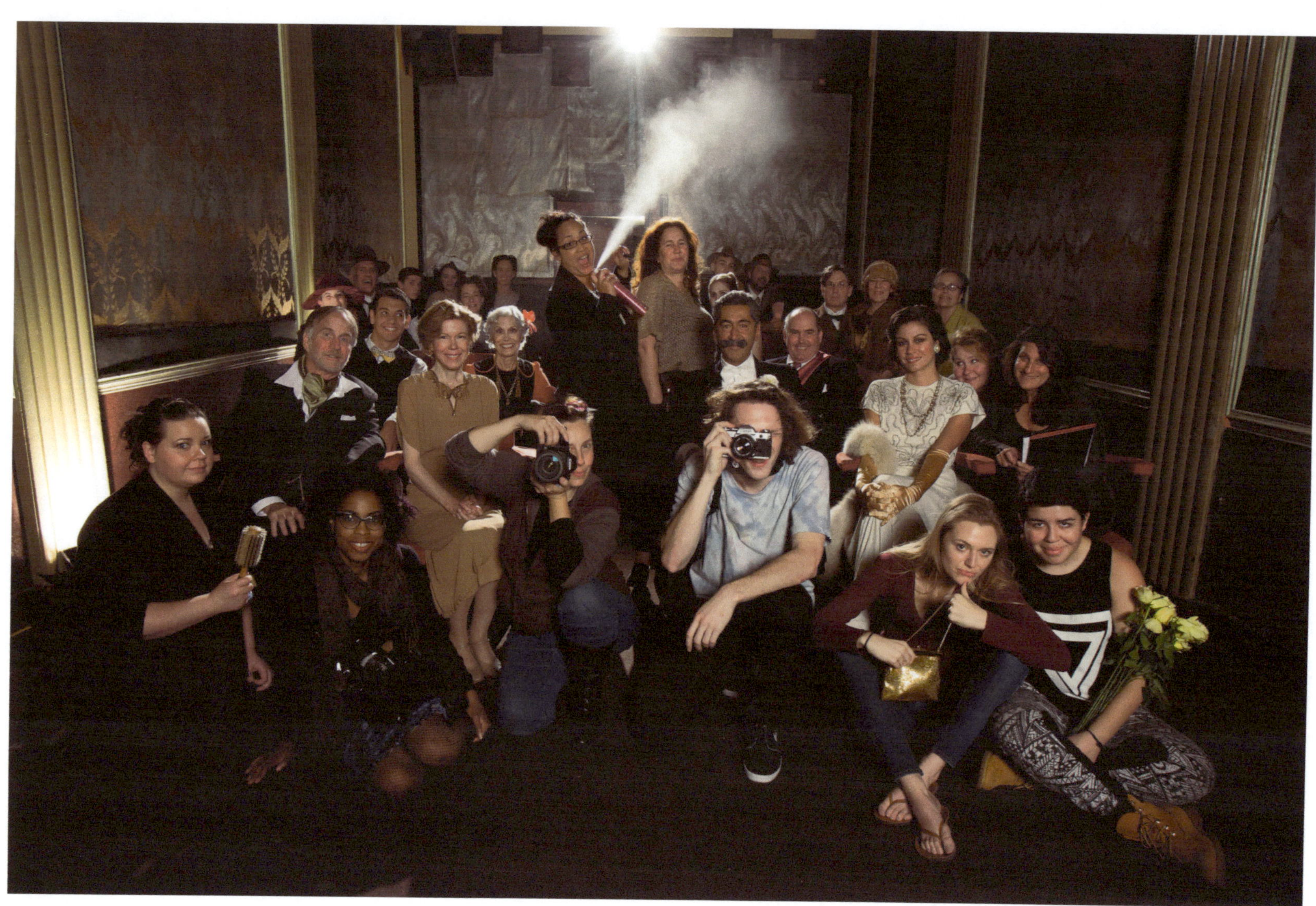

ACKNOWLEDGMENTS

We are forever grateful to the following people and organizations for their support of this project: Jerry Everard, Steve Freeborn, Friends of Historic Belltown HistoryLink, Historic Seattle, Lynn Gough and her Supercalifragilistic Hat and Fashion Shows, Marty Griswold, Nancy Guppy, Lawrence Kreisman, Project Belltown, and the Seattle Department of Neighborhoods.

PEOPLE BEHIND THE BOOK

PHOTOGRAPHER For more than twenty-five years, Staci Bernstein has honed her artistic expression through commercial work and independent community collaborations throughout the Puget Sound. As a visual storyteller, Staci has applied her razor-sharp eye toward unlocking the secrets of the past to create intimate historical characters that vividly resonate with audiences. Staci has devoted much of her life's work to supporting the artistic passion in others, as showcased through her leadership of HeroLabs, a production company specializing in video services for nonprofit organizations and the arts. Staci has also served on the board of Women in Film Seattle, founded Screenwriters Anonymous, and was the president of Northwest Screenwriters Guild. While photography remains at the forefront of her community collaborations, Staci also founded Earth Line, a modern-day fashion line inspired by medieval garments, to share her personal style with others.

PRODUCER Jane Kaplan has been a driving force behind The Rendezvous' enduring legacy for more than twenty years, providing the community with a welcoming gathering place and a public stage. The Jewelbox, a safe place for artistic expression, remains one of the most important venues in the city for Seattle's artistic community to be seen and heard. Jane's directing work has graced Seattle's stages for decades. *Belltown Exposed* represents a collision of Jane's civic leadership within the Belltown community and the vision of a passionate artistic director.

WRITERS Scot Auguston has been living and writing in Seattle for thirty years. He is known mostly as a playwright (*Ballard of Karla Fox, Murder on the Mistletoe Express*, The Penguins Series) and a shadow puppeteer (Sgt Rigsby & His Amazing Silhouettes). He is a frequent collaborator with Sandbox Radio and is the author of a collection of short tales called *The Sleepover Stories*. He works at a natural museum and an art museum.

Bruce Rutledge is the person behind Chin Music Press, a curiously bibliophilic book publisher tucked deep inside Seattle's historic Pike Place Market. There, he and his staff carry on the age-old tradition of making beautiful, engaging, and affordable books for your reading pleasure.

PHOTO SHOOT CREDITS

PRODUCERS

Staci Bernstein   Malory Graham

Jane Kaplan   Lynn Gough

VAUDVILLE

K. Brian Neel   Joselynn Tokashiki Engstrom

DRESSING ROOM

The Shanghai Pearl   Scarlett O'Hairdye

BACK ALLEY

Steve Freeborn   Wes Gonzalez

Jay Schmidtke   Elicia Sanchez

Joseph Guppy   Noa Mahoney

SPEAKEASY

Miranda Antoinette Trout   Tony Lupton

Arica Jeffery   Lily King

Victoria Brooks   Catherine DiSpigno

Slade Burgess   Evelyn Jaroz

Jerry Nash   Tani Martin-Adams

Davey Schmitt-Schrenker   Malory Graham

Devin Carlen   John Hamilton

Emma Von Berghammer-Carlen   Ken Lederman

Kevin Flick   Keith Kentop

Kaye Ostgard

Karen Meador

Zakiya Hanafi

THEATER AUDIENCE

Karen Meador   Olive Medlock

Fred Bahrimand   Zakiya Hanaffi

Kaye Ostgard   Jeff Brice

Melissa Hawthorne   Danni Krehbiel

Grace Hoffman   Andrea Wagner

Carl Sander   Stellan Min

Brian Faker   Jared Stevens

Charlie Rathbun   Zack Moore

Ronee Collins   Wilder Jolly

Brendan Alley   Kevin Jolly

Malory Graham   Slade Burgess

Wendy Medlock

MGM OFFICE

Sarah Holmes

Lacey Nelson

Talitha Anderson

Tom Bropy

Malory Graham

Ike Everard

RESTAURANT

Keith Kentop

Sailor Saint Clair

Virginia Bing

Ken Lederman

Jake Everard

CIVIL RIGHTS

Adé A Cônnére

Kiara LeBlanc

Josiah LeBlanc

Erika Lynn

Carl L. Covington

Houdini Jackson

Chase Edwards

Bruce Rutledge

GHOSTS IN BAR

Taylor Nyquist

Evan Johnson

Jennifer Krantz

Steve Freeborn

Slade Burgess

Juan Jorge Davilacampodonico

DODI

Jennifer Jasper

Andrew Bruce

Morgan Boling

Blossom Kaplan

GRUNGE

Sally Ollove

Michael Toth

Chris Clark-Johnson

Logan Billingsley

Jesse Schneider

Gretta Harley

POPS

Glenn "Pops" Freeman

Carl Covington

Madeline Kudlata

Jason Glover

James Mueller

CREW

Vanessa Blea

Lauren Hall

Virginia Bing

Scott David Strauss

Ike Everard

HAIR

Anna Yuen

Maile Hudson

Rae Lyn Barton

Madeline Flick

Tonya Carlson Jolly

MAKEUP

Stacie Thomas

Talitha Vanzo

Tonya Carlson Jolly

Dawn Warren

Madeline Flick

Sylvie Hasson

Olivia Stolber

Anna Yuen

PHOTOGRAPHERS

Jordan McGrath

Antony Lupton

Mudita Chaurasia

Shelly Gaurav Verma

Noa Mahoney

NETWORK & PARTNERING

Leanard Garfield

Lorraine McConaghy

Kimberly Jacobsen

Larry Kreisman

Paul Dorpat

Aislinn Palmer

Karin Moughamer

Joe Bopp

Ann Ferguson

Alba Juliao, *manager of Goorin Brothers Hat Shop*

THANKS

David Bernstein

Louie Raffloer

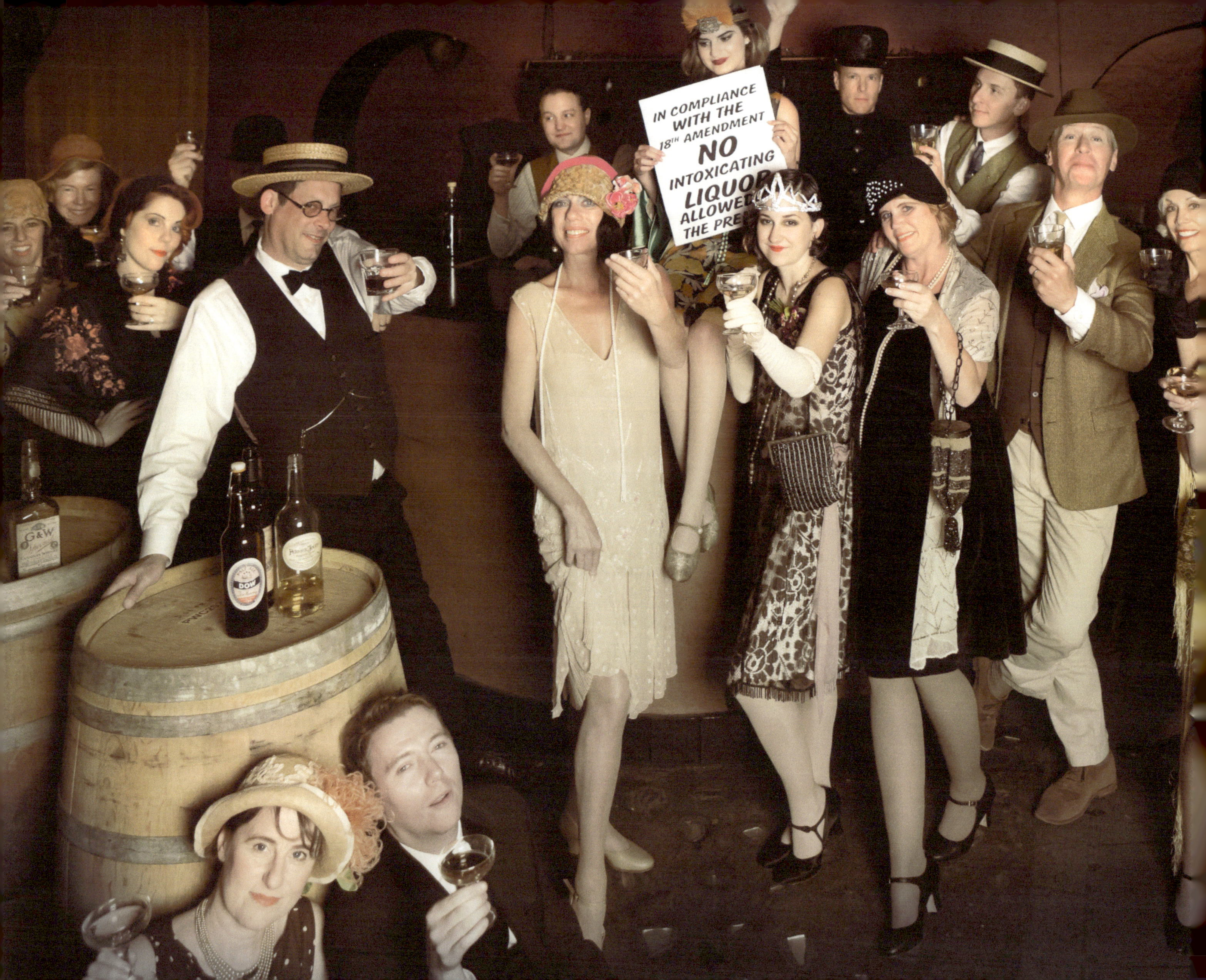

IN COMPLIANCE
WITH THE
18TH AMENDMENT
NO
INTOXICATING
LIQUOR
ALLOWED
THE PREM